Hard Press

THE GENTLEMAN FROM INDIANA

BY BOOTH TARKINGTON

Contents

CHAPTER

CHAPTER I

THE YOUNG MAN WHO CAME TO STAY

There is a fertile stretch of flat lands in Indiana where unagrarian Eastern travellers, glancing from car-windows, shudder and return their eyes to interior upholstery, preferring even the swaying caparisons of a Pullman to the monotony without. The landscape lies interminably level: bleak in winter, a desolate plain of mud and snow; hot and dusty in summer, in its flat lonesomeness, miles on miles with not one cool hill slope away from the sun. The persistent tourist who seeks for signs of man in this sad expanse perceives a reckless amount of rail fence; at intervals a large barn; and, here and there, man himself, incurious, patient, slow, looking up from the fields apathetically as the Limited flies by. Widely separated from each other are small frame railway stations—sometimes with no other building in sight, which indicates that somewhere behind the adjacent woods a few shanties and thin cottages are grouped about a couple of brick stores.

On the station platforms there are always two or three wooden packing-boxes, apparently marked for travel, but they are sacred from disturbance and remain on the platform forever; possibly the right train never comes along. They serve to enthrone a few station loafers, who look out from under their hat-brims at the faces in the car-windows with the languid scorn a permanent fixture always has for a transient, and the pity an American feels for a fellow-being who does not live in his town. Now and then the train passes a town built scatteringly about a court-house, with a mill or two humming near the tracks. This is a county-seat, and the inhabitants and the local papers refer to it confidently as "our city." The heart of the flat lands is a central area called Carlow County, and the county-seat of Carlow is a town unhappily named in honor of its first settler, William Platt, who christened it with his blood. Natives of this place have sometimes remarked, easily, that their city had a population of from five to six thousand souls. It is easy to forgive them for such statements; civic pride is a virtue.

The social and business energy of Plattville concentrates on the Square. Here, in summer-time, the gentlemen are wont to lounge from store to store in their shirt sleeves; and here stood the old, red-brick court-house, loosely fenced in a shady grove of maple and elm—"slipp'ry ellum"—called the "Court-House Yard." When the sun grew too hot for the dry-goods box whittlers in front of the stores around the Square and the occupants of the chairs in front of the Palace Hotel on the corner, they would go across and drape themselves over the court-house fence, under the trees, and leisurely carve there initials on the top board. The farmers hitched their teams to the fence, for there were usually loafers energetic enough to shout "Whoa!" if the flies worried the horses beyond patience. In the yard, amongst the weeds and tall, unkept grass, chickens foraged all day long; the fence was so low that the most matronly hen flew over with propriety; and there were gaps that accommodated the passage of itinerant pigs. Most of the latter, however, preferred the cool wallows of the less important street corners. Here and there a big dog lay asleep in the middle of the road, knowing well that the easy-going Samaritan, in his case, would pass by on the other side.

Only one street attained to the dignity of a name—Main Street, which formed the north side of the Square. In Carlow County, descriptive location is usually accomplished by designating the adjacent, as, "Up at Bardlocks'," "Down by Schofields'," "Right where Hibbards live," "Acrost from Sol. Tibbs's," or, "Other side of Jones's field." In winter, Main Street was a series of frozen gorges land hummocks; in fall and spring, a river of mud; in summer, a continuing dust heap; it was the best street in Plattville.

The people lived happily; and, while the world whirled on outside, they were content with their own. It would have moved their surprise as much as their indignation to hear themselves spoken of as a "secluded community"; for they sat up all night to hear the vote of New York, every campaign. Once when the President visited Rouen, seventy miles away, there were only few bankrupts (and not a baby amongst them) left in the deserted homes of Carlow County. Everybody had adventures; almost everybody saw the great man; and everybody was glad to get back home again. It was the longest journey some of them ever set upon, and these, elated as they were over their travels, determined to think twice ere they went that far from home another time.

On Saturdays, the farmers enlivened the commercial atmosphere of Plattville; and Miss Tibbs, the postmaster's sister and clerk, used to make a point of walking up and down Main Street as often as possible, to get a thrill in the realization of some poetical expressions that haunted her pleasingly; phrases she had employed frequently in her poems for the "Carlow County Herald." When thirty or forty country people were scattered along the sidewalks in front of the stores on Main Street, she would walk at nicely calculated angles to the different groups so as to leave as few gaps as possible between the figures, making them appear as near a solid phalanx as she could. Then she would murmur to herself, with the accent of soulful revel, "The thronged city streets," and, "Within the thronged city," or, "Where the thronging crowds were swarming and the great cathedral rose." Although she had never been beyond Carlow and the bordering counties in her life, all her poems were of city streets and bustling multitudes. She was one of those who had been unable to join the excursion to Rouen when the President was there; but she had listened avidly to her friends' descriptions of the crowds. Before that time her muse had been sylvan, speaking of "Flow'rs of May," and hinting at thoughts that overcame her when she roved the woodlands thro'; but now the inspiration was become decidedly municipal and urban, evidently reluctant to depart beyond the retail portions of a metropolis. Her verses beginning, "O, my native city, bride of Hibbard's winding stream,"— Hibbard's Creek runs west of Plattville, except in time of drought—"When thy myriad lights are shining, and thy faces, like a dream, Go flitting down thy sidewalks when their daily toil is done," were pronounced, at the time of their publication, the best poem that had ever appeared in the "Herald."

This unlucky newspaper was a thorn in the side of every patriot of Carlow County. It was a poor paper; everybody knew it was a poor paper; it was so poor that everybody admitted it was a poor paper—worse, the neighboring county of Amo possessed a better paper, the "Amo Gazette." The "Carlow County Herald" was so everlastingly bad that Plattville people bent their heads bitterly and admitted even to citizens of Amo that the "Gazette" was the better paper. The "Herald" was a weekly, issued on Saturday; sometimes it hung fire over Sunday and appeared Monday evening. In their pride, the Carlow people supported the "Herald" loyally and long; but finally subscriptions began to fall off and the "Gazette" gained them. It came to pass that the "Herald" missed fire altogether for several weeks; then it came out feebly, two small advertisements occupying the whole of the fourth page. It was breathing its last. The editor was a clay-colored gentleman with a goatee, whose one surreptitious eye betokened both indolence of disposition and a certain furtive shrewdness. He collected all the outstanding subscriptions he could, on the morning of the issue just mentioned, and, thoughtfully neglecting several items on the other side of the ledger, departed from Plattville forever.

The same afternoon a young man from the East alighted on the platform of the railway station, north of the town, and, entering the rickety omnibus that lingered there, seeking whom it might rattle to deafness, demanded to be driven to the Herald Building. It did not strike the driver that the newcomer was precisely a gay young man when he climbed into the omnibus; but, an hour later, as he stood in the doorway of the edifice he had indicated as his destination, depression seemed to have settled into the marrow of his bones. Plattville was instantly alert to the stranger's presence, and interesting conjectures were hazarded all day long at the back door of Martin's Dry-Goods Emporium, where all the clerks from the stores around the Square came to play checkers or look on at the game. (This was the club during the day; in the evening the club and the game removed to the drug, book, and wall-paper store on the corner.) At supper, the new arrival and his probable purposes were discussed over every table in the town. Upon inquiry, he had informed Judd Bennett, the driver of the omnibus, that he had come to stay. Naturally, such a declaration caused a sensation, as people did not come to Plattville to live, except through the inadvertency of being born there. In addition, the young man's appearance and attire were reported to be extraordinary. Many of the curious, among them most of the marriageable females of the place, took occasion to pass and repass the sign of the "Carlow County Herald" during the evening.

Meanwhile, the stranger was seated in the dingy office upstairs with his head bowed low on his arms. Twilight stole through the dirty window-panes and faded into darkness. Night filled the room. He did not move. The young man from the East had bought the "Herald" from an agent; had bought it without ever having been within a hundred miles of Plattville. He had vastly overpaid for it. Moreover, the price he had paid for it was all the money he had in the world.

The next morning he went bitterly to work. He hired a compositor from Rouen, a young man named Parker, who set type all night long and helped him pursue advertisements all day. The citizens shook their heads pessimistically. They had

8

about given up the idea that the "Herald" could ever amount to anything, and they betrayed an innocent, but caustic, doubt of ability in any stranger.

One day the new editor left a note on his door; "Will return in fifteen minutes."

Mr. Rodney McCune, a politician from the neighboring county of Gaines, happening to be in Plattville on an errand to his henchmen, found the note, and wrote beneath the message the scathing inquiry, "Why?"

When he discovered this addendum, the editor smiled for the first time since his advent, and reported the incident in his next issue, using the rubric, "Why Has the 'Herald' Returned to Life?" as a text for a rousing editorial on "honesty in politics," a subject of which he already knew something. The political district to which Carlow belonged was governed by a limited number of gentlemen whose wealth was ever on the increase; and "honesty in politics" was a startling conception to the minds of the passive and resigned voters, who discussed the editorial on the street corners and in the stores. The next week there was another editorial, personal and local in its application, and thereby it became evident that the new proprietor of the "Herald" was a theorist who believed, in general, that a politician's honor should not be merely of that middling healthy species known as "honor amongst politicians"; and, in particular, that Rodney McCune should not receive the nomination of his party for Congress. Now, Mr. McCune was the undoubted dictator of the district, and his followers laughed at the stranger's fantastic onset.

But the editor was not content with the word of print; he hired a horse and rode about the country, and (to his own surprise) he proved to be an adaptable young man who enjoyed exercise with a pitchfork to the farmer's profit while the farmer talked. He talked little himself, but after listening an hour or so, he would drop a word from the saddle as he left; and then, by some surprising wizardry, the farmer, thinking over the interview, decided there was some sense in what that young fellow said, and grew curious to see what the young fellow had further to say in the "Herald."

Politics is the one subject that goes to the vitals of every rural American; and a Hoosier will talk politics after he is dead.

Everybody read the campaign editorials, and found them interesting, although there was no one who did not perceive the utter absurdity of a young stranger's dropping into Carlow and involving himself in a party fight against the boss of the district. It was entirely a party fight; for, by grace of the last gerrymander, the nomination carried with it the certainty of election. A week before the convention there came a provincial earthquake; the news passed from man to man in awe-struck whispers— McCune had withdrawn his name, making the hollowest of excuses to his cohorts. Nothing was known of the real reason for his disordered retreat, beyond the fact that he had been in Plattville on the morning before his withdrawal and had issued from a visit to the "Herald" office in a state of palsy. Mr. Parker, the Rouen printer, had been present at the close of the interview; but he held his peace at the command of his employer. He had been called into the sanctum, and had found McCune, white and shaking, leaning on the desk.

"Parker," said the editor, exhibiting a bundle of papers he held in his hand, "I want you to witness a verbal contract between Mr. McCune and myself. These papers are an affidavit and copies of some records of a street-car company which obtained a charter while Mr McCune was in the State legislature. They were sent to me by a man I do not know, an anonymous friend of Mr. McCune's; in fact, a friend he seems to have lost. On consideration of our not printing these papers, Mr. McCune agrees to retire from politics for good. You understand, if he ever lifts his head again, politically, We publish them, and the courts will do the rest. Now, in case anything should happen to me——"

"Something will happen to you, all right," broke out McCune. "You can bank on that, you black——"

"Come," the editor interrupted, not unpleasantly "why should there be anything personal, in all this? I don't recognize you as my private enemy —not at all; and I think you are getting off rather easily; aren't you? You stay out of politics, and everything will be comfortable. You ought never to have been in it, you see. It's a mistake not to keep square, because in the long run somebody is sure to give you away—like the fellow who sent me these. You promise to hold to a strictly private life?"

"You're a traitor to the party," groaned the other, "but you only wait——"

The editor smiled sadly. "Wait nothing. Don't threaten, man. Go home to your wife. I'll give you three to one she'll be glad you are out of it."

"I'll give you three to one," said McCune, "that the White Caps will get you if you stay in Carlow. You want to look out for yourself, I tell you, my smart boy!"

"Good-day, Mr. McCune," was the answer. "Let me have your note of withdrawal before you leave town this afternoon." The young man paused a moment, then extended his hand, as he said: "Shake hands, won't you? I—I haven't meant to be too hard on you. I hope things will seem easier and gayer to you before long; and if—if anything should turn up that I can do for you in a private way, I'll be very glad, you know. Good-by."

The sound of the "Herald's" victory went over the State. The paper came out regularly. The townsfolk bought it and the farmers drove in for it. Old subscribers came back. Old advertisers renewed. The "Herald" began to sell in Amo, and Gaines County people subscribed. Carlow folk held up their heads when journalism was mentioned. Presently the "Herald" announced a news connection with Rouen, and with that, and the aid of "patent insides," began an era of three issues a week, appearing on Tuesdays, Thursdays, and Saturdays. The Plattville Brass Band serenaded the editor.

During the second month of the new regime of the "Herald," the working force of the paper received an addition. One night the editor found some barroom loafers tormenting a patriarchal old man who had a magnificent head and a grand white beard. He had been thrown out of a saloon, and he was drunk with the drunkenness of three weeks steady pouring. He propped himself against a wall and reproved his tormentors in Latin. "I'm walking your way, Mr. Fisbee," remarked the journalist, hooking his arm into the old man's. "Suppose we leave our friends here and go home?"

Mr. Fisbee was the one inhabitant of the town who had an unknown past; no one knew more about him than that he had been connected with a university somewhere, and had travelled in unheard-of countries before he came to Plattville. A glamour of romance was thrown about him by the gossips, to whom he ever proved a fund of delightful speculation. There was a dark, portentous secret in his life, it was agreed; an opinion not too well confirmed by the old man's appearance. His fine eyes had a pathetic habit of wandering to the horizon in a questioning fashion that had a queer sort of hopelessness in it, as if his quest were one for the Holy Grail, perhaps; and his expression was mild, vague, and sad. He had a look of race and blood; and yet, at the first glance, one saw that he was lost in dreams, and one guessed that the dreams would never be of great practicability in their application. Some such impression of Fisbee was probably what caused the editor of the "Herald" to nickname him (in his own mind) "The White Knight," and to conceive a strong, if whimsical, fancy for him.

Old Fisbee had come (from nobody knew where) to Plattville to teach, and had been principal of the High School for ten years, instructing his pupils after a peculiar fashion of his own, neglecting the ordinary courses of High School instruction to lecture on archaeology to the dumfounded scholars; growing year by year more forgetful and absent, lost in his few books and his own reflections, until, though undeniably a scholar, he had been discharged for incompetency. He was old; he had no money and no way to make money; he could find nothing to do. The blow had seemed to daze him for a time; then he began to drop in at the hotel bar, where Wilkerson, the professional drunkard, favored him with his society. The old man understood; he knew it was the beginning of the end. He sold his books in order to continue his credit at the Palace bar, and once or twice, unable to proceed to his own dwelling, spent the night in a lumber yard, piloted thither by the hardier veteran, Wilkerson.

The morning after the editor took him home, Fisbee appeared at the "Herald" office in a new hat and a decent suit of black. He had received his salary in advance, his books had been repurchased, and he had become the reportorial staff of the "Carlow County Herald"; also, he was to write various treatises for the paper. For the first few evenings, when he started home from the office, his chief walked with him, chatting heartily, until they had passed the Palace bar. But Fisbee's redemption was complete.

The old man had a daughter. When she came to Plattville, he told her what the editor of the "Herald" had done for him.

The journalist kept steadily at his work; and, as time went on, the bitterness his predecessor's swindle had left him passed away. But his loneliness and a sense of defeat grew and deepened. When the vistas of the world had opened to his first youth, he had not thought to spend his life in such a place as Plattville; but he found himself doing it, and it was no great happiness to him that the congressional representative of the district, the gentleman whom the "Herald's" opposition to McCune had sent to Washington, came to depend on his influence for renomination; nor did the realization that the editor of the "Carlow County Herald" had come to be McCune's successor as political dictator produce a perceptibly enlivening effect on the young man. The years drifted very slowly, and to him it seemed they went by while he stood far aside and could not even see them move. He did not consider the life he led an exciting one; but the other citizens of Carlow did when he undertook a war against the "White Caps." The natives were much more afraid of the "White Caps" than he was; they knew more about them and understood them better than he did.

CHAPTER II

THE STRANGE LADY

It was June. From the patent inner columns of the "Carlow County Herald" might be gleaned the information (enlivened by cuts of duchesses) that the London season had reached a high point of gaiety; and that, although the weather had grown inauspiciously warm, there was sufficient gossip for the thoughtful. To the rapt mind of Miss Selina Tibbs came a delicious moment of comparison: precisely the same conditions prevailed in Plattville.

Not unduly might Miss Selina lay this flattering unction to her soul, and well might the "Herald" declare that "Carlow events were crowding thick and fast." The congressional representative of the district was to deliver a lecture at the court-house; a circus was approaching the county-seat, and its glories would be exhibited "rain or shine"; the court had cleared up the docket by sitting to unseemly hours of the night, even until ten o'clock—one farmer witness had fallen asleep while deposing that he "had knowed this man Hender some eighteen year"—and, as excitements come indeed when they do come, and it seldom rains but it pours, the identical afternoon of the lecture a strange lady descended from the Rouen Accommodation and was greeted on the platform by the wealthiest citizen of the county. Judge Briscoe, and his daughter, Minnie, and (what stirred wonder to an itch almost beyond endurance) Mr. Fisbee! and they then drove through town on the way to the Briscoe mansion, all four, apparently, in a fluster of pleasure and exhilaration, the strange lady engaged in earnest conversation with Mr. Fisbee on the back seat.

Judd Bennett had had the best stare at her, but, as he immediately fell into a dreamy and absent state, little satisfaction could be got from him, merely an exasperating statement that the stranger seemed to have a kind of new look to her. However, by means of Miss Mildy Upton, a domestic of the Briscoe household, the community was given something a little more definite. The lady's name was Sherwood; she lived in Rouen; and she had known Miss Briscoe at the eastern school the latter had attended (to the feverish agitation of Plattville) three years before; but Mildy confessed her inadequacy in the matter of Mr. Fisbee. He had driven up in the buckboard with the others and evidently expected to stay for supper Mr. Tibbs, the postmaster (it was to the postoffice that Miss Upton brought her information) suggested, as a possible explanation, that the lady was so learned that the Briscoes had invited Fisbee on the ground of his being the only person in Plattville they esteemed wise enough to converse with her; but Miss Tibbs wrecked her brother's theory by mentioning the name of Fisbee's chief.

"You see, Solomon," she sagaciously observed, "if that were true, they would have invited him, instead of Mr. Fisbee, and I wish they had. He isn't troubled with malaria, and yet the longer he lives here the sallower-looking and sadder-looking he gets. I think the company of a lovely stranger might be of great cheer to his heart, and it will be interesting to witness the meeting between them. It may be," added the poetess, "that they *have* already met, on his travels before he settled here. It may be that they are old friends—or even more."

"Then what," returned her brother, "what is he doin' settin' up in his office all afternoon with ink on his forehead, while Fisbee goes out ridin' with her and stays for supper after_werds_?"

Although the problem of Fisbee's attendance remained a mere maze of hopeless speculation, Mildy had been present at the opening of Miss Sherwood's trunk, and here was matter for the keen consideration of the ladies, at least. Thoughtful conversations in regard to hats and linings took place across fences and on corners of the Square that afternoon; and many gentlemen wondered (in wise silence) why their spouses were absent-minded and brooded during the evening meal.

At half-past seven, the Hon. Kedge Halloway of Amo delivered himself of his lecture; "The Past and Present. What we may Glean from Them, and Their Influence on the Future." At seven the court-room was crowded, and Miss Tibbs, seated on the platform (reserved for prominent citizens), viewed the expectant throng with rapture. It is possible that she would have confessed to witnessing a sea of faces, but it is more probable that she viewed the expectant throng. The thermometer stood at eighty-seven degrees and there was a rustle of incessantly moving palm-leaf fans as, row by row, their yellow sides twinkled in the light of eight oil lamps. The stouter ladies wielded their fans with vigor. There were some very pretty faces in Mr. Halloway's audience, but it is a peculiarity of Plattville that most of those females who do not incline to stoutness incline far in the opposite direction, and the lean ladies naturally suffered less from the temperature than their sisters. The shorn lamb is cared for, but often there seems the intention to impart a moral in the refusal of Providence to temper warm weather to the full-bodied.

Old Tom Martin expressed a strong consciousness of such intention when he observed to the shocked Miss Selina, as Mr. Bill Snoddy, the stoutest citizen of the county, waddled abnormally up the aisle: "The Almighty must be gittin' a heap of fun out of Bill Snoddy to-night."

"Oh, Mr. Martin!" exclaimed Miss Tibbs, fluttering at his irreverence.

"Why, you would yourself. Miss Seliny," returned old Tom. Mr. Martin always spoke in one key, never altering the pitch of his high, dry, unctuous drawl, though, when his purpose was more than ordinarily humorous, his voice assumed a shade of melancholy. Now and then he meditatively passed his fingers through his gray beard, which followed the line of his jaw, leaving his upper lip and most of his chin smooth-shaven. "Did you ever reason out why folks laugh so much at fat people?" he continued. "No, ma'am. Neither'd anybody else."

"Why is it, Mr. Martin?" asked Miss Selina.

"It's like the Creator's sayin', 'Let there be light.' He says, 'Let ladies be lovely—'" (Miss Tibbs bowed)—"and 'Let men-folks be honest— sometimes;' and, 'Let fat people be held up to ridicule till they fall off.' You can't tell why it is; it was jest ordained that-a-way."

The room was so crowded that the juvenile portion of the assemblage was ensconced in the windows. Strange to say, the youth of Plattville were not present under protest, as their fellows of a metropolis would have been, lectures being well understood by the young of great cities to have instructive tendencies. The boys came to-night because they insisted upon coming. It was an event. Some of them had made sacrifices to come, enduring even the agony (next to hair-cutting in suffering) of having their ears washed. Conscious of parental eyes, they fronted the public with boyhood's professional expressionlessness, though they communicated with each other aside in a cipher-language of their own, and each group was a hot-bed of furtive gossip and sarcastic comment. Seated in the windows, they kept out what small breath of air might otherwise have stolen in to comfort the audience.

Their elders sat patiently dripping with perspiration, most of the gentlemen undergoing the unusual garniture of stiffly-starched collars, those who had not cultivated chin beards to obviate such arduous necessities of pomp and state, hardly bearing up under the added anxiety of cravats. However, they sat outwardly meek under the yoke; nearly all of them seeking a quiet solace of tobacco—not that they smoked; Heaven and the gallantry of Carlow County forbid—nor were there anywhere visible tokens of the comforting ministrations of nicotine to violate the eye of etiquette. It is an art of Plattville.

Suddenly there was a hum and a stir and a buzz of whispering in the room. Two gray old men and two pretty young women passed up the aisle to the platform. One old man was stalwart and ruddy, with a cordial eye and a handsome, smooth-shaven, big face. The other was bent and trembled slightly; his face was very white; he had a fine high brow, deeply lined, the brow of a scholar, and a grandly flowing white beard that covered his chest, the beard of a patriarch. One of the young women was tall and had the rosy cheeks and pleasant eyes of her father, who preceded her. The other was the strange lady.

A universal perturbation followed her progress up the aisle, if she had known it. She was small and fair, very daintily and beautifully made; a pretty Marquise whose head Greuze. should have painted Mrs. Columbus Landis, wife of the proprietor of the Palace Hotel, conferring with a lady in the next seat, applied an over-burdened adjective: "It ain't so much she's han'some, though she is, that—but don't you notice she's got a kind of smart look to her? Her bein' so teeny, kind of makes it more so, somehow, too." What stunned the gossips of the windows to awed admiration, however, was the unconcerned and stoical fashion in which she wore a long bodkin straight through her head. It seemed a large sacrifice merely to make sure one's hat remained in place.

The party took seats a little to the left and rear of the lecturer's table, and faced the audience. The strange lady chatted gaily with the other three, apparently as unconscious of the multitude of eyes fixed upon her as the gazers were innocent of rude intent. There were pretty young women in Plattville; Minnie Briscoe was the prettiest, and, as the local glass of fashion reflected, "the stylishest"; but this girl was different, somehow, in a way the critics were puzzled to discover—different, from the sparkle of her eyes and the crown of her trim sailor hat, to the edge of her snowy duck skirt.

Judd Bennett sighed a sigh that was heard in every corner of the room. As everybody immediately turned to look at him, he got up and went out.

It had long been a jocose fiction of Mr. Martin, who was a widower of thirty years' standing, that he and the gifted authoress by his side were in a state of courtship. Now he bent his rugged head toward her to whisper: "I never thought to see the day you'd have a rival in my affections. Miss Seliny, but yonder looks like it. I reckon I'll have to go up to Ben Tinkle's and buy that fancy vest he's had in stock this last twelve year or more. Will you take me back when she's left the city again; Miss Seliny?" he drawled. "I expect, maybe, Miss Sherwood is one of these here summer girls. I've heard of 'em but I never see one before. You better take warning and watch me—Fisbee won't have no clear field from now on."

The stranger leaned across to speak to Miss Briscoe and her sleeve touched the left shoulder of the old man with the patriarchal white beard. A moment later he put his right hand to that shoulder and gently moved it up and down with a caressing motion over the shabby black broadcloth her garment had touched.

"Look at that old Fisbee!" exclaimed Mr. Martin, affecting indignation. "Never be 'n half as spruced up and wide awake in all his life. He's prob'ly got her to listen to him on the decorations of Nineveh—it's my belief he was there when it was destroyed. Well, if I can't cut him out we'll get our respected young friend of the 'Herald' to do it."

"Sh!" returned Miss Tibbs. "Here he is."

The seats upon the platform were all occupied, except the two foremost ones in the centre (one on each side of a little table with a lamp, a pitcher of ice-water, and a glass) reserved for the lecturer and the gentleman who was to introduce him. Steps were audible in the hall, and every one turned to watch the door, where the distinguished pair now made their appearance in a hush of expectation over which the beating of the fans alone prevailed. The Hon. Kedge Halloway was one of the gleaners of the flesh-pots, himself, and he marched into the room unostentatiously mopping his shining expanse of brow with a figured handkerchief. He was a person of solemn appearance; a fat gold watch-chain which curved across his ponderous front, adding mysteriously to his gravity. At his side strolled a very tall, thin, rather stooping—though broad-shouldered— rather shabby young man with a sallow, melancholy face and deep-set eyes that looked tired. When they were seated, the

16

orator looked over his audience slowly and with an incomparable calm; then, as is always done, he and the melancholy young man exchanged whispers for a few moments. After this there was a pause, at the end of which the latter rose and announced that it was his pleasure and his privilege to introduce, that evening, a gentleman who needed no introduction to that assemblage. What citizen of Carlow needed an introduction, asked the speaker, to the orator they had applauded in the campaigns of the last twenty years, the statesman author of the Halloway Bill, the most honored citizen of the neighboring and flourishing county and city of Amo? And, the speaker would say, that if there were one thing the citizens of Carlow could be held to envy the citizens of Amo, it was the Honorable Kedge Halloway, the thinker, to whose widely-known paper they were about to have the pleasure and improvement of listening.

The introduction was so vehemently applauded that, had there been present a person connected with the theatrical profession, he might have been nervous for fear the introducer had prepared no encore. "Kedge is too smart to take it all to himself," commented Mr. Martin. "He knows it's half account of the man that said it."

He was not mistaken. Mr. Halloway had learned a certain perceptiveness on the stump. Resting one hand upon his unfolded notes upon the table, he turned toward the melancholy young man (who had subsided into the small of his back in his chair) and, after clearing his throat, observed with sudden vehemence that he must thank his gifted friend for his flattering remarks, but that when he said that Carlow envied Amo a Halloway, it must be replied that Amo grudged no glory to her sister county of Carlow, but, if Amo could find envy in her heart it would be because Carlow possessed a paper so sterling, so upright, so brilliant, so enterprising as the "Carlow County Herald," and a journalist so talented, so gifted, so energetic, so fearless, as its editor.

The gentleman referred to showed very faint appreciation of these ringing compliments. There was a lamp on the table beside him, against which, to the view of Miss Sherwood of Rouen, his face was silhouetted, and very rarely had it been her lot to see a man look less enthusiastic under public and favorable comment of himself. She wondered if he, also, remembered the Muggleton cricket match and the subsequent dinner oratory.

The lecture proceeded. The orator winged away to soary heights with gestures so vigorous as to cause admiration for his pluck in making use of them on such a night; the perspiration streamed down his face, his neck grew purple, and he dared the very face of apoplexy, binding his auditors with a double spell. It is true that long before the peroration the windows were empty and the boys were eating stolen, unripe fruit in the orchards of the listeners. The thieves were sure of an alibi.

The Hon. Mr. Halloway reached a logical conclusion which convinced even the combative and unwilling that the present depends largely upon the past, while the future will be determined, for the most part, by the conditions of the present. "The future," he cried, leaning forward with an expression of solemn warning, "The future is in our own hands, ladies and gentlemen of the city of Plattville. Is it not so? We will find it so. Turn it over in your minds." He leaned backward and folded his hands benevolently on his stomach and said in a searching whisper; "Ponder it." He waited for them to ponder it, and little Mr. Swanter, the druggist and bookseller, who prided himself on his politeness and who was seated directly in front, scratched his head and knit his brows to show that he was pondering it. The stillness was intense; the fans ceased to beat; Mr. Snoddy could be heard breathing dangerously. Mr. Swanter was considering the advisability of drawing a pencil from his pocket and figuring on it upon his cuff, when suddenly, with the energy of a whirlwind, the lecturer threw out his arms to their fullest extent and roared: "It is a *fact*! It is carven on stone in the gloomy caverns of *time*. It is writ in *fire* on the imperishable walls of Fate!"

After the outburst, his voice sank with startling rapidity to a tone of honeyed confidence, and he wagged an inviting forefinger at Mr. Snoddy, who opened his mouth. "Shall we take an example? Not from the marvellous, my friends; let us seek an illustration from the ordinary. Is that not better? One familiar to the humblest of us. One we can all comprehend. One from our every-day life. One which will interest even the young. Yes. The common house-fly. On a window-sill we place a bit of fly-paper, and contiguous to it, a flower upon which the happy insect likes to feed and rest. The little fly approaches. See, he hovers between the two. One is a fatal trap, an ambuscade, and the other a safe harbor and an innocuous haven. But mystery allures him. He poises, undecided. That is the present. That, my friends, is the Present! What will he do? *What* will he do? What will he *do*? Memories of the past are whispering to him: 'Choose the flower. Light on the posy.' Here we clearly see the influence of the past upon the present. But, to employ a figure of speech, the fly-paper beckons to the insect toothsomely, and, thinks he; 'Shall I give it a try? Shall I? Shall I give it a try?' The future is in his own hands to make or unmake. The past, the voice of Providence, has counselled him: 'Leave it alone, leave it alone, little fly. Go away from there.' Does he heed the warning? Does he heed it, ladies and gentlemen? Does he? Ah, no! He springs into the air, decides between the two attractions, one of them, so deadly to his interests and—*drops upon the fly-paper to perish miserably*! The future is in his hands no longer. We must lie upon the bed that we have made, nor can Providence change its unalterable decrees."

After the tragedy, the orator took a swallow of water, mopped his brow with the figured handkerchief and announced that a new point herewith presented itself for consideration. The audience sank back with a gasp of release from the strain of attention. Minnie Briscoe, leaning back, breathless like the others, became conscious that a tremor agitated her visitor. Miss Sherwood had bent her head behind the shelter of the judge's broad shoulders; was shaking slightly and had covered her face with her hands.

"What is it, Helen?" whispered Miss Briscoe, anxiously. "What is it? Is something the matter?"

"Nothing. Nothing, dear." She dropped her hands from her face. Her cheeks were deep crimson, and she bit her lip with determination.

"Oh, but there is! Why, you've tears in your eyes. Are you faint? What is it?"

"It is only—only——" Miss Sherwood choked, then cast a swift glance at the profile of the melancholy young man. The perfectly dismal decorum of this gentleman seemed to inspire her to maintain her own gravity. "It is only that it seemed such a pity about that fly," she explained. From where they sat the journalistic silhouette was plainly visible, and both Fisbee and Miss Sherwood looked toward it often, the former with the wistful, apologetic fidelity one sees in the eyes of an old setter watching his master.

When the lecture was over many of the audience pressed forward to shake the Hon. Mr. Halloway's hand. Tom Martin hooked his arm in that of the sallow gentleman and passed out with him.

"Mighty humanizin' view Kedge took of that there insect," remarked Mr. Martin. "I don't recollect I ever heard of no mournfuller error than that'n. I noticed you spoke of Halloway as a 'thinker,' without mentioning what kind. I didn't know, before, that you were as cautious a man as that."

"Does your satire find nothing sacred, Martin?" returned the other, "not even the Honorable Kedge Halloway?"

"I wouldn't presume," replied old Tom, "to make light of the catastrophe that overtook the heedless fly. When Halloway went on to other subjects I was so busy picturin' the last moments of that closin' life, stuck there in the fly-paper, I couldn't listen to him. But there's no use dwellin' on a sorrow we can't help. Look at the moon; it's full enough to cheer us up." They had emerged from the court-house and paused on the street as the stream of townsfolk divided and passed by them to take different routes leading from the Square. Not far away, some people were getting into a buckboard. Fisbee and Miss Sherwood were already on the rear seat.

"Who's with him, to-night, Mr. Fisbee?" asked Judge Briscoe in a low voice.

"No one. He is going directly to the office. To-morrow is Thursday, one of our days of publication."

"Oh, then it's all right. Climb in, Minnie, we're waiting for you." The judge offered his hand to his daughter.

"In a moment, father," she answered. "I'm going to ask him to call," she said to the other girl.

"But won't he—"

Miss Briscoe laughed. "He never comes to see me!" She walked over to where Martin and the young man were looking up at the moon, and addressed the journalist.

"I've been trying to get a chance to speak to you for a week," she said, offering him her hand; "I wanted to tell you I had a friend coming to visit me Won't you come to see us? She's here."

The young man bowed. "Thank you," he answered. "Thank you, very much. I shall be very glad." His tone had the meaningless quality of perfunctory courtesy; Miss Briscoe detected only the courtesy; but the strange lady marked the lack of intention in his words.

"Don't you include me, Minnie?" inquired Mr Martin, plaintively. "I'll try not to be too fascinatin', so as to give our young friend a show. It was love at first sight with me. I give Miss Seliny warning soon as your folks come in and I got a good look at the lady."

As the buckboard drove away, Miss Sherwood, who had been gazing steadfastly at the two figures still standing in the street, the tall ungainly old one, and the taller, loosely-held young one (he had not turned to look at her) withdrew her eyes from them, bent them seriously upon Fisbee, and asked: "What did you mean when you said no one was with him to-night?"

"That no one was watching him," he answered.

"Watching him? I don't understand."

"Yes; he has been shot at from the woods at night and——"

The girl shivered. "But who watches him?"

"The young men of the town. He has a habit of taking long walks after dark, and he is heedless of all remonstrance. He laughs at the idea of curtailing the limit of his strolls or keeping within the town when night has fallen; so the young men have organized a guard for him, and every evening one of them follows him until he goes to the office to work for the night. It is a different young man every evening, and the watcher follows at a distance so that he does not suspect."

"But how many people know of this arrangement?"

"Nearly every one in the county except the Cross-Roads people, though it is not improbable that they have discovered it."

"And has no one told him"

20

"No; it would annoy him; he would not allow it to continue. He will not even arm himself."

"They follow and watch him night after night, and every one knows and no one tells him? Oh, I must say," cried the girl, "I think these are good people."

The stalwart old man on the front seat shook out the reins and whined the whip over his roans' backs. "They are the people of your State and mine. Miss Sherwood," he said in his hearty voice, "the best people in God's world—and I'm not running for Congress, either!"

"But how about the Six-Cross-Roads people, father?" asked Minnie.

"We'll wipe them clean out some day," answered her father—"possibly judicially, possibly——"

"Surely judiciously?" suggested Miss Sherwood.

"If you care to see what a bad settlement looks like, we'll drive through there to-morrow—by daylight," said Briscoe. "Even the doctor doesn't insist on being in that neighborhood after dark. They are trying their best to get Harkless, and if they do——"

"If they do!" repeated Miss Sherwood. She clasped Fisbee's hand gently. His eyes shone and he touched her fingers with a strange, shy reverence.

"You will meet him to-morrow," he said.

She laughed and pressed his hand. "I'm afraid not. He wasn't even interested enough to look at me."

CHAPTER III

LONESOMENESS

When the rusty hands of the office clock marked half-past four, the editor-in-chief of the "Carlow County Herald" took his hand out of his hair, wiped his pen on his last notice from the White-Caps, put on his coat, swept out the close little entry, and left the sanctum for the bright June afternoon.

He chose the way to the west, strolling thoughtfully out of town by the white, hot, deserted Main Street, and thence onward by the country road into which its proud half-mile of old brick store buildings, tumbled-down frame shops and thinly painted cottages degenerated. The sun was in his face, where the road ran between the summer fields, lying waveless, low, gracious in promise; but, coming to a wood of hickory and beech and walnut that stood beyond, he might turn his down-bent-hat-brim up and hold his head erect. Here the shade fell deep and cool on the green tangle of rag and iron weed and long grass in the corners of the snake fence, although the sun beat upon the road so dose beside. There was no movement in the crisp young leaves overhead; high in the boughs there was a quick flirt of crimson where two robins hopped noiselessly. No insect raised resentment of the lonesomeness: the late afternoon, when the air is quite still, had come; yet there rested—somewhere—on the quiet day, a faint, pleasant, woody smell. It came to the editor of the "Herald" as he climbed to the top rail of the fence for a seat, and he drew a long, deep breath to get the elusive odor more luxuriously—and then it was gone altogether.

"A habit of delicacies," he said aloud, addressing the wide silence complainingly. He drew a faded tobacco-bag and a brier pipe from his coat pocket and filled and lit the pipe. "One taste—and they quit," he finished, gazing solemnly upon the shining little town down the road. He twirled the pouch mechanically about his finger, and then, suddenly regarding it, patted it caressingly. It had been a giddy little bag, long ago, satin, and gay with embroidery in the colors of the editor's university; and although now it was frayed to the verge of tatters, it still bore an air of pristine jauntiness, an air of which its owner in no wise partook. He looked from it over the fields toward the town in the clear distance and sighed softly as he put the pouch back in his pocket, and, resting his arm on his knee and his chin in his hand, sat blowing clouds of smoke out of the shade into the sunshine, absently watching the ghostly shadows dance on the white dust of the road.

A little garter snake crept under the fence beneath him and disappeared in the underbrush; a rabbit progressing timidly on his travels by a series of brilliant dashes and terror-smitten halts, came within a few yards of him, sat up with quivering nose and eyes alight with fearful imaginings— vanished, a flash of fluffy brown and white. Shadows grew longer; the brier pipe sputtered feebly in depletion and was refilled. A cricket chirped and heard answer; there was a woodland stir of breezes; and the pair of robins left the branches overhead in eager flight, vacating before the arrival of a great flock of blackbirds hastening thither ere the eventide should be upon them. The blackbirds came, chattered, gossiped, quarrelled, and beat each other with their wings above the smoker sitting on the top fence rail.

But he had remembered—it was Commencement. To-day, a thousand miles to the east, a company of grave young gentlemen sat in semi-circular rows before a central altar, while above them rose many tiers of mothers and sisters and sweethearts, listening to the final word. He could see it all very clearly: the lines of freshly shaven, boyish faces, the dainty gowns, the flowers and bright eyes above, and the light that filtered in through stained glass to fall softly over them all, with, here and there, a vivid splash of color, Gothic shaped. He could see the throngs of white-clad loungers under the elms without, under-classmen, bored by the Latin addresses and escaped to the sward and breeze of the campus; there were the troops of roistering graduates trotting about arm in arm, and singing; he heard the mandolins on the little balconies play an old refrain and the university cheering afterward; saw the old professor he had cared for most of all, with the thin white hair straggling over his silken hood, following the band in the sparse ranks of his class. And he saw his own Commencement Day—and the station at the junction where he stood the morning after, looking across the valley at the old towers for the last time; saw the broken groups of his class, standing upon the platform on the other side of the tracks, waiting for the south-bound train as he and others waited for the north-bound—and they all sang "Should auld acquaintance be forgot;" and, while they looked across at each other, singing, the shining rails between them wavered and blurred as the engine rushed in and separated them and their lives thenceforth. He filled his pipe again and spoke to the phantoms gliding over the dust—"Seven years!" He was occupied with the realization that there had been a man in his class whose ambition needed no restraint, his promise was so complete—in the strong belief of the university, a belief he could not help knowing— and that seven years to a day from his Commencement this man was sitting on a fence rail in Indiana.

Down the road a buggy came creaking toward him, gray with dust, the top canted permanently to one side, old and frayed, like the fat, shaggy, gray mare that drew it; her unchecked, despondent head lowering before her, while her incongruous tail waved incessantly, like the banner of a storming party. The editor did not hear the flop of the mare's feet nor the sound of the wheels, so deep was his reverie, till the vehicle was nearly opposite him. The red-faced and perspiring driver drew rein, and the journalist looked up and waved a long white hand to him in greeting.

"Howdy' do, Mr. Harkless?" called the man in the buggy. "Soakin' in the weather?" He spoke in shouts, though neither was hard of hearing.

"Yes; just soaking," answered Harkless; "it's such a gypsy day. How is Mr. Bowlder?"

"I'm givin' good satisfaction, thankye, and all at home. She's in town; goin' in after her now."

"Give Mrs. Bowlder my regards," said the journalist, comprehending the symbolism. "How is Hartley?"

The farmer's honest face shaded over, a second. "He's be'n steady ever sence the night you brought him out home; six weeks straight. I'm kind of bothered about to-morrow—It's show-day and he wants to come in town with us, and seems if I hadn't any call to say no. I reckon he'll have to take his chances—and us, too." He raised the reins and clucked to the gray mare; "Well, she'll be mad I ain't there long ago. Ride in with me?"

"No, I thank you. I'll walk in for the sake of my appetite."

"Wouldn't encourage it *too* much—livin' at the Palace Hotel,'" observed Bowlder. "Sorry ye won't ride." He gathered the loose ends of the reins in his hands, leaned far over the dashboard and struck the mare a hearty thwack; the tattered banner of tail jerked indignantly, but she consented to move down the road. Bowlder thrust his big head through the sun-curtain behind him and continued the conversation: "See the White-Caps ain't got ye yet."

"No, not yet." Harkless laughed.

"Reckon the boys 'druther ye stayed in town after dark," the other called back; then, as the mare stumbled into a trot, "Well, come out and see us— if ye kin spare time from the jedge's." The latter clause seemed to be an afterthought intended with humor, for Bowlder accompanied it with the loud laughter of sylvan timidity, risking a joke. Harkless nodded without the least apprehension of his meaning, and waved farewell as Bowlder finally turned his attention to the mare. When the flop, flop of her hoofs had died out, the journalist realized that the day was silent no longer; it was verging into evening.

He dropped from the fence and turned his face toward town and supper. He felt the light and life about him; heard the clatter of the blackbirds above him; heard the homing bees hum by, and saw the vista of white road and level landscape, framed on two sides by the branches of the grove, a vista of infinitely stretching fields of green, lined here and there with woodlands and flat to the horizon line, the village lying in their lap. No roll of meadow, no rise of pasture land, relieved their serenity nor shouldered up from them to be called a hill. A second great flock of blackbirds was settling down over the Plattville maples. As they hung in the fair dome of the sky below the few white clouds, it occurred to Harkless that some supping god had inadvertently peppered his custard, and now inverted and emptied his gigantic blue dish upon the earth, the innumerable little black dots seeming to poise for a moment, then floating slowly down from the heights.

A farm-bell rang in the distance, a tinkling coming small and mellow from far away, and at the lonesomeness of that sound he heaved a long, mournful sigh. The next instant he broke into laughter, for another bell rang over the fields, the court-house bell in the Square. The first four strokes were given with mechanical regularity, the pride of the custodian who operated the bell being to produce the effect of a clock-work bell such as he had once heard in the court-house at Rouen; but the fifth and sixth strokes were halting achievements, as, after four o'clock, he often lost count on the strain of the effort for precise imitation. There was a pause after the sixth, then a dubious and reluctant stroke—seven—a longer pause, followed by a final ring with desperate decision—eight! Harkless looked at his watch; it was twenty minutes of six.

As he crossed the court-house yard to the Palace Hotel, he stopped to exchange a word with the bell-ringer, who, seated on the steps, was mopping his brow with an air of hard-earned satisfaction.

"Good-evening, Schofields'," he said. "You came in strong on the last stroke, to-night."

"What we need here," responded the bell-ringer, "is more public-spirited men. I ain't kickin' on you, Mr. Harkless, no sir; but we want more men like they got in Rouen; we want men that'll git Main Street paved with block or asphalt; men that'll put in factories, men that'll act and not set round like that ole fool Martin and laugh and polly-woggle and make fun of public sperrit, day in and out. I reckon I do my best for the city."

"Oh, nobody minds Tom Martin," answered Harkless. "It's only half the time he means anything by what he says."

"That's jest what I hate about him," returned the bell-ringer in a tone of high complaint; "you can't never tell which half it is. Look at him now!" Over in front of the hotel Martin was standing, talking to the row of coatless loungers who sat with their chairs tilted back against the props of the wooden awning that projected over the sidewalk. Their faces were turned toward the court-house, and even those lost in meditative whittling had looked up to laugh. Martin, his hands in the pockets of his alpaca coat, his rusty silk hat tilted forward till the wide brim rested almost on the bridge of his nose, was addressing them in his one-keyed voice, the melancholy whine of which, though not the words, penetrated to the court-house steps.

The bell-ringer, whose name was Henry Schofield, but who was known as Schofield's Henry (popularly abbreviated to Schofields') was moved to indignation. "Look at him," he cried. "Look at him! Everlastingly goin' on about my bell! Let him talk, jest let him talk." The supper gong boomed inside the hotel and Harkless bade the bell-ringer good-night. As he moved away the latter called after him: "He don't disturb nobody. Let him talk. Who pays any 'tention to him I'd like to know?" There was a burst of laughter from the whittlers. Schofields' sat in patient silence for a full minute, as one who knew that no official is too lofty to escape the anathemas of envy. Then he sprang to his feet and shook his fist at Martin, who was disappearing within the door of the hotel. "Go to Halifax!" he shouted.

The dining-room of the Palace Hotel was a large, airy apartment, rustling with artistically perforated and slashed pink paper that hung everywhere, at this season of the year, to lend festal effect as well as to palliate the scourge of flies. There were six or seven large tables, all vacant except that at which Columbus Landis, the landlord, sat with his guests, while his wife and children ate in the kitchen by their own preference. Transient trade was light in Plattville; nobody ever came there, except occasional commercial travellers who got out of town the instant it was possible, and who said awful things if, by the exigencies of the railway time-table, they were left over night.

Behind the host's chair stood a red-haired girl in a blue cotton gown; and in her hand she languidly waved a long instrument made of clustered strips of green and white and yellow tissue paper fastened to a wooden wand; with this she amiably amused the flies except at such times as the conversation proved too interesting, when she was apt to rest it on the shoulder of one of the guests. This happened each time the editor of the "Herald" joined in the talk. As the men seated themselves they all nodded to her and said, "G'd evening, Cynthy." Harkless always called her Charmion; no one knew why. When he came in she moved around the table to a chair directly opposite him, and held that station throughout the meal, with her eyes fixed on his face. Mr. Martin noted this manoeuvre—it occurred regularly twice a day—with a stealthy smile at the girl, and her light skin flushed while her lip curled shrewishly at the old gentleman. "Oh, all right, Cynthy," he whispered to her, and chuckled aloud at her angry toss of the head.

"Schofields' seemed to be kind of put out with me this evening," he remarked, addressing himself to the company. "He's the most ungratefullest cuss I ever come up with. I was only oratin' on how proud the city ought to be of him. He fairly keeps Plattville's sportin' spirit on the gog; 'die out, wasn't for him. There's be'n more money laid on him whether he'll strike over and above the hour, or under and below, or whether he'll strike fifteen minutes before time, or twenty after, than— well, sir, we'd all forgit the language if it wasn't for Schofields' bell to keep us talkin'; that's *my* claim. Dull days, think of the talk he furnishes all over town. Think what he's done to promote conversation. Now, for instance, Anna Belle Bardlock's got a beau, they say"—here old Tom tilted back in his chair and turned an innocent eye upon a youth across the table, young William Todd, who was blushing over his griddle-cakes—"and I hear he's a good deal scared of Anna Belle and not just what you might call brash with her. They say every Sunday night he'll go up to Bardlocks' and call on Anna Belle from half-past six till nine, and when he's got into his chair he sets and looks at the floor and the crayon portraits till about seven; then he opens his tremblin' lips and says, 'Reckon Schofields' must be on his way to the court-house by this time.' And about an hour later, when Schofields' hits four or five, he'll speak up again, 'Say, I reckon he means eight.' 'Long towards nine o'clock, they say he skews around in his chair and says, 'Wonder if he'll strike before time or after,' and Anna Belle answers out loud, 'I hope after,' for politeness; but in her soul she says, 'I pray before'; and then Schofields' hits her up for eighteen or twenty, and Anna Belle's company reaches for his hat. Three Sundays ago he turned around before he went out and said, 'Do you like apple-butter?' but never waited to find out. It's the same programme every Sunday evening, and Jim

Bardlock says Anna Belle's so worn out you wouldn't hardly know her for the blithe creature she was last year—the excitement's be'n too much for her!"

Poor William Todd bent his fiery face over the table and suffered the general snicker in helpless silence. Then there was quiet for a space, broken only by the click of knives against the heavy china and the indolent rustle of Cynthia's fly-brush.

"Town so still," observed the landlord, finally, with a complacent glance at the dessert course of prunes to which his guests were helping themselves from a central reservoir, "Town so still, hardly seems like show-day's come round again. Yet there's be'n some shore signs lately: when my shavers come honeyin' up with, 'Say, pa, ain't they no urrands I can go for ye, pa? I like to run 'em for you, pa,'—'relse, 'Oh, pa, ain't they no water I can haul, or nothin', pa?'—'relse, as little Rosina T. says, this morning, 'Pa, I always pray fer *you* pa,' and pa this and pa that-you can rely either Christmas or show-day's mighty close."

William Todd, taking occasion to prove himself recovered from confusion, remarked casually that there was another token of the near approach of the circus, as ole Wilkerson was drunk again.

"There's a man!" exclaimed Mr. Martin with enthusiasm. "There's the feller for *my* money! He does his duty as a citizen more discriminatin'ly on public occasions than any man I ever see. There's Wilkerson's celebration when there's a funeral; look at the difference between it and on Fourth of July. Why, sir, it's as melancholy as a hearse-plume, and sympathy ain't the word for it when he looks at the remains, no sir; preacher nor undertaker, either, ain't *half* as blue and respectful. Then take his circus spree. He come into the store this afternoon, head up, marchin' like a grenadier and shootin' his hand out before his face and drawin' it back again, and hollering out, 'Ta, ta, ta-ra-ta, ta, ta-ta-ra'—why, the dumbest man ever lived could see in a minute show's 'comin' to-morrow and Wilkerson's playin' the trombone. Then he'd snort and goggle like an elephant. Got the biggest sense of appropriateness of any man in the county, Wilkerson has. Folks don't half appreciate him."

As each boarder finished his meal he raided the glass of wooden toothpicks and went away with no standing on the order of his going; but Martin waited for Harkless, who, not having attended to business so concisely as the others, was the last to leave the table, and they stood for a moment under the awning outside, lighting their cigars.

"Call on the judge, to-night?" asked Martin.

"No," said Harkless. "Why?"

"Didn't you see the lady with Minnie and the judge at the lecture?"

"I caught a glimpse of her. That's what Bowlder meant, then."

"I don't know what Bowlder meant, but I guess you better go out there, young man. She might not stay here long."

CHAPTER IV

THE WALRUS AND THE CARPENTER

The Briscoe buckboard rattled along the elastic country-road, the roans setting a sharp pace as they turned eastward on the pike toward home and supper.

"They'll make the eight miles in three-quarters of an hour," said the judge, proudly. He pointed ahead with his whip. "Just beyond that bend we pass through Six-Cross-Roads."

Miss Sherwood leaned forward eagerly. "Can we see 'Mr. Wimby's' house from here?"

"No, it's on the other side, nearer town; we pass it later. It's the only respectable-looking house in this township." They reached the turn of the road, and the judge touched up his colts to a sharper gait. "No need of dallying," he observed quietly. "It always makes me a little sick just to see the place. I'd hate to have a break-down here."

They came in sight of a squalid settlement, built raggedly about a blacksmith's shop and a saloon. Half-a-dozen shanties clustered near the forge, a few roofs scattered through the shiftlessly cultivated fields, four or five barns propped by fence-rails, some sheds with gaping apertures through which the light glanced from side to side, a squad of thin, "razor-back" hogs—now and then worried by gaunt hounds—and some abused-looking hens, groping about disconsolately in the mire, a broken-topped buggy with a twisted wheel settling into the mud of the middle of the road (there was always abundant mud, here, in the dryest summer), a lowering face sneering from a broken window—Six-Cross-Roads was forbidding and forlorn enough by day. The thought of what might issue from it by night was unpleasant, and the legends of the Cross-Roads, together with an unshapen threat, easily fancied in the atmosphere of the place, made Miss Sherwood shiver as though a cold draught had crossed her.

"It is so sinister!" she exclaimed. "And so unspeakably mean! This is where they live, the people who hate him, is it? The 'White-Caps'?"

"They are just a lot of rowdies," replied Briscoe. "You have your rough corners in big cities, and I expect there are mighty few parts of any country that don't have their tough neighborhoods, only Six-Cross-Roads happens to be worse than most. They choose to call themselves 'White-Caps,' but I guess it's just a name they like to give themselves. Usually White-Caps are a vigilance committee going after rascalities the law doesn't reach, or won't reach, but these fellows are not that kind. They got together to wipe out their grudges—and sometimes they didn't need any grudge and let loose their deviltries just for pure orneriness; setting haystacks afire and such like; or, where a farmer had offended them, they would put on their silly toggery and take him out at midnight and whip him and plunder his house and chase the horses and cattle into his corn, maybe. They say the women went with them on their raids."

"And he was the first to try to stop them?"

"Well, you see our folks are pretty long-suffering," Briscoe replied, apologetically. "We'd sort of got used to the meanness of the Cross-Roads. It took a stranger to stir things up—and he did. He sent eight of 'em to the penitentiary, some for twenty years."

As they passed the saloon a man stepped into the doorway and looked at them. He was coatless and clad in garments worn to the color of dust; his bare head was curiously malformed, higher on one side than on the other, and though the buckboard passed rapidly, and at a distance, this singular lopsidedness was plainly visible to the occupants, lending an ugly significance to his meagre, yellow face. He was tall, lean, hard, powerfully built. He eyed the strangers with affected languor, and then, when they had gone by, broke into sudden, loud laughter.

"That was Bob Skillett, the worst of the lot," said the judge. "Harkless sent his son and one brother to prison, and it nearly broke his heart that he couldn't swear to Bob."

When they were beyond the village and in the open road again. Miss Sherwood took a deep breath. "I think I breathe more freely," she said. "That was a hideous laugh he sent after us. I had heard of places like this before—and I don't think I care to see many of them. As I understand it, Six-Cross-Roads is entirely vicious, isn't it; and bears the same relation to the country that the slums do to a city?'"

"That's about it. They make their own whiskey. I presume; and they have their own fights amongst themselves, but they settle 'em themselves, too, and keep their own counsel and hush it up. Lige Willetts, Minnie's friend —I guess she's told you about Lige?—well, Lige Willetts will go anywhere when he's following a covey, though mostly the boys leave this part of the country alone when they're hunting; but Lige got into a thicket back of the forge one morning, and he came on a crowd of buzzards quarrelling over a heap on the ground, and he got out in a hurry. He said he was sure it was a dog; but he ran almost all the way to Plattville."

"Father!" exclaimed his daughter, leaning from the back seat. "Don't tell such stories to Helen; she'll think we're horrible, and you'll frighten her, too."

"Well, it isn't exactly a lady's story," said the judge. He glanced at his guest's face and chuckled. "I guess we won't frighten her much," he went on. "Young lady, I don't believe you'd be afraid of many things, would you? You don't look like it. Besides, the Cross-Roads isn't Plattville, and the White-Caps have been too scared to do anything much, except try to get even with the 'Herald,' for the last two years;

30

ever since it went for them. They're laying for Harkless partly for revenge and partly because they daren't do anything until he's out of the way."

The girl gave a low cry with a sharp intake of breath. "Ah! One grows tired of this everlasting American patience! Why don't the Plattville people do something before they——"

"It's just as I say," Briscoe answered; "our folks are sort of used to them. I expect we do about all we can; the boys look after him nights, and the main trouble is that we can't make him understand he ought to be more afraid of them. If he'd lived here all his life he would be. You know there's an old-time feud between the Cross-Roads and our folks; goes way back into pioneer history and mighty few know anything of it. Old William Platt and the forefathers of the Bardlocks and Tibbses and Briscoes and Schofields moved up here from North Carolina a good deal just to get away from some bad neighbors, mostly Skilletts and Johnsons—one of the Skilletts had killed old William Platt's two sons. But the Skilletts and Johnsons followed all the way to Indiana to join in making the new settlement, and they shot Platt at his cabin door one night, right where the court-house stands to-day. Then the other settlers drove them out for good, and they went seven miles west and set up a still. A band of Indians, on the way to join the Shawnee Prophet at Tippecanoe, came down on the Cross-Roads, and the Cross-Roaders bought them off with bad whiskey and sent them over to Plattville. Nearly all the Plattville men were away, fighting under Harrison, and when they came back there were only a few half-crazy women and children left. They'd hid in the woods.

"The men stopped just long enough to hear how it was, and started for the Cross-Roads; but the Cross-Roads people caught them in an ambush and not many of our folks got back.

"We really never did get even with them, though all the early settlers lived and died still expecting to see the day when Plattville would go over and pay off the score. It's the same now as it was then, good stock with us, bad stock over here; and all the country riff-raff in creation come and live with 'em when other places get too hot to hold them. Only one or two of us old folks know what the original trouble was about; but you ask a Plattville man, to-day, what he thinks of the Cross-Roads and he'll be mighty apt to say, 'I guess we'll all have to go over there some time and wipe those hoodlums out.' It's been coming to that a long time. The work the 'Herald' did has come nearer bringing us even with Six-Cross-Roads than anything else ever has. Queer, too—a man that's only lived in Plattville a few years to be settling such an old score for us. They'll do their best to get him, and if they do there'll be trouble of an illegal nature. I think our people would go over there again, but I expect there wouldn't be any ambush this time; and the pioneers, might rest easier in—" He broke off suddenly and nodded to a little old man in a buckboard, who was turning off from the road into a farm lane which led up to a trim cottage with a honeysuckle vine by the door. "That's Mrs. Wimby's husband," said the judge in an undertone.

Miss Sherwood observed that "Mrs. Wimby's husband" was remarkable for the exceeding plaintiveness of his expression. He was a weazened, blank, pale-eyed little man, with a thin, white mist of neck whisker; his coat was so large for him that the sleeves were rolled up from his wrists with several turns, and, as he climbed painfully to the ground to open the gate of the lane, it needed no perspicuous eye to perceive that his trousers had been made for a much larger man, for, as his uncertain foot left the step of his vehicle, one baggy leg of the garment fell down over his foot, completely concealing his boot and hanging some inches beneath. A faintly vexed expression crossed his face as he endeavored to arrange the disorder, but he looked up and returned Briscoe's bow, sadly, with an air of explaining that he was accustomed to trouble, and that the trousers had behaved no worse than he expected.

No more inoffensive or harmless figure than this feeble little old man could be imagined; yet his was the distinction of having received a terrible visit from his neighbors of the Cross-Roads. Mrs. Wimby was a widow, who owned a comfortable farm, and she had refused every offer of the neighboring ill-eligible bachelors to share it. However, a vagabonding tinker won her heart, and after their marriage she continued to be known as "Mrs. Wimby"; for so complete was the bridegroom's insignificance that it extended to his name, which proved quite unrememberable, and he was usually called "Widder-Woman Wimby's Husband," or, more simply, "Mr. Wimby." The bride supplied the needs of his wardrobe with the garments of her former husband, and, alleging this proceeding as the cause of their anger, the Cross-Roads raiders, clad as "White-Caps," broke into the farmhouse one night, looted it, tore the old man from his bed, and compelling his wife, who was tenderly devoted to him, to watch, they lashed him with sapling shoots till he was near to death. A little yellow cur, that had followed his master on his wanderings, was found licking the old man's wounds, and they deluged the dog with kerosene and then threw the poor animal upon a bonfire they had made, and danced around it in heartiest enjoyment.

The man recovered, but that was no palliation of the offense to the mind of a hot-eyed young man from the East, who was besieging the county authorities for redress and writing brimstone and saltpetre for his paper. The powers of the county proving either lackadaisical or timorous, he appealed to those of the State, and he went every night to sleep at a farmhouse, the owner of which had received a warning from the "White-Caps." And one night it befell that he was rewarded, for the raiders attempted an entrance. He and the farmer and the former's sons beat off the marauders and did a satisfactory amount of damage in return. Two of the "White-Caps" they captured and bound, and others they recognized. Then the State authorities hearkened to the voice of the "Herald" and its owner; there were arrests, and in the course of time there was a trial. Every prisoner proved an alibi, could have proved a dozen; but the editor of the "Herald," after virtually conducting the prosecution, went upon the stand and swore to man after man. Eight men went to the penitentiary on his evidence, five of them for twenty years. The Plattville Brass Band serenaded the editor of the "Herald" again.

There were no more raids, and the Six-Cross-Roads men who were left kept to their hovels, appalled and shaken, but, as time went by and left them unmolested, they recovered a measure of their hardiness and began to think on what they should do to the man who had brought misfortune and terror upon them. For a long time he had been publishing their threatening letters and warnings in a column which he headed: "Humor of the Day."

"Harkless don't understand the Cross-Roads," Briscoe said to Miss Sherwood as they left the Wimby farm behind; "and then he's like most of us; hardly any of us realizes that harm's ever going to come to *us*. Harkless was anxious enough about other people, but——"

The young lady interrupted him, touching his arm. "Look!" she said, "Didn't you see a child, a little girl, ahead of us on the road?"

"I noticed one a minute ago, but she's not there now," answered Briscoe.

"There was a child walking along the road just ahead, but she turned and saw us coming, and she disappeared in the most curious way; she seemed to melt into the weeds at the roadside, across from the elder-bush yonder."

The judge pulled in the horses by the elder-bush. "No child here, now," he said, "but you're right; there certainly was one, just before you spoke." The young corn was low in the fields, and there was no hiding-place in sight.

"I'm very superstitious; I am sure it was an imp," Miss Sherwood said. "An imp or a very large chameleon; she was exactly the color of the road."

"A Cross-Roads imp," said the judge, lifting the reins, "and in that case we might as well give up. I never set up to be a match for those people, and the children are as mean as their fathers, and smarter."

When the buckboard had rattled on a hundred yards or so, a little figure clad in a tattered cotton gown rose up from the weeds, not ten feet from where the judge had drawn rein, and continued its march down the road toward Plattville, capering in the dust and pursuing the buckboard with malignant gestures till the clatter of the horses was out of hearing, the vehicle out of sight.

Something over two hours later, as Mr. Martin was putting things to rights in his domain, the Dry-Goods Emporium, previous to his departure for the evening's gossip and checkers at the drug-store, he stumbled over something soft, lying on the floor behind a counter. The thing rose, and would have evaded him, but he put out his hands and pinioned it and dragged it to the show-window where the light of the fading day defined his capture. The capture shrieked and squirmed and fought earnestly. Grasped by the shoulder he held a lean, fierce-eyed, undersized girl of fourteen, clad in one ragged cotton garment, unless the coat of dust she wore over all may be esteemed another. Her cheeks were sallow, and her brow was already shrewdly lined, and her eyes were as hypocritical as they were savage. She was very thin and little, but old Tom's brown face grew a shade nearer white when the light fell upon her.

"You're no Plattville girl," he said sharply.

"You lie!" cried the child. "You lie! I am! You leave me go, will you? I'm lookin' fer pap and you're a liar!"

"You crawled in here to sleep, after your seven-mile walk, didn't you?" Martin went on.

"You're a liar," she screamed again.

"Look here," said Martin, slowly, "you go back to Six-Cross-Roads and tell your folks that if anything happens to a hair of Mr. Harkless's head every shanty in your town will burn, and your grandfather and your father and your uncles and your brothers and your cousins and your second-cousins and your third-cousins will never have the good luck to see the penitentiary. Reckon you can remember that message? But before I let you go to carry it, I guess you might as well hand out the paper they sent you over here with."

His prisoner fell into a paroxysm of rage, and struck at him.

"I'll git pap to kill ye," she shrieked. "I don' know nothin' 'bout yer Six-Cross-Roads, ner no papers, ner yer dam Mister Harkels neither, ner *you*, ye razor-backed ole devil! Pap'll kill ye; leave me go—leave me *go*!—Pap'll kill ye; I'll git him to *kill* ye!" Suddenly her struggles ceased; her eyes closed; her tense little muscles relaxed and she drooped toward the floor; the old man shifted his grip to support her, and in an instant she twisted out of his hands and sprang out of reach, her eyes shining with triumph and venom.

"Ya-hay, Mister Razor-back!" she shrilled. "How's that fer hi? Pap'll kill ye, Sunday. You'll be screechin' in hell in a week, an' we 'ull set up an' drink our apple-jack an' laff!" Martin pursued her lumberingly, but she was agile as a monkey, and ran dodging up and down the counters and mocked him, singing "Gran' mammy Tipsy-Toe," till at last she tired of the game and darted out of the door, flinging back a hoarse laugh at him as she went. He followed; but when he reached the street she was a mere shadow flitting under the courthouse trees. He looked after her forebodingly, then turned his eyes toward the Palace Hotel. The editor of the "Herald" was seated under the awning, with his chair tilted back against a post, gazing dreamily at the murky red afterglow in the west.

"What's the use of tryin' to bother him with it?" old Tom asked himself. "He'd only laugh." He noted that young William Todd sat near the editor, whittling absently. Martin chuckled. "William's turn to-night," he muttered. "Well, the boys take mighty good care of him." He locked the doors of the Emporium, tried them, and dropped the keys in his pocket.

As he crossed the Square to the drug-store, where his cronies awaited him, he turned again to look at the figure of the musing journalist. "I hope he'll go out to the judge's," he said, and shook his head, sadly. "I don't reckon Plattville's any too spry for that young man. Five years he's be'n here. Well, it's a good thing for us folks, but I guess it ain't exactly high-life for him." He kicked a stick out of his way impatiently. "Now, where'd that imp run to?" he grumbled.

The imp was lying under the court-house steps. When the sound of Martin's footsteps had passed away, she crept cautiously from her hiding-place and stole through the ungroomed grass to the fence opposite the hotel. Here she stretched herself flat in the weeds and took from underneath the tangled masses of her hair, where it was tied with a string, a rolled-up, crumpled slip of greasy paper. With this in her fingers, she lay peering under the fence, her fierce eyes fixed unwinkingly on Harkless and the youth sitting near him.

The street ran flat and gray in the slowly gathering dusk, straight to the western horizon where the sunset embers were strewn in long, dark-red streaks; the maple trees were clean-cut silhouettes against the pale rose and pearl tints of the sky above, and a tenderness seemed to tremble in the air. Harkless often vowed to himself he would watch no more sunsets in Plattville; he realized that their loveliness lent a too unhappy tone to the imaginings and introspections upon which he was thrown by the loneliness of the environment, and he considered that he had too much time in which to think about himself. For five years his introspections had monotonously hurled one word at him: "Failure; Failure! Failure!" He thought the sunsets were making him morbid. Could he have shared them, that would have been different.

His long, melancholy face grew longer and more melancholy in the twilight, while William Todd patiently whittled near by. Plattville had often discussed the editor's habit of silence, and Mr. Martin had suggested that possibly the reason Mr. Harkless was such a quiet man was that there was nobody for him to talk to. His hearers did not agree, for the population of Carlow County was a thing of pride, being greater than that of several bordering counties. They did agree, however, that Harkless's quiet was not unkind, whatever its cause, and that when it was broken it was usually broken to conspicuous effect. Perhaps it was because he wrote so much that he hated to talk.

A bent figure came slowly down the street, and William hailed it cheerfully: "Evening, Mr. Fisbee."

"A good evening, Mr. Todd," answered the old man, pausing. "Ah, Mr. Harkless, I was looking for you." He had not seemed to be looking for anything beyond the boundaries of his own dreams, but he approached Harkless, tugging nervously at some papers in his pocket. "I have completed my notes for our Saturday edition. It was quite easy; there is much doing."

"Thank you, Mr. Fisbee," said Harkless, as he took the manuscript. "Have you finished your paper on the earlier Christian symbolism? I hope the 'Herald' may have the honor of printing it." This was the form they used.

"I shall be the recipient of honor, sir," returned Fisbee. "Your kind offer will speed my work; but I fear, Mr. Harkless, I very much fear, that your kindness alone prompts it, for, deeply as I desire it, I cannot truthfully say that my essays appear to increase our circulation." He made an odd, troubled gesture as he went on: "They do not seem to read them here, Mr. Harkless, although Mr. Martin assures me that he carefully peruses my article on Chaldean decoration whenever he rearranges his exhibition windows, and I bear in mind the clipping from a Rouen paper you showed me, commenting generously upon the scholarship of the 'Herald.' But for fifteen years I have tried to improve the art feeling in Plattville, and I may say that I have worked in the face of no small discouragement. In fact," (there was a slight quaver in Fisbee's voice), "I cannot remember that I ever received the slightest word or token of encouragement till you came, Mr. Harkless. Since then I have labored with refreshed energy; still, I cannot claim that our architecture shows a change for the better, and I fear the engravings upon the walls of our people exhibit no great progress in selection. And—I—I wish also to say, Mr. Harkless, if you find it necessary to make some alterations in the form of my reportorial items for Saturday's issue, I shall perfectly understand, remembering your explanation that journalism demands it. Good-evening, Mr. Harkless. Good-evening, Mr. Todd." He plodded on a few paces, then turned, irresolutely.

"What is it, Fisbee?" asked Harkless.

Fisbee stood for a moment, as though about to speak, then he smiled faintly, shook his head, and went his way. Harkless stared after him, surprised. It suddenly struck him, with a feeling of irritation, that if Fisbee had spoken it would have been to advise him to call at Judge Briscoe's. He laughed impatiently at the notion, and, drawing his pencil and a pad from his pocket, proceeded to injure his eyes in the waning twilight by the editorial perusal of the items his staff had just left in his hands. When published, the manuscript came under a flaring heading, bequeathed by Harkless's predecessor in the chair of the "Herald," and the alteration of which he felt Plattville would refuse to sanction: "Happenings of Our City." Below, was printed in smaller type: "Improvements in the World of Business," and, beneath that, came the rubric: "Also, the Cradle, the Altar, and the Tomb."

The first of Fisbee's items was thus recorded: "It may be noted that the new sign-board of Mr. H. Miller has been put in place. We cannot but regret that Mr. Miller did not instruct the painter to confine himself to a simpler method of lettering."

"Ah, Fisbee," murmured the editor, reproachfully, "that new sign-board is almost the only improvement in the World of Business Plattville has seen this year. I wonder how many times we have used it from the first, 'It is rumored in business circles that Hervé Miller contemplates'—to the exciting, 'Under Way,' and, 'Finishing Touches.' My poor White Knight, are five years of training wasted on you?

Sometimes you make me fear it. Here is Plattville panting for our story of the hanging of the sign, and you throw away the climax like that!" He began to write rapidly, bending low over the pad in the half darkness. His narrative was an amplification of the interesting information (already possessed by every inhabitant) that Hervé Miller had put up a new sign. After a paragraph of handsome description, "Hervé is always enterprising," wrote the editor. "This is a move in the right direction. Hervé, keep it up."

He glanced over the other items meditatively, making alterations here and there. The last two Fisbee had written as follows:

"There is noticeable in the new (and somewhat incongruous) portico erected by Solomon Tibbs at the residence of Mr. Henry Tibbs Willetts, an attempt at rococo decoration which cannot fail to sadden the passer-by."

"Miss Sherwood of Rouen, whom Miss Briscoe knew at the Misses Jennings' finishing-school in New York, is a guest of Judge Briscoe's household."

Fisbee's items were written in ink; and there was a blank space beneath the last. At the bottom of the page something had been scribbled in pencil. Harkless tried vainly to decipher it, but the twilight had fallen too deep, and the writing was too faint, so he struck a match and held it close to the paper. The action betokened only a languid interest, but when he caught sight of the first of the four subscribed lines he sat up straight in his chair with an ejaculation. At the bottom of Fisbee's page was written in a dainty, feminine hand, of a type he had not seen for years:

"'The time has come,' the Walrus said,
'To talk of many things:
Of shoes—and ships—and sealing-wax—
And cabbages—and kings—'"

He put the paper in his pocket, and set off rapidly down the village street.

At his departure William Todd looked up quickly; then he got upon his feet and quietly followed the editor. In the dusk a tattered little figure rose up from the weeds across the way, and stole noiselessly after William. He was in his shirt-sleeves, his waistcoat unbuttoned and loose. On the nearest corner Mr. Todd encountered a fellow-townsman, who had been pacing up and down in front of a cottage, crooning to a protestive baby held in his arms. He had paused in his vigil to stare after Harkless.

"Whereas he bound for, William?" inquired the man with the baby.

"Briscoes'," answered William, pursuing his way.

"I reckoned he would be," commented the other, turning to his wife, who sat on the doorstep, "I reckoned so when I see that lady at the lecture last night."

The woman rose to her feet. "Hi, Bill Todd!" she said. "What you got onto the back of your vest?" William paused, put his hand behind him and encountered a paper pinned to the dangling strap of his waistcoat. The woman ran to him and unpinned the paper. It bore a writing. They took it to where the yellow lamp-light shone through the open door, and read:
"der Sir

"FoLer harkls aL yo ples an gaRd him yoR best venagesn is closteR, harkls not Got 3 das to liv

"We come in Wite."

"What ye think, William?" asked the man with the baby, anxiously. But the woman gave the youth a sharp push with her hand. "They never dast to do it!" she cried. "Never in the world! You hurry, Bill Todd. Don't you leave him out of your sight one second."

CHAPTER V

AT THE PASTURE BARS: ELDER-BUSHES MAY HAVE STINGS

The street upon which the Palace Hotel fronted formed the south side of the Square and ran west to the edge of the town, where it turned to the south for a quarter of a mile or more, then bent to the west again. Some distance from this second turn, there stood, fronting close on the road, a large brick house, the most pretentious mansion in Carlow County. And yet it was a homelike place, with its red-brick walls embowered in masses of cool Virginia creeper, and a comfortable veranda crossing the broad front, while half a hundred stalwart sentinels of elm and beech and poplar stood guard around it. The front walk was bordered by geraniums and hollyhocks; and honeysuckle climbed the pillars of the porch. Behind the house there was a shady little orchard; and, back of the orchard, an old-fashioned, very fragrant rose-garden, divided by a long grape arbor, extended to the shallow waters of a wandering creek; and on the bank a rustic seat was placed, beneath the sycamores.

From the first bend of the road, where it left the town and became (after some indecision) a country highway—called the pike—rather than a proud city boulevard, a pathway led through the fields to end at some pasture bars opposite the brick house.

John Harkless was leaning on the pasture bars. The stars were wan, and the full moon shone over the fields. Meadows and woodlands lay quiet under the old, sweet marvel of a June night. In the wide monotony of the flat lands, there sometimes comes a feeling that the whole earth is stretched out before one. To-night it seemed to lie so, in the pathos of silent beauty, all passive and still; yet breathing an antique message, sad, mysterious, reassuring. But there had come a divine melody adrift on the air. Through the open windows it floated. Indoors some one struck a peal of silver chords, like a harp touched by a lover, and a woman's voice was lifted. John Harkless leaned on the pasture bars and listened with upraised head and parted lips.

"To thy chamber window roving, love hath led my feet."

The Lord sent manna to the children of Israel in the wilderness. Harkless had been five years in Plattville, and a woman's voice singing Schubert's serenade came to him at last as he stood by the pasture bars of Jones's field and listened and rested his dazzled eyes on the big, white face of the moon.

How long had it been since he had heard a song, or any discourse of music other than that furnished by the Plattville Band—not that he had not taste for a brass band! But music that he loved always gave him an ache of delight and the twinge of reminiscences of old, gay days gone forever. To-night his memory leaped to the last day of a June gone seven years; to a morning when the little estuary waves twinkled in the bright sun about the boat in which he sat, the trim launch that brought a cheery party ashore from their schooner to the Casino landing at Winter Harbor, far up on the Maine coast.

It was the happiest of those last irresponsible days before he struck into his work in the world and became a failure. To-night he saw the picture as plainly as if it were yesterday; no reminiscence had risen so keenly before his eyes for years: pretty Mrs. Van Skuyt sitting beside him— pretty Mrs. Van Skuyt and her roses! What had become of her? He saw the crowd of friends waiting on the pier for their arrival, and the dozen or so emblazoned classmates (it was in the time of brilliant flannels) who suddenly sent up a volley of college cheers in his honor—how plainly the dear, old, young faces rose up before him to-night, the men from whose lives he had slipped! Dearest and jolliest of the faces was that of Tom Meredith, clubmate, classmate, his closest friend, the thin, red-headed third baseman; he could see Tom's mouth opened at least a yard, it seemed, such was his frantic vociferousness. Again and again the cheers rang out, "Harkless! Harkless!" on the end of them. In those days everybody (particularly his classmates) thought he would be minister to England in a few years, and the orchestra on the Casino porch was playing "The Conquering Hero," in his honor, and at the behest of Tom Meredith, he knew.

There were other pretty ladies besides Mrs. Van Skuyt in the launch-load from the yacht, but, as they touched the pier, pretty girls, or pretty women, or jovial gentlemen, all were overlooked in the wild scramble the college men made for their hero. They haled him forth, set him on high, bore him on their shoulders, shouting "Skal to the Viking!" and carried him up the wooded bluff to the Casino. He heard Mrs. Van Skuyt say, "Oh, we're used to it; we've put in at several other places where he had friends!" He struggled manfully to be set down, but his triumphal procession swept on. He heard bystanders telling each other, "It's that young Harkless, 'the Great Harkless,' they're all so mad about"; and while it pleased him a little to hear such things, they always made him laugh a great deal. He had never understood his popularity: he had been chief editor of the university daily, and he had done a little in athletics, and the rest of his distinction lay in college offices his mates had heaped upon him without his being able to comprehend why they did it. And yet, somehow, and in spite of himself, they had convinced him that the world was his oyster; that it would open for him at a touch. He could not help seeing how the Freshmen looked at him, how the Sophomores jumped off the narrow campus walks to let him pass; he could not help knowing that he was the great man of his time, so that "The Great Harkless" came to be one of the traditions of the university. He remembered the wild progress they made for him up the slope that morning at Winter Harbor, how the people baked on, and laughed, and clapped their hands. But at the veranda edge he had noticed a little form disappearing around a corner of the building; a young girl running away as fast as she could.

"See there!" he said, as the tribe set him down, "You have frightened the populace." And Tom Meredith stopped shouting long enough to answer, "It's my little cousin, overcome with emotion. She's been counting the hours till you came—been hearing of you from me and others for a good while; and hasn't been able to talk or think of anything else. She's only fifteen, and the crucial moment is too much for her—the Great Harkless has arrived, and she has fled."

He remembered other incidents of his greatness, of the glory that now struck him as rarely comical; be hoped he hadn't taken it too seriously then, in the flush of his youth. Maybe, after all, he had been a, big-headed boy, but he must have bottled up his conceit tightly enough, or the other boys would have detected it and abhorred him. He was inclined to believe that he had not been very much set up by the pomp they made for him. At all events, that day at Winter Harbor had been beautiful, full of the laughter of friends and music; for there was a musicale at the Casino in the afternoon.

But the present hour grew on him as he leaned on the pasture bars, and suddenly his memories sped; and the voice that was singing Schubert's serenade across the way touched him with the urgent, personal appeal that a present beauty always had for him. It was a soprano; and without tremolo, yet came to his ear with a certain tremulous sweetness; it was soft and slender, but the listener knew it could be lifted with fullness and power if the singer would. It spoke only of the song, yet the listener thought of the singer. Under the moon thoughts run into dreams, and he dreamed that the owner of the voice, she who quoted "The Walrus and the Carpenter" on Fisbee's notes, was one to laugh with you and weep with you; yet her laughter would be tempered with sorrow, and her tears with laughter.

When the song was ended, he struck the rail he leaned upon a sharp blow with his open hand. There swept over him a feeling that he had stood precisely where he stood now, on such a night, a thousand years ago, had heard that voice and that song, had listened and been moved by the song, and the night, just as he was moved now.

He had long known himself for a sentimentalist; he had almost given up trying to cure himself. And he knew himself for a born lover; he had always been in love with some one. In his earlier youth his affections had been so constantly inconstant that he finally came to settle with his self-respect by recognizing in himself a fine constancy that worshipped one woman always—it was only the shifting image of her that changed! Somewhere (he dreamed, whimsically indulgent of the fancy; yet mocking himself for it) there was a girl whom he had never seen, who waited till he should come. She was Everything. Until he found her, he could not help adoring others who possessed little pieces and suggestions of her—her brilliancy, her courage, her short upper lip, "like a curled roseleaf," or her dear voice, or her pure profile. He had no recollection of any lady who had quite her eyes.

He had never passed a lovely stranger on the street, in the old days, without a thrill of delight and warmth. If he never saw her again, and the vision only lasted the time it takes a lady to cross the sidewalk from a shop door to a carriage, he was always a little in love with her, because she bore about her, somewhere, as did every pretty girl he ever saw, a suggestion of the far-away divinity. One does not pass lovely strangers in the streets of Plattville. Miss Briscoe was pretty, but not at all in the way that Harkless dreamed. For five years the lover in him that had loved so often had been starved of all but dreams. Only at twilight and dusk in the summer, when, strolling, he caught sight of a woman's skirt, far up the village street—half-outlined in the darkness under the cathedral arch of meeting branches—this romancer of petticoats could sigh a true lover's sigh, and, if he kept enough distance between, fly a yearning fancy that his lady wandered there.

Ever since his university days the image of her had been growing more and more distinct. He had completely settled his mind as to her appearance and her voice. She was tall, almost too tall, he was sure of that; and out of his consciousness there had grown a sweet and vivacious young face that he knew was hers. Her hair was light-brown with gold lustres (he reveled in the gold lustres, on the proper theory that when your fancy is painting a picture you may as well go in for the whole thing and make it sumptuous), and her eyes were gray. They were very earnest, and yet they sparkled and laughed to him companionably; and sometimes he had smiled back upon her. The Undine danced before him through the lonely years, on fair nights in his walks, and came to sit by his fire on winter evenings when he stared alone at the embers.

And to-night, here in Plattville, he heard a voice he had waited for long, one that his fickle memory told him he had never heard before. But, listening, he knew better— he had heard it long ago, though when and how, he did not know, as rich and true, and ineffably tender as now. He threw a sop to his common sense. "Miss Sherwood is a little thing" (the image was so surely tall) "with a bumpy forehead and spectacles," he said to himself, "or else a provincial young lady with big eyes to pose at you." Then he felt the ridiculousness of looking after his common sense on a moonlight night in June; also, he knew that he lied.

The song had ceased, but the musician lingered, and the keys were touched to plaintive harmonies new to him. He had come to Plattville before "Cavalleria Rusticana" was sung at Rome, and now, entranced, he heard the "Intermezzo" for the first time. Listening to this, he feared to move lest he should wake from a summer-night's dream.

A ragged little shadow flitted down the path behind him, and from a solitary apple-tree, standing like a lonely ghost in the middle of the field, came the *woo* of a screech owl—twice. It was answered—twice— from a clump of elder-bushes that grew in a fence-corner fifty yards west of the pasture bars. Then the barrel of a squirrel rifle issued, lifted out of the white elder-blossoms, and lay along the fence. The music in the house across the way ceased, and Harkless saw two white dresses come out through the long parlor windows to the veranda.

"It will be cooler out here," came the voice of the singer clearly through the quiet. "What a night!"

John vaulted the bars and started to cross the road. They saw him from the veranda, and Miss Briscoe called to him in welcome. As his tall figure stood out plainly in the bright light against the white dust, a streak of fire leaped from the elder-blossoms and there rang out the sharp report of a rifle. There were two screams from the veranda. One white figure ran into the house. The other, a little one with a gauzy wrap streaming behind, came flying out into the moonlight—straight to Harkless. There was a second report; the rifle-shot was answered by a revolver. William Todd had risen up, apparently from nowhere, and, kneeling by the pasture bars, fired at the flash of the rifle.

"Jump fer the shadder, Mr. Harkless," he shouted; "he's in them elders," and then: "Fer God's sake, comeback!"

Empty-handed as he was, the editor dashed for the treacherous elder-bush as fast as his long legs could carry him; but, before he had taken six strides, a hand clutched his sleeve, and a girl's voice quavered from close behind him:

"Don't run like that, Mr. Harkless; I can't keep up!" He wheeled about, and confronted a vision, a dainty little figure about five feet high, a flushed and lovely face, hair and draperies disarranged and flying. He stamped his foot with rage. "Get back in the house!" he cried.

"You mustn't go," she panted. "It's the only way to stop you."

"Go back to the house!" he shouted, savagely.

"Will you come?"

"Fer God's sake," cried William Todd, "come back! Keep out of the road." He was emptying his revolver at the clump of elder, the uproar of his firing blasting the night. Some one screamed from the house:

"Helen! Helen!"

John seized the girl's wrists roughly; her gray eyes flashed into his defiantly. "Will you go?" he roared.

"No!"

He dropped her wrists, caught her up in his arms as if she had been a kitten, and leaped into the shadow of the trees that leaned over the road from the yard. The rifle rang out again, and the little ball whistled venomously overhead. Harkless ran along the fence and turned in at the gate.

A loose strand of the girl's hair blew across his cheek, and in the moon her head shone with gold. She had light-brown hair and gray eyes and a short upper lip like a curled rose-leaf. He set her down on the veranda steps. Both of them laughed wildly.

"But you came with me!" she gasped triumphantly.

"I always thought you were tall," he answered; and there was afterward a time when he had to agree that this was a somewhat vague reply.

CHAPTER VI

JUNE

Judge Briscoe smiled grimly and leaned on his shot-gun in the moonlight by the veranda. He and William Todd had been trampling down the elder-bushes, and returning to the house, found Minnie alone on the porch. "Safe?" he said to his daughter, who turned an anxious face upon him. "They'll be safe enough now, and in our garden."

"Maybe I oughtn't to have let them go," she returned, nervously.

"Pooh! They're all right; that scalawag's half-way to Six-Cross-Roads by this time, isn't he, William?"

"He tuck up the fence like a scared rabbit," Mr. Todd responded, looking into his hat to avoid meeting the eyes of the lady. "I didn't have no call to toller, and he knowed how to run, I reckon. Time Mr. Harkless come out the yard again, he was near out o' sight, and we see him take across the road to the wedge-woods, near half-a-mile up. Somebody else with him then —looked like a kid. Must 'a' cut acrost the field to join him. They're fur enough towards home by this."

"Did Miss Helen shake hands with you four or five times?" asked Briscoe, chuckling.

"No. Why?"

"Because Harkless did. My hand aches, and I guess William's does, too; he nearly shook our arms off when we told him he'd been a fool. Seemed to do him good. I told him he ought to hire somebody to take a shot at him every morning before breakfast—not that it's any joking matter," the old gentleman finished, thoughtfully.

"I should say not," said William, with a deep frown and a jerk of his head toward the rear of the house. "*He* jokes about it enough. Wouldn't even promise to carry a gun after this. Said he wouldn't know how to use it. Never shot one off since he was a boy, on the Fourth of July. This is the third time he's be'n shot at this year, but he says the others was at a— a—what'd he call it?"

"'A merely complimentary range,'" Briscoe supplied. He handed William a cigar and bit the end off another himself. "Minnie, you better go in the house and read, I expect—unless you want to go down the creek and join those folks."

"*Me!*" she responded. "I know when to stay away, I guess. Do go and put that terrible gun up."

45

"No," said Briscoe, lighting his cigar, deliberately. "It's all safe; there's no question of that; but maybe William and I better go out and take a smoke in the orchard as long as they stay down at the creek."

In the garden, shafts of white light pierced the bordering trees and fell where June roses lifted their heads to breathe the mild night breeze, and here, through summer spells, the editor of the "Herald" and the lady who had run to him at the pasture bars strolled down a path trembling with shadows to where the shallow creek tinkled over the pebbles. They walked slowly, with an air of being well-accustomed friends and comrades, and for some reason it did not strike either of them as unnatural or extraordinary. They came to a bench on the bank, and he made a great fuss dusting the seat for her with his black slouch hat. Then he regretted the hat—it was a shabby old hat of a Carlow County fashion.

It was a long bench, and he seated himself rather remotely toward the end opposite her, suddenly realizing that he had walked very close to her, coming down the narrow garden path. Neither knew that neither had spoken since they left the veranda; and it had taken them a long time to come through the little orchard and the garden. She rested her chin on her hand, leaning forward and looking steadily at the creek. Her laughter had quite gone; her attitude seemed a little wistful and a little sad. He noted that her hair curled over her brow in a way he had not pictured in the lady of his dreams; this was so much lovelier. He did not care for tall girls; he had not cared for them for almost half an hour. It was so much more beautiful to be dainty and small and piquant. He had no notion that he was sighing in a way that would have put a furnace to shame, but he turned his eyes from her because he feared that if he looked longer he might blurt out some speech about her beauty. His glance rested on the bank; but its diameter included the edge of her white skirt and the tip of a little, white, high-heeled slipper that peeped out beneath it; and he had to look away from that, too, to keep from telling her that he meant to advocate a law compelling all women to wear crisp, white gowns and white slippers on moonlight nights.

She picked a long spear of grass from the turf before her, twisted it absently in her fingers, then turned to him slowly. Her lips parted as if to speak. Then she turned away again. The action was so odd, and somehow, as she did it, so adorable, and the preserved silence was such a bond between them, that for his life he could not have helped moving half-way up the bench toward her.

"What is it?" he asked; and he spoke in a whisper he might have used at the bedside of a dying friend. He would not have laughed if he had known he did so. She twisted the spear of grass into a little ball and threw it at a stone in the water before she answered.

"Do you know, Mr. Harkless, you and I haven't 'met,' have we? Didn't we forget to be presented to each other?"

"I beg your pardon. Miss Sherwood. In the perturbation of comedy I forgot."

46

"It was melodrama, wasn't it?" she said. He laughed, but she shook her head.

"Comedy," he answered, "except your part of it, which you shouldn't have done. It was not arranged in honor of 'visiting ladies.' But you mustn't think me a comedian. Truly, I didn't plan it. My friend from Six-Cross-Roads must be given the credit of devising the scene-though you divined it!"

"It was a little too picturesque, I think. I know about Six-Cross-Roads. Please tell me what you mean to do."

"Nothing. What should I?"

"You mean that you will keep on letting them shoot at you, until they— until you—" She struck the bench angrily with her hand.

"There's no summer theatre in Six-Cross-Roads; there's not even a church. Why shouldn't they?" he asked gravely. "During the long and tedious evenings it cheers the poor Cross-Reader's soul to drop over here and take a shot at me. It whiles away dull care for him, and he has the additional exercise of running all the way home."

"Ah!" she cried indignantly, "they told me you always answered like this!"

"Well, you see the Cross-Roads efforts have proved so purely hygienic for me. As a patriot I have sometimes felt extreme mortification that such bad marksmanship should exist in the county, but I console myself with the thought that their best shots are unhappily in the penitentiary."

"There are many left. Can't you understand that they will organize again and come in a body, as they did before you broke them up? And then, if they come on a night when they know you are wandering out of town——"

"You have not the advantage of an intimate study of the most exclusive people of the Cross-Roads, Miss Sherwood. There are about twenty gentlemen who remain in that neighborhood while their relatives sojourn under discipline. If you had the entree over there, you would understand that these twenty could not gather themselves into a company and march the seven miles without physical debate in the ranks. They are not precisely amiable people, even amongst themselves. They would quarrel and shoot each other to pieces long before they got here."

"But they worked in a company once."

"Never for seven miles. Four miles was their radius. Five would see them all dead."

She struck the bench again. "Oh, you laugh at me! You make a joke of your own life and death, and laugh at everything! Have five years of Plattville taught you to do that?"

"I laugh only at taking the poor Cross-Roaders too seriously. I don't laugh at your running into fire to help a fellow-mortal."

"I knew there wasn't any risk. I knew he had to stop to load before he shot again."

"He did shoot again. If I had known you before to-night—I—" His tone changed and he spoke gravely. "I am at your feet in worship of your philanthropy. It's so much finer to risk your life for a stranger than for a friend."

"That is rather a man's point of view, isn't it?"

"You risked yours for a man you had never seen before."

"Oh, no! I saw you at the lecture; I heard you introduce the Honorable Mr. Halloway."

"Then I don't understand your wishing to save me."

She smiled unwillingly, and turned her gray eyes upon him with troubled sunniness, and, under the kindness of her regard, he set a watch upon his lips, though he knew it might not avail him. He had driveled along respectably so far, he thought, but he had the sentimental longings of years, starved of expression, culminating in his heart. She continued to look at him, wistfully, searchingly, gently. Then her eyes traveled over his big frame from his shoes (a patch of moonlight fell on them; they were dusty; he drew them under the bench with a shudder) to his broad shoulders (he shook the stoop out of them). She stretched her small hands toward him in contrast, and broke into the most delicious low laughter in the world. At this sound he knew the watch on his lips was worthless. It was a question of minutes till he should present himself to her eyes as a sentimental and susceptible imbecile. He knew it. He was in wild spirits.

"Could you realize that one of your dangers might be a shaking?" she cried. "Is your seriousness a lost art?" Her laughter ceased suddenly. "Ah, no. I understand. Thiers said the French laugh always, in order not to weep. I haven't lived here five years. I should laugh too, if I were you."

"Look at the moon," he responded. "We Plattvillains own that with the best of metropolitans, and, for my part, I see more of it here. You do not appreciate us. We have large landscapes in the heart of the city, and what other capital possesses advantages like that? Next winter the railway station is to have a new stove for the waiting-room. Heaven itself is one of our suburbs—it is so close that all one has to do is to die. You insist upon my being French, you see, and I know you are fond of nonsense. How did you happen to put 'The Walrus and the Carpenter' at the bottom of a page of Fisbee's notes?"

"Was it? How were you sure it was I?"

"In Carlow County!"

"He might have written it himself."

"Fisbee has never in his life read anything lighter than cuneiform inscriptions."

"Miss Briscoe——"

"She doesn't read Lewis Carroll; and it was not her hand. What made you write it on Fisbee's manuscript?"

"He was with us this afternoon, and I teased him a little about your heading. 'Business and the Cradle, the Altar, and the Tomb,' isn't it? And he said it had always troubled him, but that you thought it good. So do I. He asked me if I could think of anything that you might like better, to put in place of it, and I wrote, 'The time has come,' because it was the only thing I could think of that was as appropriate and as fetching as your headlines. He was perfectly dear about it. He was so serious; he said he feared it wouldn't be acceptable. I didn't notice that the paper he handed me to write on was part of his notes, nor did he, I think. Afterward, he put it back in his pocket. It wasn't a message."

"I'm not so sure he did not notice. He is very wise. Do you know, somehow, I have the impression that the old fellow wanted me to meet you."

"How dear and good of him!" She spoke earnestly, and her face was suffused with a warm light. There was no doubt about her meaning what she said.

"It was," John answered, unsteadily. "He knew how great was my need of a few moments' companionableness with—with——"

"No," she interrupted. "I meant dear and good to me, because I think he was thinking of me, and it was for my sake he wanted us to meet."

It would have been hard to convince a woman, if she had overheard this speech, that Miss Sherwood's humility was not the calculated affectation of a coquette. Sometimes a man's unsuspicion is wiser, and Harkless knew that she was not flirting with him. In addition, he was not a fatuous man; he did not extend the implication of her words nearly so far as she would have had him.

"But I had met you," said he, "long ago."

"What!" she cried, and her eyes danced. "You actually remember?"

"Yes; do you?" he answered. "I stood in Jones's field and heard you singing, and I remembered. It was a long time since I had heard you sing:

"'I was a ruffler of Flanders,
And fought for a florin's hire.
You were the dame of my captain
And sang to my heart's desire.'

"But that is the balladist's notion. The truth is that you were a lady at the Court of Clovis, and I was a heathen captive. I heard you sing a Christian hymn—and asked for baptism." By a great effort he managed to look as if he did not mean it.

But she did not seem over-pleased with his fancy, for, the surprise fading from her face, "Oh, that was the way you remembered!" she said.

"Perhaps it was not that way alone. You won't despise me for being mawkish to-night?" he asked. "I haven't had the chance for so long."

The night air wrapped them warmly, and the balm of the little breezes that stirred the foliage around them was the smell of damask roses from the garden. The creek tinkled over the pebbles at their feet, and a drowsy bird, half-wakened by the moon, crooned languorously in the sycamores. The girl looked out at the flashing water through downcast lashes. "Is it because it is so transient that beauty is pathetic?" she said; "because we can never come back to it in quite the same way? I am a sentimental girl. If you are born so, it is never entirely teased out of you, is it? Besides, to-night is all a dream. It isn't real, you know. You couldn't be mawkish."

Her tone was gentle as a caress, and it made him tingle to his finger-tips. "How do you know?" he asked in a low voice.

"I just know. Do you think I'm very 'bold and forward'?" she said, dreamily.

"It was your song I wanted to be sentimental about. I am like one 'who through long days of toil'—only that doesn't quite apply—'and nights devoid of ease'—but I can't claim that one doesn't sleep well here; it is Plattville's specialty—like one who

"'Still heard in his soul the music
Of wonderful melodies.'"

"Those blessed old lines!" she said. "Once a thing is music or poetry, all the hand-organs and elocutionists in the world cannot ruin it, can they? Yes; to live here, out of the world, giving up the world, doing good and working for others, working for a community as you do——"

50

"I am not quite shameless," he interrupted, smilingly. "I was given a life sentence for incompetency, and I've served five years of it, which have been made much happier than my deserts."

"No," she persisted, "that is your way of talking of yourself; I know you would always 'run yourself down,' if one paid any attention to it. But to give up the world, to drop out of it without regret, to come here and do what you have done, and to live the life that must be so desperately dry and dull for a man of your sort, and yet to have the kind of heart that makes wonderful melodies sing in itself—oh!" she cried, "I say that is fine!"

"You do not understand," he returned, sadly, wishing, before her, to be unmercifully just to himself. "I came here because I couldn't make a living anywhere else. And the 'wonderful melodies'—I have known you only one evening—and the melodies—" He rose to his feet and took a few steps toward the garden. "Come," he said. "Let me take you back. Let us go before I—" he finished with a helpless laugh.

She stood by the bench, one hand resting on it; she stood all in the tremulant shadow. She moved one step toward him, and a single, long sliver of light pierced the sycamores and fell upon her head. He gasped.

"What was it about the melodies?" she said.

"Nothing! I don't know how to thank you for this evening that you have given me. I—I suppose you are leaving to-morrow. No one ever stays here.—I——"

"What about the melodies?"

He gave it up. "The moon makes people insane!" he cried.

"If that is true," she returned, "then you need not be more afraid than I, because 'people' is plural. What were you saying about——"

"I *had* heard them—in my heart. When I heard your voice to-night, I knew that it was you who sang them there—had been singing them for me always."

"So!" she cried, gaily. "All that debate about a pretty speech!" Then, sinking before him in a deep courtesy, "I am beholden to you," she said. "Do you think that no man ever made a little flattery for me before to-night?"

At the edge of the orchard, where they could keep an unseen watch on the garden and the bank of the creek. Judge Briscoe and Mr. Todd were ensconced under an apple-tree, the former still armed with his shot-gun. When the two young people got up from their bench, the two men rose hastily, and then sauntered slowly toward them. When they met, Harkless shook each of them cordially by the hand, without seeming to know it.

"We were coming to look for you," explained the judge. "William was afraid to go home alone; thought some one might take him for Mr. Harkless and shoot him before he got into town. Can you come out with young Willetts in the morning, Harkless," he went on, "and go with the ladies to see the parade? And Minnie wants you to stay to dinner and go to the show with them in the afternoon."

Harkless seized his hand and shook it fervently, and then laughed heartily, as he accepted the invitation.

At the gate, Miss Sherwood extended her hand to him and said politely, and with some flavor of mockery: "Good-night, Mr. Harkless. I do not leave to-morrow. I am very glad to have met you."

"We are going to keep her all summer if we can," said Minnie, weaving her arm about her friend's waist. "You'll come in the morning?"

"Good-night, Miss Sherwood," he returned, hilariously. "It has been such a pleasure to meet you. Thank you so much for saving my life. It was very good of you indeed. Yes, in the morning. Good-night—good-night." He shook hands with them all again, including Mr. Todd, who was going with him.

He laughed most of the way home, and Mr. Todd walked at his side in amazement. The Herald Building was a decrepit frame structure on Main Street; it had once been a small warehouse and was now sadly in need of paint. Closely adjoining it, in a large, blank-looking yard, stood a low brick cottage, over which the second story of the warehouse leaned in an effect of tipsy affection that had reminded Harkless, when he first saw it, of an old Sunday-school book wood-cut of an inebriated parent under convoy of a devoted child. The title to these two buildings and the blank yard had been included in the purchase of the "Herald"; and the cottage was Harkless's home.

There was a light burning upstairs in the "Herald" office. From the street a broad, tumble-down stairway ran up on the outside of the building to the second floor, and at the stairway railing John turned and shook his companion warmly by the hand.

"Good-night, William," he said. "It was plucky of you to join in that muss, to-night. I shan't forget it."

"I jest happened to come along," replied the other, drowsily; then, with a portentous yawn, he asked: "Ain't ye goin' to bed?"

"No; Parker wouldn't allow it."

52

"Well," observed William, with another yawn, which bade fair to expose the veritable soul of him, "I d'know how ye stand it. It's closte on eleven o'clock. Good-night."

John went up the steps, singing aloud:

"For to-night we'll merry, merry be,
For to-night we'll merry, merry be,"

and stopped on the sagging platform at the top of the stairs and gave the moon good-night with a wave of the hand and friendly laughter. At that it suddenly struck him that he was twenty-nine years of age; that he had laughed a great deal that evening; that he had laughed and laughed over things not in the least humorous, like an excited schoolboy making his first formal call; that he had shaken hands with Miss Briscoe when he left her, as if he should never see her again; that he had taken Miss Sherwood's hand twice in one very temporary parting; that he had shaken the judge's hand five times, and William's four!

"Idiot!" he cried. "What has happened to me?" Then he shook his fist at the moon and went in to work—he thought.

CHAPTER VII

MORNING: "SOME IN RAGS AND SOME IN TAGS AND SOME IN VELVET GOWNS"

The bright sun of circus-day shone into Harkless's window, and he awoke to find himself smiling. For a little while he lay content, drowsily wondering why he smiled, only knowing that there was something new. It was thus, as a boy, he had wakened on his birthday mornings, or on Christmas, or on the Fourth of July, drifting happily out of pleasant dreams into the consciousness of long-awaited delights that had come true, yet lying only half-awake in a cheerful borderland, leaving happiness undefined.

The morning breeze was fluttering at his window blind; a honeysuckle vine tapped lightly on the pane. Birds were trilling, warbling, whistling. From the street came the rumbling of wagons, merry cries of greeting, and the barking of dogs. What was it made him feel so young and strong and light-hearted? The breeze brought him the smell of June roses, fresh and sweet with dew, and then he knew why he had come smiling from his dreams. He would go a holiday-making. With that he leaped out of bed, and shouted loudly: "Zen! Hello, Xenophon!"

In answer, an ancient, very black darky put his head in at the door, his warped and wrinkled visage showing under his grizzled hair like charred paper in a fall of pine ashes. He said: "Good-mawn', suh. Yessuh. Hit's done pump' full. Good-mawn', suh."

A few moments later, the colored man, seated on the front steps of the cottage, heard a mighty splashing within, while the rafters rang with stentorian song:

"He promised to buy me a bunch o' blue ribbon,
He promised to buy me a bunch o' blue ribbon,
He promised to buy me a bunch o' blue ribbon,

     To tie up my bonny brown hair
"Oh dear! What can the matter be?
Oh dear! What can the matter be?
Oh dear! What can the matter be?

     Johnnie's so long at the Fair!"

At the sound of this complaint, delivered in a manly voice, the listener's jaw dropped, and his mouth opened and stayed open. "*Him!*" he muttered, faintly. "*Singin'!*"

"Well, the old Triangle knew the music of our tread;
How the peaceful Seminole would tremble in his bed!"

sang the editor. "I dunno huccome it," exclaimed the old man, "an' dat ain' hyer ner dar; but, bless Gawd! de young man' happy!" A thought struck him suddenly, and he scratched his head. "Maybe he goin' away," he said, querulously. "What become o' ole Zen?" The splashing ceased, but not the voice, which struck into a noble marching chorus. "Oh, my Lawd," said the colored man, "I pray you listen at dat!"

"Soldiers marching up the street,
They keep the time;
They look sublime!
Hear them play Die Wacht am Rhein!
They call them Schneider's Band.
Tra la la la, la!"

The length of Main Street and all the Square resounded with the rattle of vehicles of every kind. Since earliest dawn they had been pouring into the village, a long procession on every country road. There were great red and blue farm wagons, drawn by splendid Clydesdales; the elders of the family on the front seat and on boards laid from side to side in front, or on chairs placed close behind, while, in the deep beds back of these, children tumbled in the straw, or peeped over the sides, rosy-cheeked and laughing, eyes alight with blissful anticipations. There were more pretentious two-seated cut-unders and stout buckboards, loaded down with merrymakers, four on a seat meant for two; there were rattle-trap phaetons and comfortable carry-alls drawn by steady spans; and, now and then, mule teams bringing happy negroes, ready to squander all on the first Georgia watermelons and cider. Every vehicle contained heaping baskets of good things to eat (the previous night had been a woeful Bartholomew for Carlow chickens) and underneath, where the dogs paced faithfully, swung buckets and fodder for the horses, while colts innumerable trotted dose to the maternal flanks, viewing the world with their big, new eyes in frisky surprise.

Here and there the trim side-bar buggy of some prosperous farmer's son, escorting his sweetheart, flashed along the road, the young mare stepping out in pride of blood to pass the line of wagons, the youth who held the reins, resplendent in Sunday best and even better, his scorched brown face glowing with a fine belief in the superiority of both his steed and his lady; the latter beaming out upon life and rejoicing in the light-blue ribbons on her hat, the light-blue ribbon around her waist, the light-blue, silk half-mittens on her hands, and the beautiful red coral necklace about her neck and the red coral buttons that fastened her gown in the back.

The air was full of exhilaration; everybody was laughing and shouting and calling greetings; for Carlow County was turning out, and from far and near the country people came; nay, from over the county line, clouds of dust rising from every thoroughfare and highway, and sweeping into town to herald their coming.

Dibb Zane, the "sprinkling contractor," had been at work with the town water-cart since the morning stars were bright, but he might as well have watered the streets with his tears, which, indeed, when the farmers began to come in, bringing their cyclones of dust, he drew nigh unto, after a spell of profanity as futile as his cart.

"Tief wie das Meer soll deine Liebe sein,"

hummed the editor in the cottage. His song had taken on a reflective tone as that of one who cons a problem, or musically ponders which card to play. He was kneeling before an old trunk in his bedchamber. From one compartment he took a neatly folded pair of duck trousers and a light-gray tweed coat; from another, a straw hat with a ribbon of bright colors. They had lain in the trunk a long time undisturbed; and he examined them musingly. He shook the coat and brushed it; then he laid the garments upon his bed, and proceeded to shave himself carefully, after which he donned the white trousers, the gray coat, and, rummaging in the trunk again, found a gay pink cravat, which he fastened about his tall collar (also a resurrection from the trunk) with a pearl pin. After that he had a long, solemn time arranging his hair with a pair of brushes. When at last he was suited, and his dressing completed, he sallied forth to breakfast.

Xenophon stared after him as he went out of the gate whistling heartily. The old darky lifted his hands, palms outward.

"Lan' name, who dat!" he exclaimed aloud. "Who dat in dem pan-jingeries? He jine' de circus?" His hands fell upon his knees, and he got to his feet pneumatically, shaking his head with foreboding. "Honey, honey, hit' baid luck, baid luck sing 'fo' breakfus. Trouble 'fo' de day be done. Trouble, honey, gre't trouble. Baid luck, baid luck!"

Along the Square the passing of the editor in his cool equipment evoked some gasps of astonishment; and Mr. Tibbs and his sister rushed from the postoffice to stare after him.

"He looks just beautiful, Solomon," said Miss Tibbs.

"But what's the name for them kind of clothes?" inquired her brother. "'Seems to me there's a special way of callin' 'em. 'Seems as if I see a picture of 'em, somewheres. Wasn't it on the cover of that there long-tennis box we bought and put in the window, and the country people thought it was a seining outfit?"

"It was a game, the catalogue said," observed Miss Selina. "Wasn't it?"

"It was a mighty pore investment," the postmaster answered.

As Harkless approached the hotel, a decrepit old man, in a vast straw hat and a linen duster much too large for him, came haltingly forward to meet him. He was Widow-

56

Woman Wimby's husband. And, as did every one else, he spoke of his wife by the name of her former martial companion.

"Be'n a-lookin' fer you, Mr. Harkless," he said in a shaking spindle of a voice, as plaintive as his pale little eyes. "Mother Wimby, she sent some roses to ye. Cynthy's fixin' 'em on yer table. I'm well as ever I am; but her, she's too complaining to come in fer show-day. This morning, early, we see some the Cross-Roads folks pass the place towards town, an' she sent me in to tell ye. Oh, I knowed ye'd laugh. Says she, 'He's too much of a man to be skeered,' says she, 'these here tall, big men always 'low nothin' on earth kin hurt 'em,' says she, 'but you tell him to be keerful,' says she; an' I see Bill Skillett an' his brother on the Square lessun a half-an-hour ago, 'th my own eyes. I won't keep ye from yer breakfast.—Eph Watts is in there, eatin'. He's come back; but I guess I don't need to warn ye agin' him. He seems peaceable enough. It's the other folks you got to look out fer."

He limped away. The editor waved his hand to him from the door, but the old fellow shook his head, and made a warning, friendly gesture with his arm.

Harkless usually ate his breakfast alone, as he was the latest riser in Plattville. (There were days in the winter when he did not reach the hotel until eight o'clock.) This morning he found a bunch of white roses, still wet with dew and so fragrant that the whole room was fresh and sweet with their odor, prettily arranged in a bowl on the table, and, at his plate, the largest of all with a pin through the stem. He looked up, smilingly, and nodded at the red-haired girl. "Thank you, Charmion," he said. "That's very pretty."

She turned even redder than she always was, and answered nothing, vigorously darting her brush at an imaginary fly on the cloth. After several minutes she said abruptly, "You're welcome."

There was a silence, finally broken by a long, gasping sigh. Astonished, he looked at the girl. Her eyes were set unfathomably upon his pink tie; the wand had dropped from her nerveless hand, and she stood rapt and immovable. She started violently from her trance. "Ain't you goin' to finish your coffee?" she asked, plying her instrument again, and, bending over him slightly, whispered: "Say, Eph Watts is over there behind you."

At a table in a far corner of the room a large gentleman in a brown frock coat was quietly eating his breakfast and reading the "Herald." He was of an ornate presence, though entirely neat. A sumptuous expanse of linen exhibited itself between the lapels of his low-cut waistcoat, and an inch of bediamonded breastpin glittered there, like an ice-ledge on a snowy mountain side. He had a steady, blue eye and a dissipated, iron-gray mustache. This personage was Mr. Ephraim Watts, who, following a calling more fashionable in the eighteenth century than in the latter decades of the nineteenth, had shaken the dust of Carlow from his feet some three years previously, at the strong request of the authorities. The "Herald" had been particularly insistent upon his deportation, and, in the local phrase, Harkless had "run him out of town." Perhaps it was because the "Herald's" opposition (as the editor explained at the time) had been merely moral and impersonal, and the editor had always confessed to a liking for the unprofessional qualities of Mr. Watts, that there was but slight embarrassment when the two gentlemen met to-day. His breakfast finished, Harkless went over to the other and extended his hand. Cynthia held her breath and clutched the back of a chair. However, Mr. Watts made no motion toward his well-known hip pocket. Instead, he rose, flushed slightly, and accepted the hand offered him.

"I'm glad to see you, Mr. Watts," said the journalist, cordially. "Also, if you are running with the circus and calculate on doing business here to-day, I'll have to see that you are fired out of town before noon. How are you? You're looking extremely well."

"Mr. Harkless," answered Watts, "I cherish no hard feelings, and I never said but what you done exactly right when I left, three years ago. No, sir; I'm not here in a professional way at all, and I don't want to be molested. I've connected myself with an oil company, and I'm down here to look over the ground. It beats poker and fan-tan hollow, though there ain't as many chances in favor of the dealer, and in oil it's the farmer that gets the rake-off. I've come back, but in an enterprising spirit this time, to open up a new field and shed light and money in Carlow. They told me never to show my face here again, but if you say I stay, I guess I stay. I always was sure there was oil in the county, and I want to prove it for everybody's benefit. Is it all right?"

"My dear fellow," laughed the young man, shaking the gambler's hand again, "it is all right. I have always been sorry I had to act against you. Everything is all right! Stay and bore to Corea if you like. Did ever you see such glorious weather?"

"I'll let you in on some shares," Watts called after him as he turned away. He nodded in reply and was leaving the room when Cynthia detained him by a flourish of the fly-brush. "Say," she said,—she always called him "Say"—"You've forgot your flower."

He came back, and thanked her. "Will you pin it on for me, Charmion?"

"I don't know what call you got to speak to me out of my name," she responded, looking at the floor moodily.

"Why?" he asked, surprised.

"I don't see why you want to make fun of me."

"I beg your pardon, Cynthia," he said gravely. "I didn't mean to do that. I haven't been considerate. I didn't think you'd be displeased. I'm very sorry. Won't you pin it on my coat?"

Her face was lifted in grateful pleasure, and she began to pin the rose to his lapel. Her hands were large and red and trembled. She dropped the flower, and, saying huskily, "I don't know as I could do it right," seized violently upon a pile of dishes and hurried from the room.

Harkless rescued the rose, pinned it on his coat himself, and, observing internally, for the hundredth time, that the red-haired waitress was the queerest creature in the village, set forth gaily upon his holiday.

When he reached the brick house on the pike he discovered a gentleman sunk in an easy and contemplative attitude in a big chair behind the veranda railing. At the click of the gate the lounger rose and disclosed the stalwart figure and brown, smiling, handsome face of Mr. Lige Willetts, an habitual devotee of Minnie Briscoe, and the most eligible bachelor of Carlow. "The ladies will be down right off," he said, greeting the editor's finery with a perceptible agitation and the editor himself with a friendly shake of the hand. "Mildy says to wait out here."

But immediately there was a faint rustling within the house: the swish of draperies on the stairs, a delicious whispering when light feet descend, tapping, to hearts that beat an answer, the telegraphic message, "We come! We come! We are near! We are near!" Lige Willetts stared at Harkless. He had never thought the latter good-looking until he saw him step to the door to take Miss Sherwood's hand and say in a strange, low, tense voice, "Good-morning," as if he were announcing, at the least: "Every one in the world except us two, died last night. It is a solemn thing, but I am very happy."

They walked, Minnie and Mr. Willetts a little distance in front of the others. Harkless could not have told, afterward, whether they rode, or walked, or floated on an air-ship to the court-house. All he knew distinctly was that a divinity in a pink shirt waist, and a hat that was woven of gauzy cloud by mocking fairies to make him stoop hideously to see under it, dwelt for the time on earth and was at his side, dazzling him in the morning sunshine. Last night the moon had lent her a silvery glamour; she had something of the ethereal whiteness of night-dews in that watery light, a nymph to laugh from a sparkling fountain, at the moon or, as he thought, remembering her courtesy for his pretty speech, perhaps a little lady of King Louis's court, wandering down the years from Fontainebleau and appearing to clumsy mortals sometimes, of a June night when the moon was in their heads.

But to-day she was of the clearest color, a pretty girl, whose gray eyes twinkled to his in gay companionship. He marked how the sunshine was spun into the fair shadows of her hair and seemed itself to catch a lustre, rather than to impart it, and the light of the June day drifted through the gauzy hat, touching her face with a delicate and tender flush that came and went like the vibrating pink of early dawn. She had the divinest straight nose, tip-tilted the faintest, most alluring trifle, and a dimple cleft her chin, "the deadliest maelstrom in the world!" He thrilled through and through. He had been only vaguely conscious of the dimple in the night. It was not until he saw her by daylight that he really knew it was there.

The village hummed with life before them. They walked through shimmering airs, sweeter to breathe than nectar is to drink. She caught a butterfly, basking on a jimson weed, and, before she let it go, held it out to him in her hand. It was a white butterfly. He asked which was the butterfly.

"Bravo!" she said, tossing the captive craft above their heads and watching the small sails catch the breeze; "And so you can make little flatteries in the morning, too. It is another courtesy you should be having from me, if it weren't for the dustiness of it. Wait till we come to the board walk."

She had some big, pink roses at her waist. "In the meantime," he answered, indicating these, "I know very well a lad that would be blithe to accept a pretty token of any lady's high esteem."

"But you have one, already, a very beautiful one." She gave him a genial up-and-down glance from head to foot, half quizzical, but so quick he almost missed it. And then he was glad he had found the straw hat with the youthful ribbon, and all his other festal vestures. "And a very becoming flower a white rose is," she continued, "though I am a bold girl to be blarneying with a young gentleman I met no longer ago than last night."

"But why shouldn't you blarney with a gentleman, when you began by saving his life?"

"Or, rather, when the gentleman had the politeness to gallop about the county with me tucked under his arm?" She stood still and laughed softly, but consummately, and her eyes closed tight with the mirth of it. She had taken one of the roses from her waist, and, as she stood, holding it by the long stem, its petals lightly pressed her lips.

"You may have it—in exchange," she said. He bent down to her, and she began to fasten the pink rose in place of the white one on his coat. She did not ask him, directly or indirectly, who had put the white one there for him, because she knew by the way it was pinned that he had done it himself. "Who is it that ev'ry morning brings me these lovely flow'rs?" she burlesqued, as he bent over her.

"'Mr. Wimby,'" he returned. "I will point him out to you. You must see him, and, also, Mr. Bodeffer, the oldest inhabitant—and crossest."

"Will you present them to me?"

"No; they might talk to you and take some of my time with you away from me." Her eyes sparkled into his for the merest fraction of a second, and she laughed half mockingly. Then she dropped his lapel and they proceeded. She did not put the white rose in her belt, but carried it.

The Square was heaving with a jostling, goodnatured, happy, and constantly increasing crowd that overflowed on Main Street in both directions; and the good nature of this crowd was augmented in the ratio that its size increased. The streets were a confusion of many colors, and eager faces filled every window opening on Main Street or the Square. Since nine o'clock all those of the courthouse had been occupied, and here most of the damsels congregated to enjoy the spectacle of the parade, and their swains attended, gallantly posting themselves at coignes of less vantage behind the ladies. Some of the faces that peeped from the dark, old courthouse windows were pretty, and some of them were not pretty; but nearly all of them were rosy-cheeked, and all were pleasant to see because of the good cheer they showed. Some of the gallants affected the airy and easy, entertaining the company with badinage and repartee; some were openly bashful. Now and then one of the latter, after long deliberation, constructed a laborious compliment for his inamorata, and, after advancing and propounding half of it, again retired into himself, smit with a blissful palsy. Nearly all of them conversed in tones that might have indicated that they were separated from each other by an acre lot or two.

Here and there, along the sidewalk below, a father worked his way through the throng, a licorice-bedaubed cherub on one arm, his coat (borne with long enough) on the other; followed by a mother with the other children hanging to her skirts and tagging exasperatingly behind, holding red and blue toy balloons and delectable batons of spiral-striped peppermint in tightly closed, sadly sticky fingers.

A thousand cries rent the air; the strolling mountebanks and gypsying booth-merchants; the peanut vendors; the boys with palm-leaf fans for sale; the candy sellers; the popcorn peddlers; the Italian with the toy balloons that float like a cluster of colored bubbles above the heads of the crowd, and the balloons that wail like a baby; the red-lemonade man, shouting in the shrill voice that reaches everywhere and endures forever: "Lemo! Lemo! Ice-cole lemo! Five cents, a nickel, a half-a-dime, the twentiethpotofadollah! Lemo! Ice-cole lemo!"—all the vociferating harbingers of the circus crying their wares. Timid youth, in shoes covered with dust through which the morning polish but dimly shone, and unalterably hooked by the arm to blushing maidens, bought recklessly of peanuts, of candy, of popcorn, of all known sweetmeats, perchance; and forced their way to the lemonade stands; and there, all shyly, silently sipped the crimson-stained ambrosia. Everywhere the hawkers dinned, and everywhere was heard the plaintive squawk of the toy balloon.

But over all rose the nasal cadence of the Cheap John, reeking oratory from his big wagon on the corner: "Walk up, walk up, walk up, ladies and gents! Here we are! Here we are! Make hay while we gather the moss. Walk up, one and all. Here I put this solid gold ring, sumptuous and golden, eighteen carats, eighteen golden carats of the priceless mother of metals, toiled fer on the wild Pacific slope, eighteen garnteed, I put this golden ring, rich and golden, in the package with the hangkacheef, the elegant and blue-ruled note-paper, self-writing pens, pencil and penholder. Who takes the lot? Who takes it, ladies and gents?"

His tongue curled about his words; he seemed to love them. "Fer a quat-of-a-dollah! Don't turn away, young man—you feller in the green necktie, there. We all see the young lady on your arm is a-langrishing fer the golden ring and the package. Faint heart never won fair wummin'. There you are, sir, and you'll never regret it. Go—and be happy! Now, who's the next man to git solid with his girl fer a quat-of-a-dollah? Life is a mysterus and unviolable shadder, my friends; who kin read its orgeries? To-day we are here—but to-morrow we may be in jail. Only a quat-of-a-dollah! We are Seventh-Day Adventists, ladies and gents, a-givin' away our belongings in the awful face of Michael, fer a quat-of-a-dollah. The same price fer each-an-devery individual, lady and gent, man, wummin, wife and child, and happiness to one and all fer a quat-of-a-dollah!"

Down the middle of the street, kept open between the waiting crowd, ran barefoot boys, many of whom had not slept at home, but had kept vigil in the night mists for the coming of the show, and, having seen the muffled pageant arrive, swathed, and with no pomp and panoply, had returned to town, rioting through jewelled cobwebs in the morning fields, happy in the pride of knowledge of what went on behind the scenes. To-night, or to-morrow, the runaways would face a woodshed reckoning with outraged ancestry; but now they caracoled in the dust with no thought of the grim deeds to be done upon them.

In the court-house yard, and so sinning in the very eye of the law, two swarthy, shifty-looking gentlemen were operating (with some greasy walnut shells and a pea) what the fanciful or unsophisticated might have been pleased to call a game of chance; and the most intent spectator of the group around them was Mr. James Bardlock, the Town Marshal. He was simply and unofficially and earnestly interested. Thus the eye of Justice may not be said to have winked upon the nefariousness now under its vision; it gazed with strong curiosity, an itch to dabble, and (it must be admitted) a growing hope of profit. The game was so direct and the player so sure. Several countrymen had won small sums, and one, a charmingly rustic stranger, with a peculiar accent (he said that him and his goil should now have a smoot' old time off his winninks—though the lady was not manifested), had won twenty-five dollars with no trouble at all. The two operators seemed depressed, declaring the luck against them and the Plattville people too brilliant at the game.

It was wonderful how the young couples worked their way arm-in-arm through the thickest crowds, never separating. Even at the lemonade stands they drank holding the glasses in their outer hands—such are the sacrifices demanded by etiquette. But, observing the gracious outpouring of fortune upon the rustic with the rare accent, a youth in a green tie disengaged his arm—for the first time in two hours—from that of a girl upon whose finger there shone a ring, sumptuous and golden, and, conducting her to a corner of the yard, bade her remain there until he returned. He had to speak to Hartly Bowlder, he explained.

Then he plunged, red-faced and excited, into the circle about the shell manipulators, and offered, to lay a wager.

"Hol' on there, Hen Fentriss," thickly objected a flushed young man beside him, "'iss my turn."

"I'm first. Hartley," returned the other. "You can hold yer bosses a minute, I reckon."

"Plenty fer each and all, chents," interrupted one of the shell-men. "Place yer spondulicks on de little ball. Wich is de next lucky one to win our money? Chent bets four sixty-five he seen de little ball go under de middle shell. Up she comes! Dis time *we* wins; Plattville can't win *every* time. Who's de next chent?"

Fentriss edged slowly out of the circle, abashed, and with rapidly whitening cheeks. He paused for a moment, outside, slowly realizing that all his money had gone in one wild, blind whirl—the money he had earned so hard and saved so hard, to make a holiday for his sweetheart and himself. He stole one glance around the building to where a patient figure waited for him. Then he fled down a side alley and soon was out upon the country road, tramping soddenly homeward through the dust, his chin sunk in his breast and his hands clenched tight at his sides. Now and then he stopped and bitterly hurled a stone at a piping bird on a fence, or gay Bob White in the fields. At noon the patient figure was still waiting in the corner of the court-house yard, meekly twisting the golden ring upon her finger.

But the flushed young man who had spoken thickly to her deserter drew an envied roll of bankbills from his pocket and began to bet with tipsy caution, while the circle about the gamblers watched with fervid interest, especially Mr. Bardlock, Town Marshal.

From far up Main Street came the cry "She's a-comin'! She's a-comin'!" and, this announcement of the parade proving only one of a dozen false alarms, a thousand discussions took place over old-fashioned silver timepieces as to when "she" was really due. Schofields' Henry was much appealed to as an arbiter in these discussions, from a sense of his having a good deal to do with time in a general sort of way; and thus Schofields' came to be reminded that it was getting on toward ten o'clock, whereas, in the excitement of festival, he had not yet struck nine. This, rushing forthwith to do, he did; and, in the elation of the moment, seven or eight besides. Miss Helen Sherwood was looking down on the mass of shifting color from a second-story window—whither many an eye was upturned in wonder—and she had the pleasure of seeing Schofields' emerge on the steps beneath her, when the bells had done, and heard the cheers (led by Mr. Martin) with which the laughing crowd greeted his appearance after the performance of his feat.

She turned beamingly to Harkless. "What a family it is!" she laughed. "Just one big, jolly family. I didn't know people could be like this until I came to Plattville."

"That is the word for it," he answered, resting his hand on the casement beside her. "I used to think it was desolate, but that was long ago." He leaned from the window to look down. In his dark cheek was a glow Carlow folk had never seen there; and somehow he seemed less thin and tired; indeed, he did not seem tired at all, by far the contrary; and he carried himself upright (when he was not stooping to see under the hat), though not as if he thought about it. "I believe they are the best people I know," he went on. "Perhaps it is because they have been so kind to me; but they are kind to each other, too; kind, good people——"

"I know," she said, nodding—a flower on the gauzy hat set to vibrating in a tantalizing way. "I know. There are fat women who rock and rock on piazzas by the sea, and they speak of country people as the 'lower classes.' How happy this big family is in not knowing it is the lower classes!" "We haven't read Nordau down here," said John. "Old Tom Martin's favorite work is 'The Descent of Man.' Miss Tibbs admires Tupper, and 'Beulah,' and some of us possess the works of E. P. Roe—and why not?"

"Yes; what of it," she returned, "since you escape Nordau? I think the conversation we hear from the other windows is as amusing and quite as loud as most of that I hear in Rouen during the winter; and Rouen, you know, is just like any other big place nowadays, though I suppose there are Philadelphians, for instance, who would be slow to believe a statement like that."

"Oh, but they are not all of Philadelphia——" He left the sentence, smilingly.

"And yet somebody said, 'The further West I travel the more convinced I am the Wise Men came from the East.'"

"Yes," he answered. "'From' is the important word in that."

"It was a girl from Southeast Cottonbridge, Massachusetts," said Helen, "who heard I was from Indiana and asked me if I didn't hate to live so far away from things." There was a pause, while she leaned out of the window with her face aside from him. Then she remarked carelessly, "I met her at Winter Harbor."

"Do you go to Winter Harbor?" he asked.

"We have gone there every summer until this one, for years. Have you friends who go there?"

"I had—once. There was a classmate of mine from Rouen——"

"What was his name? Perhaps I know him." She stole a glance at him. His face had fallen into sad lines, and he looked like the man who had come up the aisle with the Hon. Kedge Halloway. A few moments before he had seemed another person entirely.

64

"He's forgotten me, I dare say. I haven't seen him for seven years; and that's a long time, you know. Besides, he's 'out in the world,' where remembering is harder. Here in Plattville we don't forget."

"Were you ever at Winter Harbor?"

"I was—once. I spent a very happy day there long ago, when you must have been a little girl. Were you there in—"

"Listen!" she cried. "The procession is coming. Look at the crowd!" The parade had seized a psychological moment.

There was a fanfare of trumpets in the east. Lines of people rushed for the street, and, as one looked down on the straw hats and sunbonnets and many kinds of finer head apparel, tossing forward, they seemed like surf sweeping up the long beaches.

She was coming at last. The boys whooped in the middle of the street; some tossed their arms to heaven, others expressed their emotion by somersaults; those most deeply moved walked on their hands. In the distance one saw, over the heads of the multitude, tossing banners and the moving crests of triumphal cars, where "cohorts were shining in purple and gold." She *was* coming. After all the false alarms and disappointments, she was coming!

There was another flourish of music. Immediately all the band gave sound, and then, with blare of brass and the crash of drums, the glory of the parade burst upon Plattville. Glory in the utmost! The resistless impetus of the march-time music; the flare of royal banners, of pennons on the breeze; the smiling of beautiful Court Ladies and great, silken Nobles; the swaying of howdahs on camel and elephant, and the awesome shaking of the earth beneath the elephant's feet, and the gleam of his small but devastating eye (every one declared he looked the alarmed Mr. Snoddy full in the face as he passed, and Mr. Snoddy felt not at all reassured when Tom Martin severely hinted that it was with the threatening glance of a rival); then the badinage of the clown, creaking along in his donkey cart; the terrific recklessness of the spangled hero who was drawn by in a cage with two striped tigers; the spirit of the prancing steeds that drew the rumbling chariots, and the grace of the helmeted charioteers; the splendor of the cars and the magnificence of the paintings with which they were adorned; the ecstasy of all this glittering, shining, gorgeous pageantry needed even more than walking on your hands to express.

Last of all came the tooting calliope, followed by swarms of boys as it executed, "Wait till the clouds roll by, Jennie" with infinite dash and gusto.

When it was gone, Miss Sherwood's intent gaze relaxed—she had been looking on as eagerly as any child,—and she turned to speak to Harkless and discovered that he was no longer in the room; instead, she found Minnie and Mr. Willetts, whom he had summoned from another window.

"He was called away," explained Lige. "He thought he'd be back before the parade was over, and said you were enjoying it so much he didn't want to speak to you."

"Called away?" she said, inquiringly.

Minnie laughed. "Oh, everybody sends for Mr. Harkless."

"It was a farmer, name of Bowlder," added Mr. Willetts. "His son Hartley's drinking again, and there ain't any one but Harkless can do anything with him. You let him tackle a sick man to nurse, or a tipsy one to handle, and I tell you," Mr. Willetts went on with enthusiasm, "he is at home. It beats me,—and lots of people don't think college does a man any good! Why, the way he cured old Fis——"

"See!" cried Minnie, loudly, pointing out of the window. "Look down there. Something's happened."

There was a swirl in the crowd below. Men were running around a corner of the court-house, and the women and children were harking after. They went so fast, and there were so many of them, that immediately that whole portion of the yard became a pushing, tugging, pulling, squirming jam of people.

"It's on the other side," said Lige. "We can see from the hall window. Come quick, before these other folks fill it up."

They followed him across the building, and looked down on an agitated swarm of faces. Five men were standing on the entrance steps to the door below, and the crowd was thickly massed beyond, leaving a little semicircle clear about the steps. Those behind struggled to get closer, and leaped in the air to catch a glimpse of what was going on. Harkless stood alone on the top step, his hand resting on the shoulder of the pale and contrite and sobered Hartley. In the clear space, Jim Bardlock was standing with sheepishly hanging head, and between him and Harkless were the two gamblers of the walnut shells. The journalist held in his hand the implements of their profession.

"Give it all up," he was saying in his steady voice. "You've taken eighty-six dollars from this boy. Hand it over."

The men began to edge closer to the crowd, giving little, swift, desperate, searching looks from left to right, and right to left, moving nervously about, like weasels in a trap. "Close up there tight," said Harkless, sharply. "Don't let them out."

"W'y can't we git no square treatment here?" one of the gamblers whined; but his eyes, blazing with rage, belied the plaintive passivity of his tone. "We been running no skin. Wy d'ye say we gotter give up our own money? You gotter prove it was a skin. We risked our money fair."

"Prove it! Come up here, Eph Watts. Friends," the editor turned to the crowd, smiling, "friends, here's a man we ran out of town once, because he knew too much about things of this sort. He's come back to us again and he's here to stay. He'll give us an object-lesson on the shell game."

"It's pretty simple," remarked Mr. Watts. "The best way is to pick up the ball with your second finger and the back part of your thumb as you pretend to lay the shell down over it: this way." He illustrated, and showed several methods of manipulation, with professional sang-froid; and as he made plain the easy swindle by which many had been duped that morning, there arose an angry and threatening murmur.

"You all see," said Harkless, raising his voice a little, "what a simple cheat it is—and old as Pharaoh. Yet a lot of you stood around and lost your own money, and stared like idiots, and let Hartley Bowlder lose eighty-odd dollars on a shell racket, and not one of you lifted a hand. How hard did you work for what these two cheap crooks took from you? Ah!" he cried, "it is because you were greedy that they robbed you so easily. You know it's true. It's when you want to get something for nothing that the 'confidence men' steal the money you sweat for and make the farmer a laughing stock. And *you*, Jim Bardlock, Town Marshal!—you, who confess that you 'went in the game sixty cents' worth, yourself—" His eyes were lit with wrath as he raised his accusing hand and levelled it at the unhappy municipal.

The Town Marshal smiled uneasily and deprecatingly about him, and, meeting only angry glances, hearing only words of condemnation, he passed his hand unsteadily over his fat mustache, shifted from one leg to the other and back again, looked up, looked down, and then, an amiable and pleasure-loving man, beholding nothing but accusation and anger in heaven and earth, and wishing nothing more than to sink into the waters under the earth, but having no way of reaching them, finding his troubles quite unbearable, and unable to meet the manifold eye of man, he sought relief after the unsagacious fashion of a larger bird than he. His burly form underwent a series of convulsions not unlike sobs, and he shut his eyes tightly and held them so, presenting a picture of misery unequalled in the memory of any spectator. Harkless's outstretched hand began to shake. "You!" he tried to continue—"you, a man elected to——"

There came from the crowd the sound of a sad, high-keyed voice, drawling: "That's a nice vest Jim's got on, but it ain't hardly the feathers fitten for an ostrich, is it?"

The editor's gravity gave way; he broke into a ringing laugh and turned again to the shell-men. "Give up the boy's money. Hurry."

"Step down here and git it," said the one who had spoken.

There was a turbulent motion in the crowd, and a cry arose, "Run 'em out! Ride 'em on a rail! Tar and feathers! Run 'em out o' town!"

"I wouldn't dilly-dally long if I were you," said Harkless, and his advice seemed good to the shell-men. A roll of bills, which he counted and turned over to the elder Bowlder, was sullenly placed in his hand. The fellow who had not yet spoken clutched the journalist's sleeve with his dirty hand.

"We hain't done wit' youse," he said, hoarsely. "Don't belief it, not fer a minute, see?"

The Town Marshal opened his eyes briskly, and placing a hand on each of the gamblers, said: "I hereby do arrest your said persons, .and declare you my prisoners." The cry rose again, louder: "Run 'em out! String 'em up! Hang them! Hang them!" and a forward rush was made.

"This way, Jim. Be quick," said Harkless, quietly, bending down and jerking one of the gamblers half-way up the steps. "Get through the hall to the other side and then run them to the lock-up. No one will stop you that way. Watts and I will hold this door." Bardlock hustled his prisoners through the doorway, and the crowd pushed up the steps, while Harkless struggled to keep the vestibule clear until Watts got the double doors closed. "Stand back, here!" he cried; "it's all over. Don't be foolish. The law is good enough for us. Stand back, will you!"

He was laughing a little, shoving them back with open hand and elbow, when a small, compact group of men suddenly dashed up the steps together, and a heavy stick swung out over their heads. A straw hat with a gay ribbon sailed through the air. The journalist's long arms went out swiftly from his body in several directions, the hands not open, but clenched and hard. The next instant he and Mr. Watts stood alone on the steps, and a man with a bleeding, blaspheming mouth dropped his stick and tried to lose himself in the crowd. Mr. Watts was returning something he had not used to his hip-pocket.

"Prophets of Israel!" exclaimed William Todd, ruefully, "it wasn't Eph Watts's pistol. Did you see Mr. Harkless? I was up on them steps when he begun. I don't believe he needs as much takin' care of as we think."

"Wasn't it one of them Cross-Roads devils that knocked his hat off?" asked Judd Bennett. "I thought I see Bob Skillett run up with a club."

Harkless threw open the doors behind him; the hall was empty. "You may come in now," he said. "This isn't my court-house."

CHAPTER VIII

GLAD AFTERNOON: THE GIRL BY THE BLUE TENT-POLE

They walked slowly back along the pike toward the brick house. The white-ruffed fennel reached up its dusty yellow heads to touch her skirts as she passed, and then drooped, satisfied, against the purple iron-weed at the roadside. In the noonday silence no cricket chirped nor locust raised its lorn monotone; the tree shadows mottled the road with blue, and the level fields seemed to pant out a dazzling breath, the transparent "heat-waves" that danced above the low corn and green wheat.

He was stooping very much as they walked; he wanted to be told that he could look at her for a thousand years. Her face was rarely and exquisitely modelled, but, perhaps, just now the salient characteristic of her beauty (for the salient characteristic seemed to be a different thing at different times) was the coloring, a delicate glow under the white skin, that bewitched him in its seeming a reflection of the rich benediction of the noonday sun that blazed overhead.

Once he had thought the way to the Briscoe homestead rather a long walk; but now the distance sped malignantly; and strolled they never so slow, it was less than a "young bird's flutter from a wood." With her acquiescence he rolled a cigarette, and she began to hum lightly the air of a song, a song of an ineffably gentle, slow movement.

That, and a reference of the morning, and, perhaps, the smell of his tobacco mingling with the fragrance of her roses, awoke again the keen reminiscence of the previous night within him. Clearly outlined before him rose the high, green slopes and cool cliff-walls of the coast of Maine, while his old self lazily watched the sharp little waves through half-closed lids, the pale smoke of his cigarette blowing out under the rail of a waxen deck where he lay cushioned. And again a woman pelted his face with handfuls of rose-petals and cried: "Up lad and at 'em! Yonder is Winter Harbor." Again he sat in the oak-raftered Casino, breathless with pleasure, and heard a young girl sing the "Angel's Serenade," a young girl who looked so bravely unconscious of the big, hushed crowd that listened, looked so pure and bright and gentle and good, that he had spoken of her as "Sir Galahad's little sister." He recollected he had been much taken with this child; but he had not thought of her from that time to this, he supposed; had almost forgotten her. No! Her face suddenly stood out to his view as though he saw her with his physical eye—a sweet and vivacious child's face with light-brown hair and gray eyes and a short upper lip. . . . And the voice. . . .

He stopped short and struck his palms together. "You are Tom Meredith's little cousin!"

"The Great Harkless!" she answered, and stretched out her hand to him.

"I remember you!"

"Isn't it time?"

"Ah, but I never forgot you," he cried. "I thought I had. I didn't know who it was I was remembering. I thought it was fancy, and it was memory. I never forgot your voice, singing—and I remembered your face too; though I thought I didn't." He drew a deep breath. "*That* was why——"

"Tom Meredith has not forgotten you," she said, as he paused.

"Would you mind shaking hands once more?" he asked. She gave him her hand again. "With all my heart. Why?"

"I'm making a record at it. Thank you."

"They called me 'Sir Galahad's little sister' all one summer because the Great John Harkless called me that. You danced with me in the evening."

"Did I?"

"Ah," she said, shaking her head, "you were too busy being in love with Mrs. Van Skuyt to remember a waltz with only me! I was allowed to meet you as a reward for singing my very best, and you—you bowed with the indulgence of a grandfather, and asked me to dance."

"Like a grandfather? How young I was then! How time changes us!"

"I'm afraid my conversation did not make a great impression upon you," she continued.

"But it did. I am remembering very fast. If you will wait a moment, I will tell you some of the things you said."

The girl laughed merrily. Whenever she laughed he realized that it was becoming terribly difficult not to tell her how adorable she was. "I wouldn't risk it, if I were you," she warned him, "because I didn't speak to you at all. I shut my lips tight and trembled all over every bit of the time I was dancing with you. I did not sleep that night, because I was so unhappy, wondering what the Great Harkless would think of me. I knew he thought me unutterably stupid because I couldn't talk to him. I wanted to send him word that I knew I had bored him. I couldn't bear for him not to know that I knew I had. But he was not thinking of me in any way. He had gone to sea again in a big boat, the ungrateful pirate, cruising with Mrs. Van Skuyt."

70

"How time *does* change us!" said John. "You are wrong, though; I did think of you; I have al——"

"Yes," she interrupted, tossing her head in airy travesty of the stage coquette, "you think so—I mean you say so—now. Away with you and your blarneying!"

And so they went through the warm noontide, and little he cared for the heat that wilted the fat mullein leaves and made the barefoot boy, who passed by, skip gingerly through the burning dust with anguished mouth and watery eye. Little he knew of the locust that suddenly whirred his mills of shrillness in the maple-tree, and sounded so hot, hot, hot; or those others that railed at the country quiet from the dim shade around the brick house; or even the rain-crow that sat on the fence and swore to them in the face of a sunny sky that they should see rain ere the day were done.

Little the young man recked of what he ate at Judge Briscoe's good noon dinner: chicken wing and young roas'n'-ear; hot rolls as light as the fluff of a summer cloudlet; and honey and milk; and apple-butter flavored like spices of Arabia; and fragrant, flaky cherry-pie; and cool, rich, yellow cream. Lige Willetts was a lover, yet he said he asked no better than to Just go on eating that cherry-pie till a sweet death overtook him; but railroad sandwiches and restaurant chops might have been set before Harkless for all the difference it would have made to him.

At no other time is a man's feeling of companionship with a woman so strong as when he sits at table with her-not at a "decorated" and becatered and bewaitered table, but at a homely, appetizing, wholesome home table like old Judge Briscoe's. The very essence of the thing is domesticity, and the implication is utter confidence and liking. There are few greater dangers for a bachelor. An insinuating imp perches on his shoulder, and, softly tickling the bachelor's ear with the feathers of an arrow-shaft, whispers: "Pretty nice, isn't it, eh? Rather pleasant to have that girl sitting there, don't you think? Enjoy having her notice your butter-plate was empty? Think it exhilarating to hand her those rolls? Looks nice, doesn't she? Says 'Thank you' rather prettily? Makes your lonely breakfast seem mighty dull, doesn't it? How would you like to have her pour your coffee for you to-morrow, my boy? How would it seem to have such pleasant company all the rest of your life? Pretty cheerful, eh?"

When Miss Sherwood passed the editor the apple-butter, the casual, matter-of-course way she did it entranced him in a strange, exquisite wonderment. He did not set the dish down when she put it in his hand, but held it straight out before him, just looking at it, until Mr. Willetts had a dangerous choking fit, for which Minnie was very proud of Lige; no one could have suspected that it was the veil of laughter. When Helen told John he really must squeeze a lemon into his iced tea, he felt that his one need in life was to catch her up in his arms and run away with her, not anywhere in particular, but just run and run and run away.

After dinner they went out to the veranda and the gentlemen smoked. The judge set his chair down on the ground, tilted back in it with his feet on the steps, and blew a wavery domed city up in the air. He called it solid comfort. He liked to sit out from under the porch roof, he said; he wanted to see more of the sky. The others moved their chairs down to join him in the celestial vision. There had blown across the heaven a feathery, thin cloud or two, but save for these, there was nothing but glorious and tender, brilliant blue. It seemed so clear and close one marvelled the little church spire in the distance did not pierce it; yet, at the same time, the eye ascended miles and miles into warm, shimmering ether. Far away two buzzards swung slowly at anchor, half-way to the sun.

"'O bright, translucent, cerulean hue,
Let my wide wings drift on in you,'"

said Harkless, pointing them out to Helen.

"You seem to get a good deal of fun out of this kind of weather," observed Lige, as he wiped his brow and shifted his chair out of the sun.

"I expect you don't get such skies as this up in Rouen," said the judge, looking at the girl from between half-closed eyelids.

"It's the same Indiana sky, I think," she answered.

"I guess maybe in the city you don't see as much of it, or think as much about it. Yes, they're the Indiana skies," the old man went on.

> Skies as blue
> As the eyes of children when they smile at you.'

"There aren't any others anywhere that ever seemed much like them to me. They've been company for me all my life. I don't think there are any others half as beautiful, and I know there aren't any as sociable. They were always so." He sighed gently, and Miss Sherwood fancied his wife must have found the Indiana skies as lovely as he had, in the days of long ago. "Seems to me they *are* the softest and bluest and kindest in the world."

"I think they are," said Helen, "and they are more beautiful than the 'Italian skies,' though I doubt if many of us Hoosiers realize it; and— certainly no one else does."

The old man leaned over and patted her hand. Harkless gasped. "'Us Hoosiers!'" chuckled the judge. "You're a great Hoosier, young lady! How much of your life have you spent in the State? 'Us Hoosiers!'"

"But I'm going to be a good one," she answered, gaily, "and if I'm good enough, when I grow up maybe I'll be a great one."

The buckboard had been brought around, and the four young people climbed in, Harkless driving. Before they started, the judge, standing on the horse-block in front of the gate, leaned over and patted Miss Sherwood's hand again. Harkless gathered up the reins.

"You'll make a great Hoosier, all right," said the old man, beaming upon the girl. "You needn't worry about that, I guess, my dear."

When he said "my dear," Harkless spoke to the horses.

"Wait," said the judge, still holding the girl's hand. "You'll make a great Hoosier, some day; don't fret. You're already a very beautiful one." Then he bent his white head and kissed her, gallantly. John said: "Good afternoon, judge"; the whip cracked like a pistol-shot, and the buckboard dashed off in a cloud of dust.

"Every once in a while, Harkless," the old fellow called after them, "you must remember to look at the team."

The enormous white tent was filled with a hazy yellow light, the warm, dusty, mellow light that thrills the rejoicing heart because it is found nowhere in the world except in the tents of a circus—the canvas-filtered sunshine and sawdust atmosphere of show day. Through the entrance the crowd poured steadily, coming from the absorptions of the wild-animal tent to feast upon greater wonders; passing around the sawdust ellipse that contained two soul-cloying rings, to find seats whence they might behold the splendors so soon to be unfolded. Every one who was not buying the eternal lemonade was eating something; and the faces of children shone with gourmand rapture; indeed, very often the eyes of them were all you saw, half-closed in palate-gloating over a huge apple, or a bulky oblong of popcorn, partly unwrapped from its blue tissue-paper cover; or else it might be a luscious pink crescent of watermelon, that left its ravisher stained and dripping to the brow.

Here, as in the morning, the hawkers raised their cries in unintermittent shrillness, offering to the musically inclined the Happy Evenings Song-book, alleged to contain those treasures, all the latest songs of the day, or presented for the consideration of the humorous the Lawrence Lapearl Joke-book, setting forth in full the art of comical entertainment and repartee. (Schofields' Henry bought two of these—no doubt on the principle that two were twice as instructive as one—intending to bury himself in study and do battle with Tom Martin on his own ground.)

Here swayed the myriad palm-leaf fans; here paraded blushing youth and rosy maiden, more relentlessly arm-in-arm than ever; here crept the octogenarian, Mr. Bodeffer, shaking on cane and the shoulder of posterity; here waddled Mr. Snoddy, who had hurried through the animal tent for fear of meeting the elephant; here marched sturdy yeomen and stout wives; here came William Todd and his Anna Belle, the good William hushed with the embarrassments of love, but looking out warily with the white of his eye for Mr. Martin, and determined not to sit within a hundred yards of him; here rolled in the orbit of habit the bacchanal, Mr. Wilkerson, who politely answered in kind all the uncouth roarings and guttural ejaculations of jungle and fen that came from the animal tent; in brief, here came with lightest hearts the population of Carlow and part of Amo.

Helen had found a true word: it was a big family. Jim Bardlock, broadly smiling and rejuvenated, shorn of depression, paused in front of the "reserve" seats, with Mrs. Bardlock on his arm, and called loudly to a gentleman on a tier about the level of Jim's head: "How are ye? I reckon we were a *little* too smart fer 'em, this morning, huh?" Five or six hundred people—every one within hearing—fumed to look at Jim; but the gentleman addressed was engaged in conversation with a lady and did not notice.

"Hi! Hi, there! *Say*! Mr. Harkless!" bellowed Jim, informally. The people turned to look at Harkless. His attention was arrested and his cheek grew red.

"*What is it?*" he asked, a little confused and a good deal annoyed.

"I don't hear what ye say," shouted Jim, putting his hand to his ear.

"*What is it?*" repeated the young man. "I'll kill that fellow to-night," he added to Lige Willetts. "Some one ought to have done it long ago."

"What?"

"I *say*, WHAT IS IT?"

"I only wanted to say me and you certainly did fool these here Hoosiers this morning, huh? Hustled them two fellers through the court-house, and nobody never thought to slip round to the other door and head us off. Ha, ha! We were jest a *leetle* too many fer 'em, huh?"

From an upper tier of seats the rusty length of Mr. Martin erected itself joint by joint, like an extension ladder, and he peered down over the gaping faces at the Town Marshal. "Excuse me," he said sadly to those behind him, but his dry voice penetrated everywhere, "I got up to hear Jim say 'We' again."

Mr. Bardlock joined in the laugh against himself, and proceeded with his wife to some seats, forty or fifty feet distant. When he had settled himself comfortably, he shouted over cheerfully to the unhappy editor: "Them shell-men got it in fer you, Mr. Harkless."

"Ain't that fool shet up *yit*?" snarled the aged Mr. Bodeffer, indignantly. He was sitting near the young couple, and the expression of his sympathy was distinctly audible to them and many others. "Got no more regards than a brazing calf-disturbin' a feller with his sweetheart!"

"The both of 'em says they're goin' to do fer you," bleated Mr. Bardlock. "Swear they'll git their evens with ye."

Mr. Martin rose again. "Don't git scared and leave town, Mr. Harkless," he called out; "Jim'll protect you."

Vastly to the young man's relief the band began to play, and the equestrians and equestriennes capered out from the dressing-tent for the "Grand Entrance," and the performance commenced. Through the long summer afternoon it went on: wonders of horsemanship and horsewomanship; hair-raising exploits on wires, tight and slack; giddy tricks on the high trapeze; feats of leaping and tumbling in the rings; while the tireless musicians blatted inspiringly through it all, only pausing long enough to allow that uproarious jester, the clown, to ask the ring-master what he would do if a young lady came up and kissed him on the street, and to exploit his hilarities during the short intervals of rest for the athletes.

When it was over, John and Helen found themselves in the midst of a densely packed crowd, and separated from Miss Briscoe and Lige. People were pushing and shoving, and he saw her face grow pale. He realized with a pang of sympathy how helpless he would feel if he were as small as she, and at his utmost height could only see big, suffocating backs and huge shoulders pressing down from above. He was keeping them from crowding heavily upon her with all his strength, and a royal feeling of protectiveness came over him. She was so little. And yet, without the remotest hint of hardness, she gave him such a distinct impression of poise and equilibrium, she seemed so able to meet anything that might come, to understand it—even to laugh at it—so Americanly capable and sure of the event, that in spite of her pale cheek he could not feel quite so protective as he wished to feel.

He managed to get her to one of the tent-poles, and placed her with her back to it. Then he set one of his own hands against it over her head, braced himself and stood, keeping a little space about her, ruggedly letting the crowd surge against him as it would; no one should touch her in rough carelessness.

"Thank you. It was rather trying in there," she said, and looked up into his eyes with a divine gratitude.

"Please don't do that," he answered in a low voice.

"Do what?"

"Look like that."

She not only looked like that, but more so. "Young man, young man," she said, "I fear you're wishful of turning a girl's head."

The throng was thick around them, garrulous and noisy, but they two were more richly alone together, to his appreciation, than if they stood on some far satellite of Mars. He was not to forget that moment, and he kept the picture of her, as she leaned against the big blue tent-pole, there, in his heart: the clear gray eyes lifted to his, the delicate face with the color stealing back to her cheeks, and the brave little figure that had run so straight to him out of the night shadows. There was something about her, and in the moment, that suddenly touched him with a saddening sweetness too keen to be borne; the forget-me-not finger of the flying hour that could not come again was laid on his soul, and he felt the tears start from his heart on their journey to his eyes. He knew that he should always remember that moment. She knew it, too. She put her hand to her cheek and turned away from him a little tremulously. Both were silent.

They had been together since early morning. Plattville was proud of him. Many a friendly glance from the folk who jostled about them favored his suit and wished both of them well, and many lips, opening to speak to Harkless in passing, closed when their owners (more tactful than Mr. Bardlock) looked a second time.

Old Tom Martin, still perched alone On his high seat, saw them standing by the tent-pole, and watched them from under his rusty hat brim. "I reckon it's be'n three or four thousand years since I was young," he sighed to himself; then, pushing his hat still further down over his eyes: "I don't believe I'd ort to rightly look on at that." He sighed again as he rose, and gently spoke the name of his dead wife: "Marjie,— it's be'n lonesome, sometimes. I reckon you're mighty tired waitin' for me, ever since sixty-four—yet maybe not; Ulysses S. Grant's over on your side now, and perhaps you've got acquainted with him; you always thought a good deal more of him than you did of me."

"Do you see that tall old man up there?" said Helen, nodding her head toward Martin. "I think I should like to know him. I'm sure I like him."

"That is old Tom Martin."

"I know."

"I was sorry and ashamed about all that conspicuousness and shouting. It must have been very unpleasant for you; it must have been so, for a stranger. Please try to forgive me for letting you in for it."

"But I liked it. It was 'all in the family,' and it was so jolly and good-natured, and that dear old man was so bright. Do you know," she said softly, "I don't think I'm such a stranger—I—I think I love all these people a great deal—in spite of having known them only two days."

At that a wild exhilaration possessed him. He wanted to shake hands with everybody in the tent, to tell them all that he loved them with his whole heart, but, what was vastly more important, *she* loved them a great deal —in spite of having known them only two days!

He made the horses prance on the homeward drive, and once, when she told him that she had read a good many of his political columns in the "Herald," he ran them into a fence. After this it occurred to him that they were nearing their destination and had come at a perversely sharp gait; so he held the roans down to a snail's pace (if it be true that a snail's natural gait is not a trot) for the rest of the way, while they talked of Tom Meredith and books and music, and discovered that they differed widely about Ibsen.

They found Mr. Fisbee in the yard, talking to Judge Briscoe. As they drove up, and before the horses had quite stopped, Helen leaped to the ground and ran to the old scholar with both her hands outstretched to him. He looked timidly at her, and took the hands she gave him; then he produced from his pocket a yellow telegraph envelope, watching her anxiously as she received it. However, she seemed to attach no particular importance to it, and, instead of opening it, leaned toward him, still holding one of his hands.

"These awful old men!" Harkless groaned inwardly as he handed the horses over to the judge. "I dare say *he*'ll kiss her, too." But, when the editor and Mr. Willetts had gone, it was Helen who kissed Fisbee.

"They're coming out to spend the evening, aren't they?" asked Briscoe, nodding to the young men as they set off down the road.

"Lige has to come whether he wants to or not," Minnie laughed, rather consciously; "It's his turn to-night to look after Mr. Harkless."

"I guess he won't mind coming," said the judge.

"Well," returned his daughter, glancing at Helen, who stood apart, reading the telegram to Fisbee, "I know if he follows Mr. Harkless he'll get here pretty soon after supper—as soon as the moon comes up, anyway."

The editor of the "Herald" was late to his supper that evening. It was dusk when he reached the hotel, and, for the first time in history, a gentleman sat down to meat in that house of entertainment in evening dress. There was no one in the diningroom when he went in; the other boarders had finished, and it was Cynthia's "evening out," but the landlord came and attended to his guests' wants himself, and chatted with him while he ate.

"There's a picture of Henry Clay," remarked Landis, in obvious relevancy to his companion's attire, "there's a picture of Henry Clay somewheres about the house in a swallow-tail coat. Governor Ray spoke here in one in early times, Bodeffer says, except it was higher built up 'n yourn about the collar, and had brass buttons, I think. Ole man Wimby was here to-night," the landlord continued, changing the subject. "He waited around fer ye a good while. He's be'n mighty wrought up sence the trouble this morning, an' wanted to see ye bad. I don't know 'f you seen it, but that feller 't knocked your hat off was mighty near tore to pieces in the crowd before he got away. 'Seems some the boys re-*cog*-nized him as one the Cross-Roads Skillets, and sicked the dogs on him, and he had a pretty mean time of it. Wimby says the Cross-Roads folks'll be worse 'n ever, and, says he, 'Tell him to stick close to town,' says he. 'They'll do anything to git him now,' says he, 'and *resk* anything.' I told him you wouldn't take no stock in it, but, see here, don't you put nothin' too mean fer them folks. I tell you, Mr. Harkless, plenty of us are scared fer ye."

The good fellow was so earnest that when the editor's meal was finished and he would have departed, Landis detained him almost by force until the arrival of Mr. Willetts, who, the landlord knew, was his allotted escort' for the evening. When Lige came (wearing a new tie, a pink one he had hastened to buy as soon as his engagements had allowed him the opportunity), Mr. Landis hissed a savage word of reproach for his tardiness in his ear, and whisperingly bade him not let the other out of reach that night, to which Willetts replied with a nod implying his trustworthiness; and the young men set off in the darkness.

Harkless wondered if his costume were not an injustice to his companion, but he did not regret it; he would wear his best court suit, his laces and velvets, for deference to that lady. It was a painful thing to remember his dusty rustiness of the night before, the awful Carlow cut of his coat, and his formless black cravat; the same felt hat he wore again to-night, perforce, but it was brushed—brushed almost to holes in spots, and somehow he had added a touch of shape to it. His dress-coat was an antique; fashions had changed, no doubt; he did not know; possibly she would recognize its vintage—but it was a dress-coat.

Lige walked along talking; Harkless answering "Yes" and "No" at random. The woodland-spiced air was like champagne to him; the road under foot so elastic and springy that he felt like a thoroughbred before a race; he wanted to lift his foot knee-high at every step, he had so much energy to spare. In the midst of a speech of Lige's about the look of the wheat he suddenly gave out a sigh so deep, so heartfelt, so vibrant, so profound, that Willetts turned with astonishment; but when his eye reached his companion's face, Harkless was smiling. The editor extended his hand.

"Shake hands, Lige," he cried.

The moon peeped over the shoulder of an eastern wood, and the young men suddenly descried their long shadows stretching in front of them. Harkless turned to look at the silhouetted town, the tree-tops and roofs and the Methodist church spire, silvered at the edges.

"Do you see that town, Willetts?" he asked, laying his fingers on his companion's sleeve. "That's the best town in the United States!"

78

"I always kind of thought you didn't much like it," said the other, puzzled. "Seemed to me you always sort of wished you hadn't settled here."

A little further on they passed Mr. Fisbee. He was walking into the village with his head thrown back, a strange thing for him. They gave him a friendly greeting and passed on.

"Well, it beats me!" observed Lige, when the old man was out of hearing. "He's be'n there to supper again. He was there all day yesterday, and with 'em at the lecture, and at the deepo day before and he looks like another man, and dressed up— for him—to beat thunder——What do you expect makes him so thick out there all of a sudden?"

"I hadn't thought about it. The judge and he have been friends a good while, haven't they?"

"Yes, three or four years; but not like this. It beats *me*! He's all upset over Miss Sherwood, I think. Old enough to be her grandfather, too, the old——"

His companion stopped him, dropping a hand on his shoulder.

"Listen!"

They were at the corner of the Briscoe picket fence, and a sound lilted through the stillness—a touch on the keys that Harkless knew. "Listen," he whispered.

It was the "Moonlight Sonata" that Helen was playing. "It's a pretty piece," observed Lige after a time. John could have choked him, but he answered: "Yes, it is seraphic."

"Who made it up?" pursued Mr. Willetts.

"Beethoven."

"Foreigner, I expect. Yet in some way or another makes me think of fishing down on the Wabash bend in Vigo, and camping out nights like this; it's a mighty pretty country around there—especially at night."

The sonata was finished, and then she sang—sang the "Angel's Serenade." As the soft soprano lifted and fell in the modulations of that song there was in its timbre, apart from the pure, amber music of it, a questing, seeking pathos, and Willetts felt the hand on his shoulder tighten and then relax; and, as the song ended, he saw that his companion's eyes were shining and moist.

CHAPTER IX

NIGHT: IT IS BAD LUCK TO SING BEFORE BREAKFAST

There was a lace of faint mists along the creek and beyond, when John and Helen reached their bench (of course they went back there), and broken roundelays were croaking from a bayou up the stream, where rakish frogs held carnival in resentment of the lonesomeness. The air was still and close. Hundreds of fire-flies coquetted with the darkness amongst the trees across the water, glinting from unexpected spots, shading their little lanterns for a second to glow again from other shadows. The sky was a wonderful olive green; a lazy cloud drifted in it and lapped itself athwart the moon.

"The dead painters design the skies for us each day and night, I think," Helen said, as she dropped a little scarf from her shoulders and leaned back on the bench. "It must be the only way to keep them happy and busy 'up there.' They let them take turns, and those not on duty, probably float around and criticise."

"They've given a good man his turn to-night," said John; "some quiet colorist, a poetic, friendly soul, no Turner—though I think I've seen a Turner sunset or two in Plattville."

"It was a sculptor's sunset this evening. Did you see it?—great massy clouds piled heap on heap, almost with violence. I'm sure it was Michelangelo. The judge didn't think it meant Michelangelo; he thought it meant rain."

"Michelangelo gets a chance rather often, doesn't he, considering the number of art people there must be over there? I believe I've seen a good many sunsets of his, and a few dawns, too; the dawns not for a long time— I used to see them more frequently toward the close of senior year, when we sat up all night talking, knowing we'd lose one another soon, and trying to hold on as long as we could."

She turned to him with a little frown. "Why have you never let Tom Meredith know you were living so near him, less than a hundred miles, when he has always liked and admired you above all the rest of mankind? I know that he has tried time and again to hear of you, but the other men wrote that they knew nothing—that it was thought you had gone abroad. I had heard of you, and so must he have seen your name in the Rouen papers— about the 'White-Caps,' and in politics—but he would never dream of connecting the Plattville Mr. Harkless with *his* Mr. Harkless, though *I* did, just a little, and rather vaguely. I knew, of course, when you came into the lecture. But why haven't you written to my cousin?"

"Rouen seems a long way from here," he answered quietly. "I've only been there once—half a day on business. Except that, I've never been further away than Amo or Gainesville, for a convention or to make a speech, since I came here."

"Wicked!" she exclaimed, "To shut yourself up like this! I said it was fine to drop out of the world; but why have you cut off your old friends from you? Why haven't you had a relapse, now and then, and come over to hear Ysaye play and Melba sing, or to see Mansfield or Henry Irving, when we have had them? And do you think you've been quite fair to Tom? What right had you to assume that he had forgotten you?"

"Oh, I didn't exactly mean forgotten," he said, pulling a blade of grass to and fro between his fingers, staring at it absently. "It's only that I have dropped out of the world, you know. I kept track of every one, saw most of my friends, or corresponded, now and then, for a year or so after I left college; but people don't miss you much after a while. They rather expected me to do a lot of things, in a way, you know, and I wasn't doing them. I was glad to get away. I always had an itch for newspaper work, and I went on a New York paper. Maybe it was the wrong paper; at least, I wasn't fit for it. There was something in the side of life I saw, too, not only on the paper, that made me heart-sick; and then the rush and fight and scramble to be first, to beat the other man. Probably I am too squeamish. I saw classmates and college friends diving into it, bound to come out ahead, dear old, honest, frank fellows, who had been so happy-go-lucky and kind and gay, growing too busy to meet and be good to any man who couldn't be good to them, asking (more delicately) the eternal question, 'What does it get me?' You might think I bad-met with unkindness; but it was not so; it was the other way more than I deserved. But the cruel competition, the thousands fighting for places, the multitude scrambling for each ginger-bread baton, the cold faces on the streets—perhaps it's all right and good; of course it has to be—but I wanted to get out of it, though I didn't want to come here. That was chance. A new man bought the paper I was working for, and its policy changed. Many of the same men still wrote for it, facing cheerfully about and advocating a tricky theory, vehement champions of a set of personal schemers and waxy images."

He spoke with feeling; but now, as though a trifle ashamed of too much seriousness, and justifiably afraid of talking like one of his own editorials, he took a lighter tone. "I had been taken on the paper through a friend and not through merit, and by the same undeserved, kindly influence, after a month or so I was set to writing short political editorials, and was at it nearly two years. When the paper changed hands the new proprietor indicated that he would be willing to have me stay and write the other way. I refused; and it became somewhat plain to me that I was beginning to be a failure.

"A cousin of mine, the only relative I had, died in Chicago, and I went to his funeral. I happened to hear of the Carlow 'Herald' through an agent there, the most eloquent gentleman I ever met. I was younger, and even more thoughtless than now, and I had a little money and I handed it over for the 'Herald.' I wanted to run a paper myself, and to build up a power! And then, though I only lived here the first few years of my life and all the rest of it had been spent in the East, I was born in Indiana, and, in a way, the thought of coming back to a life-work in my native State appealed to me. I always had a dim sort of feeling that the people out in these parts knew more—had more sense and were less artificial, I mean— and were kinder, and tried less to be somebody else, than almost any other people anywhere. And I believe it's so. It's dull, here in Carlow, of course—that is, it used to be. The agent explained that I could make the paper a daily at once, with an enormous circulation in the country. I was very, very young. Then I came here and saw what I had got. Possibly it is because I am sensitive that I never let Tom know. They expected me to amount to something; but I don't believe his welcome would be less hearty to a failure—he is a good heart."

"Failure!" she cried, and clapped her hands and laughed.

"I'm really not very tragic about it, though I must seem consumed with self-pity," he returned, smiling. "It is only that I have dropped out of the world while Tom is still in it."

"Dropped out of the world!'" she echoed, impatiently. "Can't you see you've dropped into it? That you——"

"Last night I was honored by your praise of my graceful mode of quitting it!"

"And so you wish me to be consistent!" she retorted scornfully. "What becomes of your gallantry when *we* abide by reason?"

"True enough; equality is a denial of privilege."

"And privilege is a denial of equality. I don't like that at all." She turned a serious, suddenly illuminated face upon him and spoke earnestly. "It's my hobby, I should tell you, and I'm very tired of that nonsense about 'women always sounding the personal note.' It *should* be sounded as we would sound it. And I think we could bear the loss of 'privilege'—"

He laughed and raised a protesting hand. "But *we* couldn't."

"No, you couldn't; it's the ribbon of superiority in your buttonhole. I know several women who manage to live without men to open doors for them, and I think I could bear to let a man pass before me now and then, or wear his hat in an office where I happened to be; and I could get my own ice at a dance, I think, possibly with even less fuss and scramble than I've sometimes observed in the young men who have done it for me. But you know you would never let us do things for ourselves, no matter what legal equality might be declared, even when we get representation for our taxation. You will never be able to deny yourselves giving us our 'privilege.' I hate being waited on. I'd rather do things for myself."

She was so earnest in her satire, so full of scorn and so serious in her meaning, and there was such a contrast between what she said and her person; she looked so preeminently the pretty marquise, all silks and softness, the little exquisite, so essentially to be waited on and helped, to have cloaks thrown over the dampness for her to tread upon, to be run about for—he could see half a dozen youths rushing about for her ices, for her carriage, for her chaperone, for her wrap, at dances—that to save his life he could not repress a chuckle. He managed to make it inaudible, however; and it was as well that he did.

"I understand your love of newspaper work," she went on, less vehemently, but not less earnestly. "I have always wanted to do it myself, wanted to immensely. I can't think of any more fascinating way of earning one's living. And I know I could do it. Why don't you make the 'Herald' a daily?"

To hear her speak of "earning one's living" was too much for him. She gave the impression of riches, not only for the fine texture and fashioning of her garments, but one felt that luxuries had wrapped her from her birth. He had not had much time to wonder what she did in Plattville; it had occurred to him that it was a little odd that she could plan to spend any extent of time there, even if she had liked Minnie Briscoe at school. He felt that she must have been sheltered and petted and waited on all her life; one could not help yearning to wait on her.

He answered inarticulately, "Oh, some day," in reply to her question, and then burst into outright laughter.

"I might have known you wouldn't take me seriously," she said with no indignation, only a sad wistfulness. "I am well used to it. I think it is because I am not tall; people take big girls with more gravity. Big people are nearly always listened to."

"Listened to?" he said, and felt that he must throw himself on his knees before her. "You oughtn't to mind being Titania. She was listened to, you——"

She sprang to her feet and her eyes flashed. "Do you think personal comment is ever in good taste?" she cried fiercely, and in his surprise he almost fell off the bench. "If there is one thing I cannot bear, it is to be told that I am '*small*' I am not! Every one who isn't a giantess isn't '*small*'. I *hate* personalities! I am a great deal over five feet, a great deal more than that. I——"

"Please, *please*," he said, "I didn't——"

"Don't say you are sorry," she interrupted, and in spite of his contrition he found her angry voice delicious, it was still so sweet, hot with indignation, but ringing, not harsh. "Don't say you didn't mean it; because you did! You can't unsay it, you cannot alter it! Ah!" She drew in her breath with a sharp sigh, and covering her face with her hands, sank back upon the bench. "I will not cry," she said, not so firmly as she thought she did.

"My blessed child!" he cried, in great distress and perturbation, "What have I done? I—I——"

"Call me 'small' all you like!" she answered. "I don't care. It isn't that. You mustn't think me such an imbecile." She dropped her hands from her face and shook the tears from her eyes with a mournful laugh. He saw that her hands were clenched tightly and her lip trembled. "I will not cry!" she said in a low voice.

"Somebody ought to murder me; I ought to have thought—personalities *are* hideous——"

"Don't! It wasn't that."

"I ought to be shot——"

"Ah, please don't say that," she said, shuddering; "please don't, not even as a joke—after last night."

"But I ought to be for hurting you, indeed——"

She laughed sadly, again. "It wasn't that. I don't care what you call me. I am small. You'll try to forgive me for being such a baby? I didn't mean anything I said. I haven't acted so badly since I was a child."

"It's my fault, all of it. I've tired you out. And I let you get into that crush at the circus—" he was going on, remorsefully.

"*That!*" she interrupted. "I don't think I would have missed the circus." He had a thrilling hope that she meant the tent-pole; she looked as if she meant that, but he dared not let himself believe it.

"No," he continued; "I have been so madly happy in being with you that I've fairly worn out your patience. I've haunted you all day, and I have——"

"All that has nothing to do with it," she said, slowly. "Just after you left, this afternoon, I found that I could not stay here. My people are going abroad, to Dresden, at once, and I must go with them. That's what almost made me cry. I leave to-morrow morning."

He felt something strike at his heart. In the sudden sense of dearth he had no astonishment that she should betray such agitation over her departure from a place she had known so little, and friends who certainly were not part of her life. He rose to his feet, and, resting his arm against a sycamore, stood staring away from her at nothing.

She did not move. There was a long silence.

84

He had wakened suddenly; the skies had been sapphire, the sward emerald, Plattville a Camelot of romance; to be there, enchantment—and now, like a meteor burned out in a breath, the necromancy fell away and he gazed into desolate years. The thought of the Square, his dusty office, the bleak length of Main Street, as they should appear to-morrow, gave him a faint physical sickness. To-day it had all been touched to beauty; he had felt fit to live and work there a thousand years—a fool's dream, and the waking was to emptiness. He should die now of hunger and thirst in that Sahara; he hoped the Fates would let it be soon—but he knew they would not; knew that this was hysteria, that in his endurance he should plod on, plod, plod dustily on, through dingy, lonely years.

There was a rumble of thunder far out on the western prairie. A cold breath stole through the hot stillness, and an arm of vapor reached out between the moon and the quiet earth. Darkness fell. The man and the girl kept silence between them. They might have been two sad guardians of the black little stream that splashed unseen at their feet. Now and then an echo of far away lightning faintly illumined them with a green light. Thunder rolled nearer, ominously; the gods were driving their chariots over the bridge. The chill breath passed, leaving the air again to its hot inertia.

"I did not want to go," she said, at last, with tears just below the surface of her voice. "I wanted to stay here, but he—they wouldn't—I can't."

"Wanted to stay here?" he said, huskily, not turning. "Here?"

"Yes."

"In Rouen, you mean?"

"In Plattville."

"In Plattville?" He turned now, astounded.

"Yes; wouldn't you have taken me on the 'Herald'?" She rose and came toward him. "I could have supported myself here if you would—and I've studied how newspapers are made; I know I could have earned a wage. We could have made it a daily." He searched in vain for a trace of raillery in her voice; there was none; she seemed to intend her words to be taken literally.

"I don't understand," he said. "I don't know what you mean."

"I mean that I want to stay here; that I ought to stay here; that my conscience tells me I should—but I can't and it makes me very unhappy. That was why I acted so badly."

"Your conscience!" he cried.

"Oh, I know what a jumble and puzzle it must seem to you."

"I only know one thing; that you are going away to-morrow morning, and that I shall never see you again."

The darkness had grown heavy. They could not see each other; but a wan glimmer gave him a fleeting, misty view of her; she stood half-turned away from him, her hand to her cheek in the uncertain fashion of his great moment of the afternoon; her eyes-he saw in the flying picture that he caught—were adorably troubled and her hand trembled. She had been irresistible in her gaiety; but now that a mysterious distress assailed her, the reason for which he had no guess, she was so divinely pathetic; and seemed such a rich and lovely and sad and happy thing to have come into his life only to go out of it; and he was so full of the prophetic sense of loss of her—it seemed so much like losing everything—that he found too much to say to be able to say anything.

He tried to speak, and choked a little. A big drop of rain fell on his bare head. Neither of them noticed the weather or cared for it. They stood with the renewed blackness hanging like a thick drapery between them.

"Can—can you—tell me why you think you ought not to go?" he whispered, finally, with a great effort.

"No; not now. But I know you would think I am right in wanting to stay," she cried, impulsively. "I know you would, if you knew about it—but I can't, I can't. I must go in the morning."

"I should always think you right," he answered in an unsteady tone, "Always!" He went over to the bench, fumbled about for his hat, and picked it up.

"Come," he said, gently, "I am going now."

She stood quite motionless for a full minute or longer; then, without a word, she moved toward the house. He went to her with hands extended to find her, and his fingers touched her sleeve. Then together and silently they found the garden-path; and followed its dim length. In the orchard he touched her sleeve again and led the way.

As they came out behind the house she detained him. Stopping short, she shook his hand from her arm. She spoke in a single breath, as if it were all one word:

"Will you tell me why you go? It is not late. Why do you wish to leave me, when I shall not see you again?"

"The Lord be good to me!" he broke out, all his long-pent passion of dreams rushing to his lips, now that the barrier fell. "Don't you see it is because I can't bear to let

86

you go? I hoped to get away without saying it. I want to be alone. I want to be with myself and try to realize. I didn't want to make a babbling idiot of myself—but I am! It is because I don't want another second of your sweetness to leave an added pain when you've gone. It is because I don't want to hear your voice again, to have it haunt me in the loneliness you will leave—but it's useless, useless! I shall hear it always, just as I shall always see your face, just as I have heard your voice and seen your face these seven years—ever since I first saw you, a child at Winter Harbor. I forgot for a while; I thought it was a girl I had made up out of my own heart, but it was you—you always! The impression I thought nothing of at the time, just the merest touch on my heart, light as it was, grew and grew deeper until it was there forever. You've known me twenty-four hours, and I understand what you think of me for speaking to you like this. If I had known you for years and had waited and had the right to speak and keep your respect, what have I to offer you? I, couldn't even take care of you if you went mad as I and listened. I've no excuse for this raving. Yes, I have!"

He saw her in another second of lightning, a sudden, bright one. Her back was turned to him; she had taken a few startled steps from him.

"Ah," he cried, "you are glad enough, now, to see me go! I knew it. I wanted to spare myself that. I tried not to be a hysterical fool in your eyes." He turned aside and his head fell on his breast. "God help me," he said, "what will this place be to me now?"

The breeze had risen; it gathered force; it was a chill wind, and there rose a wailing on the prairie. Drops of rain began to fall.

"You will not think a question implied in this," he said more composedly, and with an unhappy laugh at himself. "I believe you will not think me capable of asking you if you care——"

"No," she answered; "I—I do not love you."

"Ah! Was it a question, after all? I—you read me better than I do, perhaps—but if I asked, I knew the answer."

She made as if to speak again, but words refused her.

After a moment, "Good-by," he said, very steadily. "I thank you for the charity that has given me this little time with you—it will always be— precious to me—I shall always be your servant." His steadiness did not carry him to the end of his sentence. "Good-by."

She started toward him and stopped, without his seeing her. She answered nothing; but stretched out her hand to him and then let it fall quickly.

"Good-by," he said again. "I shall go out the orchard gate. Please tell them good-night for me. Won't you speak to me? Good-by."

He stood waiting while the rising wind blew their garments about them. She leaned against the wall of the house. "Won't you say good-by and tell me you can forget my——"

She did not speak.

"No!" he cried, wildly. "Since you don't forget it! I have spoiled what might have been a pleasant memory for you, and I know it. You were already troubled, and I have added, and you won't forget it, nor shall I—nor shall I! Don't say good-by—I can say it for both of us. God bless you— and good-by, good-by, good-by!"

He crushed his hat down over his eyes and ran toward the orchard gate. For a moment lightning flashed repeatedly; she saw him go out the gate and disappear into sudden darkness. He ran through the field and came out on the road. Heaven and earth were revealed again for a dazzling white second. From horizon to horizon rolled clouds contorted like an illimitable field of inverted haystacks, and beneath them enormous volumes of pale vapor were tumbling in the west, advancing eastward with sinister swiftness. She ran to a little knoll at the corner of the house and saw him set his face to the storm. She cried aloud to him with all her strength and would have followed, but the wind took the words out of her mouth and drove her back cowering to the shelter of the house.

Out on the road the dust came lashing and stinging him like a thousand nettles; it smothered him, and beat upon him so that he covered his face with his sleeve and fought into the storm shoulder foremost, dimly glad of its rage, scarcely conscious of it, keeping westward on his way to nowhere. West or east, south or north—it was all one to him. The few heavy drops that fell boiling into the dust ceased to come; the rain withheld while the wind-kings rode on earth. On he went in spite of them. On and on, running blindly when he could run at all. At least, the wind-kings were company. He had been so long alone. He could remember no home that had ever been his since he was a little child, neither father nor mother, no one who belonged to him or to whom he belonged, except one cousin, an old man who was dead. For a day his dreams had found in a girl's eyes the precious thing that is called home—oh, the wild fancy! He laughed aloud.

There was a startling answer; a lance of living fire hurled from the sky, riving the fields before his eyes, while crash on crash of artillery numbed his ears. With that his common-sense awoke and he looked about him. He was almost two miles from town; the nearest house was the Briscoes' far down the road. He knew the rain would come now. There was a big oak near him at the roadside. He stepped under its sheltering branches and leaned against the great trunk, wiping the perspiration and dust from his face. A moment of stunned quiet had succeeded the peal of thunder. It was followed by several moments of incessant lightning that played along the road and danced in the fields. From that intolerable brightness he turned his head and saw, standing against the fence, five feet away, a man, leaning over the top rail and looking at him.

The same flash staggered brilliantly before Helen's eyes as she crouched against the back steps of the brick house. It scarred a picture like a marine of big waves: the tossing tops of the orchard trees; for in the same second the full fury of the storm was loosed, wind and rain and hail. It drove her against the kitchen door with cruel force; the latch lifted, the door blew open violently, and she struggled to close it in vain. The house seemed to rock. A lamp flickered toward her from the inner doorway and was blown out.

"Helen! Helen!" came Minnie's voice, anxiously. "Is that you? We were coming to look for you. Did you get wet?"

Mr. Willetts threw his weight against the door and managed to close it. Then Minnie found her friend's hand and led her through the dark hall to the parlor where the judge sat, placidly reading by a student-lamp.

Lige chuckled as they left the kitchen. "I guess you didn't try too hard to shut that door, Harkless," he said, and then, when they came into the lighted room, "Why, where *is* Harkless?" he asked. "Didn't he come with us from the kitchen?"

"No," answered Helen, faintly; "he's gone." She sank upon the sofa and drew her hand across her eyes as if to shade them from too sudden light.

"Gone!" The judge dropped his book and stared across the table at the girl. "Gone! When?"

"Ten minutes—five—half an hour—I don't know. Before the storm commenced."

"Oh!" The old gentleman appeared to be reassured. "Probably he had work to do and wanted to get in before the rain."

But Lige Willetts was turning pale. He swallowed several times with difficulty. "Which way did he go? He didn't come around the house; we were out there till the storm broke."

"He went by the orchard gate. When he got to the road he turned that way." She pointed to the west.

"He must have been crazy!" exclaimed the judge. "What possessed the fellow?"

"I couldn't stop him. I didn't know how." She looked at her three companions, slowly and with growing terror, from one face to another. Minnie's eyes were wide and she had unconsciously grasped Lige's arm; the young man was looking straight before him; the judge got up and walked nervously back and forth. Helen rose to her feet swiftly and went toward the old man, her hands pressed to her bosom.

"Ah!" she cried out, sharply, "I had forgotten *that*! You don't think they—you don't think——"

"I know what I think," Lige broke in; "I think I'd ought to be hanged for letting him out of my sight. Maybe it's all right; maybe he turned and started right back for town—and got there. But I had no business to leave him, and if I can I'll catch up with him yet." He went to the front door, and, opening it, let in a tornado of wind and flood of water that beat him back; sheets of rain blew in horizontally, in spite of the porch beyond.

Briscoe followed him. "Don't be a fool, Lige," he said. "You hardly expect to go out in that." Lige shook his head; it needed them both to get the door closed. The young man leaned against it and passed his sleeve across his wet brow. "I hadn't ought to have left him."

"Don't scare the girls," whispered the other; then in a louder tone: "All I'm afraid of is that he'll get blown to pieces or catch his death of cold. That's all there is to worry about. Those scalawags wouldn't try it again so soon after last night. I'm not bothering about that; not at all. That needn't worry anybody."

"But this morning——"

"Pshaw! He's likely home and dry by this time—all foolishness; don't be an old woman." The two men reentered the room and found Helen clinging to Minnie's hand on the sofa. She looked up at them quickly.

"Do you think—do you—what do you—" Her voice shook so that she could not go on.

The judge pinched her cheek and patted it. "I think he's home and dry, but I think he got wet first; that's what I think. Never you fear, he's a good hand at taking care of himself. Sit down, Lige. You can't go for a while." Nor could he. It was long before he could venture out; the storm raged and roared without abatement; it was Carlow's worst since 'Fifty-one, the old gentleman said. They heard the great limbs crack and break outside, while the thunder boomed and the wind ripped at the eaves till it seemed the roof must go. Meanwhile the judge, after some apology, lit his pipe and told long stories of the storms of early days and of odd freaks of the wind. He talked on calmly, the picture of repose, and blew rings above his head, but Helen saw that one of his big slippers beat an unceasing little tattoo on the carpet. She sat with fixed eyes, in silence, holding Minnie's hand tightly; and her face was colorless, and grew whiter as the slow hours dragged by.

Every moment Mr. Willetts became more restless, though assuring the ladies he had no anxiety regarding Mr. Harkless; it was only his own dereliction of duty that he regretted; the boys would have the laugh on him, he said. But he visibly chafed more and more under the judge's stories; and constantly rose to peer out of the window into the wrack and turmoil, or uneasily shifted in his chair. Once or twice he struck his hands together with muttered ejaculations. At last there was a lull in the fury without, and, as soon as it was perceptible, he declared his intention of making his way into town; he had ought to have went before, he declared, apprehensively; and then, with immediate amendment, of course he would find the editor at work in the "Herald" office; there wasn't the slightest doubt of that; he agreed with the judge, but he better see about it. He would return early in the morning to bid Miss Sherwood good-by; hoped she'd come back, some day; hoped it wasn't her last visit to Plattville. They gave him an umbrella and he plunged out into the night, and as they stood watching him for a moment from the door, the old man calling after him cheery good-nights and laughing messages to Harkless, they could hear his feet slosh into the puddles and see him fight with his umbrella when he got out into the road.

Helen's room was over the porch, the windows facing north, looking out upon the pike and across the fields beyond. "Please don't light the lamp, Minnie," she said, when they had gone upstairs. "I don't need a light." Miss Briscoe was flitting about the room, hunting for matches. In the darkness she came to her friend, and laid a kind, large hand on Helen's eyes, and the hand became wet. She drew Helen's head down on her shoulder and sat beside her on the bed.

"Sweetheart, you mustn't fret," she soothed, in motherly fashion. "Don't you worry, dear. He's all right. It isn't your fault, dear. They wouldn't come on a night like this."

But Helen drew away and went to the window, flattening her arm against the pane, her forehead pressed against her arm. She had let him go; she had let him go alone. She had forgotten the danger that always beset him. She had been so crazy, she had seen nothing, thought of nothing. She had let him go into that, and into the storm, alone. Who knew better than she how cruel they were? She had seen the fire leap from the white blossom and heard the ball whistle, the ball they had meant for his heart, that good, great heart. She had run to him the night before—why had she let him go into the unknown and the storm to-night? But how could she have stopped him? How could she have kept him, after what he had said? She peered into the night through distorting tears.

The wind had gone down a little, but only a little, and the electrical flashes danced all around the horizon in magnificent display, sometimes far away, sometimes dazingly near, the darkness trebly deep between the intervals when the long sweep of flat lands lay in dazzling clearness, clean-cut in the washed air to the finest detail of stricken field and heaving woodland. A staggering flame clove earth and sky; sheets of light came following it, and a frightful uproar shook the house and rattled the casements, but over the crash of thunder Minnie heard her friend's loud scream and saw her spring back from the window with both hands, palm outward, pressed to her face. She leaped to her and threw her arms about her.

"What is it?"

"Look!" Helen dragged her to the window. "At the next flash—the fence beyond the meadow——"

"What was it? What was it like?" The lightning flashed incessantly. Helen tried to point; her hand only jerked from side to side.

"*Look!*" she cried.

"I see nothing but the lightning," Minnie answered, breathlessly.

"Oh, the *fence*! The fence—and in the field!"

"*Helen*! What was it *like*?"

"Ah-ah!" she panted, "a long line of white—horrible white——"

"What *like*?" Minnie turned from the window and caught the other's wrist in a fluttering clasp.

"Minnie, Minnie! Like long white gowns and cowls crossing the fence." Helen released her wrist, and put both hands on Minnie's cheeks, forcing her around to face the pane. "You must look—you must look," she cried.

"They wouldn't do it, they wouldn't—it *isn't*!" Minnie cried. "They couldn't come in the storm. They wouldn't do it in the pouring rain!"

"Yes! Such things would mind the rain!" She burst into hysterical laughter, and Minnie, almost as unnerved, caught her about the waist. "They would mind the rain. They would fear a storm! Ha, ha, ha! Yes—yes! And I let him go—I let him go!"

Pressing close together, shuddering, clasping each other's waists, the two girls peered out at the flickering landscape.

"*Look!*"

Up from the distant fence that bordered the northern side of Jones's field, a pale, pelted, flapping thing reared itself, poised, and seemed, just as the blackness came again, to drop to the ground.

"Did you *see*?"

92

But Minnie had thrown herself into a chair with a laugh of wild relief. "My darling girl!" she cried. "Not a line of white things—just one—Mr. Jones's old scarecrow! And we saw it blown down!"

"No, no, no! I saw the others; they were in the field beyond. I saw them! When I looked the first time they were nearly all on the fence. This time we saw the last man crossing. Ah! I let him go alone!"

Minnie sprang up and enfolded her. "No; you dear, imagining child, you're upset and nervous—that's all the matter in the world. Don't worry; don't, child, it's all right. Mr. Harkless is home and safe in bed long ago. I know that old scarecrow on the fence like a book; you're so unstrung you fancied the rest. He's all right; don't you bother, dear."

The big, motherly girl took her companion in her arms and rocked her back and forth soothingly, and petted and reassured her, and then cried a little with her, as a good-hearted girl always will with a friend. Then she left her for the night with many a cheering word and tender caress. "Get to sleep, dear," she called through the door when she had closed it behind her. "You must, if you have to go in the morning—it just breaks my heart. I don't know how we'll bear it without you. Father will miss you almost as much as I will. Good-night. Don't bother about that old white scarecrow. That's all it was. Good-night, dear, good-night."

"Good-night, dear," answered a plaintive little voice. Helen's hot cheek pressed the pillow and tossed from side to side. By and by she turned the pillow over; it had grown wet. The wind blew about the eaves and blew itself out; she hardly heard it. Sleep would not come. She got up and laved her burning eyes. Then she sat by the window. The storm's strength was spent at last; the rain grew lighter and lighter, until there was but the sound of running water and the drip, drip on the tin roof of the porch. Only the thunder rumbling in the distance marked the storm's course; the chariots of the gods rolling further and further away, till they finally ceased to be heard altogether. The clouds parted majestically, and then, between great curtains of mist, the day-star was seen shining in the east.

The night was hushed, and the peace that falls before dawn was upon the wet, flat lands. Somewhere in the sodden grass a swamped cricket chirped. From an outlying flange of the village a dog's howl rose mournfully; was answered by another, far away, and by another and another. The sonorous chorus rose above the village, died away, and quiet fell again.

Helen sat by the window, no comfort touching her heart. Tears coursed her cheeks no longer, but her eyes were wide and staring, and her lips parted, for the hush was broken by the far clamor of the court-house bell ringing in the night. It rang, and rang, and rang, and rang. She could not breathe. She threw open the window. The bell stopped. All was quiet once more. The east was growing gray.

Suddenly out of the stillness there came the sound of a horse galloping over a wet road. He was coming like mad. Some one for a doctor? No; the horse-hoofs grew louder, coming out from the town, coming this way, coming faster and faster, coming *here*. There was a splashing and trampling in front of the house and a sharp "Whoa!" In the dim gray of first dawn she made out a man on a foam-flecked horse. He drew up at the gate.

A window to the right of hers went screeching up. She heard the judge clear his throat before he spoke.

"What is it? That's you, isn't it, Wiley? What is it?" He took a good deal of time and coughed between the sentences. His voice was more than ordinarily quiet, and it sounded husky. "What is it, Wiley?"

"Judge, what time did Mr. Harkless leave here last night and which way did he go?"

There was a silence. The judge turned away from the window. Minnie was standing just outside his door. "It must have been about half-past nine, wasn't it, father?" she called in a shaking voice. "And, you know, Helen thought he went west."

"Wiley!" The old man leaned from the sill again.

"Yes!" answered the man on horseback.

"Wiley, he left about half-past nine—just before the storm. They think he went west."

"Much obliged. Willetts is so upset he isn't sure of anything."

"Wiley!" The old man's voice shook; Minnie began to cry aloud. The horseman wheeled about and turned his animal's head toward town. "Wiley!"

"Yes."

"Wiley, they haven't—you don't think they've got him?"

"By God, judge," said the man on horseback, "I'm afraid they have!"

94

CHAPTER X

THE COURT-HOUSE BELL

The court-house bell ringing in the night! No hesitating stroke of Schofields' Henry, no uncertain touch, was on the rope. A loud, wild, hurried clamor pealing out to wake the country-side, a rapid *clang! clang! clang!* that struck clear in to the spine.

The court-house bell had tolled for the death of Morton, of Garfield, of Hendricks; had rung joy-peals of peace after the war and after political campaigns; but it had rung as it was ringing now only three times; once when Hibbard's mill burned, once when Webb Landis killed Sep Bardlock and intrenched himself in the lumber-yard and would not be taken till he was shot through and through, and once when the Rouen accommodation was wrecked within twenty yards of the station.

Why was the bell ringing now? Men and women, startled into wide wakefulness, groped to windows—no red mist hung over town or country. What was it? The bell rang on. Its loud alarm beat increasingly into men's hearts and quickened their throbbing to the rapid measure of its own. Vague forms loomed in the gloaming. A horse, wildly ridden, splashed through the town. There were shouts; voices called hoarsely. Lamps began to gleam in the windows. Half-clad people emerged from their houses, men slapping their braces on their shoulders as they ran out of doors. Questions were shouted into the dimness.

Then the news went over the town.

It was cried from yard to yard, from group to group, from gate to gate, and reached the furthermost confines. Runners shouted it as they sped by; boys panted it, breathless; women with loosened hair stumbled into darkling chambers and faltered it out to new-wakened sleepers; pale girls clutching wraps at their throats whispered it across fences; the sick, tossing on their hard beds, heard it. The bell clamored it far and near; it spread over the country-side; it flew over the wires to distant cities. The White-Caps had got Mr. Harkless!

Lige Willetts had lost track of him out near Briscoes', it was said, and had come in at midnight seeking him. He had found Parker, the "Herald" foreman, and Ross Schofield, the typesetter, and Bud Tipworthy, the devil, at work in the printing-room, but no sign of Harkless, there or in the cottage. Together these had sought for him and had roused others, who had inquired at every house where he might have gone for shelter, and they had heard nothing. They had watched for his coming during the slackening of the storm and he had not come, and there was nowhere he could have gone. He was missing; only one thing could have happened.

They had roused up Warren Smith, the prosecutor, the missing editor's most intimate friend in Carlow, and Homer, the sheriff, and Jared Wiley, the deputy. William Todd had rung the alarm. The first thing to do was to find him. After that there would be trouble—if not before. It looked as if there would be trouble before. The men tramping up to the muddy Square in their shirt-sleeves were bulgy about the right hips; and when Homer Tibbs joined Lum Landis at the hotel corner, and Landis saw that Homer was carrying a shot-gun, Landis went back for his. A hastily sworn posse galloped out Main Street. Women and children ran into neighbors' yards and began to cry. Day was coming; and, as the light grew, men swore and savagely kicked at the palings of fences that they passed.

In the foreglow of dawn they gathered in the Square and listened to Warren Smith, who made a speech from the court-house fence and warned them to go slow. They answered him with angry shouts and hootings, but he made his big voice heard, and bade them do nothing rash; no facts were known, he said; it was far from certain that harm had been done, and no one knew that the Six-Cross-Roads people had done it—even if something had happened to Mr. Harkless. He declared that he spoke in Harkless's name. Nothing could distress *him* so much as for them to defy the law, to take it out of the proper hands. Justice would be done.

"Yes it will!" shouted a man below him, brandishing the butt of a raw-hide whip above his head. "And while you jaw on about it here, he may be tied up like a dog in the woods, shot full of holes by the men you never lifted a finger to hender, because you want their votes when you run for circuit judge. What are we doin' *here*? What's the good of listening to you?"

There was a yell at this, and those who heard the speaker would probably have started for the Cross-Roads without further parley, had not a rumor sprung up, which passed so rapidly from man to man that within five minutes it was being turbulently discussed in every portion of the crowd. The news came that the two shell-gamblers had wrenched a bar out of a window under cover of the storm, had broken jail, and were at large. Their threats of the day before were remembered now, with convincing vividness. They had sworn repeatedly to Bardlock and to the sheriff, and in the hearing of others, that they would "do" for the man who took their money from them and had them arrested. The prosecuting attorney, quickly perceiving the value of this complication in holding back the mob that was already forming, called Homer from the crowd and made him get up on the fence and confess that his prisoners had escaped—at what time he did not know, probably toward the beginning of the storm, when it was noisiest.

"You see," cried the attorney, "there is nothing as yet of which we can accuse the Cross-Roads. If our friend has been hurt, it is much more likely that these crooks did it. They escaped in time to do it, and we all know they were laying for him. You want to be mighty careful, fellow-citizens. Homer is already in telegraphic communication with every town around here, and we'll have those men before night. All you've got to do is to control yourselves a little and go home quietly." He could see that his words (except those in reference to returning home—no one was going home) made an impression. There rose a babble of shouting and argument and swearing that grew continually louder, and the faces the lawyer looked down on were creased with perplexity, and shadowed with an anger that settled darker and darker.

Mr. Ephraim Watts, in spite of all confusion, clad as carefully as upon the preceding day, deliberately climbed the fence and stood by the lawyer and made a single steady gesture with his hand. He was listened to at once, as his respect for the law was less notorious than his irreverence for it, and he had been known in Carlow as a customarily reckless man. They wanted illegal and desperate advice, and quieted down to hear it. He spoke in his professionally calm voice.

"Gentlemen, it seems to me that Mr. Smith and Mr. Ribshaw" (nodding to the man with the rawhide whip) "are both right. What good are we doing here? What we want to know is what's happened to Mr. Harkless. It looks just now like the shell-men might have done it. Let's find out what they done. Scatter and hunt for him. 'Soon as anything is known for certain, Hibbard's mill whistle will blow three times. Keep on looking till it does. *Then*" he finished, with a barely perceptible scornful smile at the attorney, "*then* we can decide on what had ought to be done."

Six-Cross-Roads lay dark and steaming in the sun that morning. The forge was silent, the saloon locked up, the roadway deserted, even by the pigs. The broken old buggy stood rotting in the mud without a single lean, little old man or woman—such were the children of the Cross-Roads—to play about it. The fields were empty, and the rag-stuffed windows blank, under the baleful glance of the horsemen who galloped by at intervals, muttering curses, not always confining themselves to muttering them. Once, when the deputy sheriff rode through alone, a tattered black hound, more wolf than dog, half-emerged, growling, from beneath one of the tumble-down barns, and was jerked back into the darkness by his tail, with a snarl fiercer than his own, while a gun-barrel shone for a second as it swung for a stroke on the brute's head. The hound did not yelp or whine when the blow fell. He shut his eyes twice, and slunk sullenly back to his place.

The shanties might have received a volley or two from some of the mounted bands, exasperated by futile searching, had not the escape of Homer's prisoners made the guilt of the Cross-Roads appear doubtful in the minds of many. As the morning waned, the advocates of the theory that the gamblers had made away with Harkless grew in number. There came a telegram from the Rouen chief of police that he had a clew to their whereabouts; he thought they had succeeded in reaching Rouen, and it began to be generally believed that they had escaped by the one-o'clock freight, which had stopped to take on some empty cars at a side-track a mile northwest of the town, across the fields from the Briscoe house. Toward noon a party went out to examine the railroad embankment.

Men began to come back into the village for breakfast by twos and threes, though many kept on searching the woods, not feeling the need of food, or caring if they did. Every grove and clump of underbrush, every thicket, was ransacked; the waters of the creek, shallow for the most part, but swollen overnight, were dragged at every pool. Nothing was found; there was not a sign.

The bar of the hotel was thronged all morning as the returning citizens rapidly made their way thither, and those who had breakfasted and were going out again paused for internal, as well as external, reinforcement. The landlord, himself returned from a long hunt, set up his whiskey with a lavish hand.

"He was the best man we had, boys," said Landis, as he poured the little glasses full. "We'd ort of sent him to the legislative halls of Washington long ago. He'd of done us honor there; but we never thought of doin' anything fer him; jest set 'round and let him build up the town and give him empty thankyes. Drink hearty, gentlemen," he finished, gloomily, "I don't grudge no liquor to-day—except to Lige Willetts."

"He was a good man," said young William Todd, whose nose was red, not from the whiskey. "I've about give up."

Schofields' Henry drew his sleeve across his eyes. "He was the only man in this whole city that didn't jab and nag at me when I done my best," he exclaimed, with an increasing break in his utterance. "Many a good word I've had from him when nobody in town done nothin' but laugh an' rile an' badger me about my—my bell." And Schofields' Henry began to cry openly.

"He was a great hand with the chuldern," said one man. "Always have something to say to 'em to make 'em laugh when he went by. 'Talk more to them 'n he would to grown folks. Yes, sir."

"They knowed *him* all right," added another. "I reckon all of us did, little and big."

"It's goin' to seem mighty empty around here," said Ross Schofield. "What's goin' to become o' the 'Herald' and the party in this district? Where's the man to run either of 'em now. Like as not," he concluded desperately, "the election'll go against us in the fall."

Dibb Zane choked over his four fingers. "We might's well bust up this dab-dusted ole town ef he's gone."

"I don't know what's come over that Cynthy Tipworthy," said the landlord. "She's waited table on him last two year, and her brother Bud works at the 'Herald' office. She didn't say a word—only looked and looked and looked —like a crazy woman; then her and Bud went off together to hunt in the woods. They just tuck hold of each other's hands like——"

"That ain't nothin'," Homer Tibbs broke in. "You'd ort to've saw old Miz Hathaway, that widder woman next door to us, when she heard it. He had helped her to git her pension; and she tuck on worse 'n' anything I ever hear—lot worse 'n' when Hathaway died."

"I reckon there ain't many crazier than them two Bowlders, father and son," said the postmaster, wiping the drops from his beard as he set his glass on the bar. "They rid into town like a couple of wild Indians, the old man beatin' that gray mare o' theirn till she was one big welt, and he ain't natcherly no cruel man, either. I reckon Lige Willetts better keep out of Hartley's way."

"I keep out of no man's way," cried a voice behind him. Turning, they saw Lige standing on the threshold of the door that led to the street. In his hand he held the bridle of the horse he had ridden across the sidewalk, and that now stood panting, with lowered head, half through the doorway, beside his master. Lige was hatless, splashed with mud from head to foot; his jaw was set, his teeth ground together; his eyes burned under red lids, and his hair lay tossed and damp on his brow. "I keep out of no man's way," he repeated, hoarsely.

"I heard you, Mr. Tibbs, but I've got too much to do, while you loaf and gas and drink over Lum Landis's bar—I've got other business than keeping out of Hartley Bowlder's way. I'm looking for John Harkless. He was the best man we had in this ornery hole, and he was too good for us, and so we've maybe let him get killed, and maybe I'm to blame. But I'm going to find him, and if he's hurt—damn *me*! I'm going to have a hand on the rope that lifts the men that did it, if I have to go to Rouen to put it there! After that I'll answer for my fault, not before!"

He threw himself on his horse and was gone. Soon the room was emptied, as the patrons of the bar returned to the search, and only Mr. Wilkerson and the landlord remained, the bar being the professional office, so to speak, of both.

Wilkerson had a chair in a corner, where he sat chanting a funeral march in a sepulchral murmur, allowing a parenthetical *hic* to punctuate the dirge in place of the drum. Whenever a batch of newcomers entered, he rose to drink with them; and, at such times, after pouring off his liquor with a rich melancholy, shedding tears after every swallow, he would make an exploring tour of the room on his way back to his corner, stopping to look under each chair inquiringly and ejaculate: "Why, where kin he be!" Then, shaking his head, he would observe sadly: "Fine young man, he was, too; fine young man. Pore fellow! I reckon we hain't a-goin' to git him."

At eleven o'clock, Judge Briscoe dropped wearily from his horse at his own gate, and said to a wan girl who came running down the walk to meet him: "There is nothing, yet. I sent the telegram to your mother—to Mrs. Sherwood."

Helen turned away without answering. Her face was very white and looked pinched about the mouth. She went back to where old Fisbee sat on the porch, his white head held between his two hands; he was rocking himself to and fro. She touched him gently, but he did not look up. She spoke to him.

"There isn't anything—yet. He sent the telegram to mamma. I shall stay with you, now, no matter what you say." She sat beside him and put her head down on his shoulder, and though for a moment he appeared not to notice it, when Minnie came out on the porch, hearing her father at the door, the old scholar had put his arm about the girl and was stroking her fair hair softly.

Briscoe glanced at them, and raised a warning finger to his daughter, and they went tiptoeing into the house, where the judge dropped heavily upon a sofa with an asthmatic sigh; he was worn and tired. Minnie stood before him with a look of pale inquiry, and he shook his head.

"No use to tell *them*; but I can't see any hope," he answered her, biting nervously at the end of a cigar. "I expect you better bring me some coffee in here; I couldn't take another step to save me. I'm too old to tear around the country horseback before breakfast, like I have to-day."

"Did you send her telegram?" Minnie asked, as he drank the coffee she brought him. She had interpreted "coffee" liberally, and, with the assistance of Mildy Upton (whose subdued nose was frankly red and who shed tears on the raspberries), had prepared an appetizing table at his elbow.

"Yes," responded the judge, "and I'm glad she sent it. I talked the other way yesterday, what little I said—it isn't any of our business—but I don't think any too much of those people, somehow. She thinks she belongs with Fisbee, and I guess she's right. That young fellow must have got along with her pretty well, and I'm afraid when she gives up she'll be pretty bad over it; but I guess we all will. It's terribly sudden, somehow, though it's only what everybody half expected would come; only we thought it would come from over yonder." He nodded toward the west. "But she's got to stay here with us. Boarding at Sol Tibbs's with that old man won't do; and she's no girl to live in two rooms. You fix it up with her— you make her stay."

"She must," answered his daughter as she knelt beside him and patted his coat and handed him several things to eat at the same time. "Mr. Fisbee will help me persuade her, now that she's bound to stay in spite of him and the Sherwoods, too. I think she is perfectly grand to do it. I've always thought she was grand—ever since she took me under her wing at school when I was terribly 'country' and frightened; but she was so sweet and kind she made me forget. She was the pet of the school, too, always doing things for the other girls, for everybody; looking out for people simply heads and heads bigger than herself, and so recklessly generous and so funny about it; and always thoughtful and—and—pleasant——"

Minnie was speaking sadly, mechanically; but suddenly she broke off with a quick sob, sprang up and went to the window; then, turning, cried out:

"I don't believe it! He knew how to take care of himself too well. He'd have got away from them."

Her father shook his head. "Then why hasn't he turned up? He'd have gone home after the storm if something bad wasn't the matter."

"But nothing—nothing *that* bad could have happened. They haven't found— any— anything."

"But why hasn't he come back, child?"

"Well, he's lying hurt somewhere, that's all."

"Then why haven't they found him?"

"I don't care!" she cried, and choked with the words and tossed her dishevelled hair from her temples; "it isn't true. Helen won't believe it —why should I? It's only a few hours since he was right here in our yard, talking to us all. I won't believe it till they've searched every stick and stone of Six-Cross-Roads and found him."

"It wasn't the Cross-Roads," said the old gentleman, pushing the table away and relaxing his limbs on the sofa. "They probably didn't have anything to do with it. We thought they had at first, but everybody's about come to believe it was those two devils that he had arrested yesterday."

"Not the Cross-Roads!" echoed Minnie, and she began to tremble violently. "Haven't they been out there yet?"

"What use? They are out of it, and they can thank God they are!"

"They are not!" she cried excitedly. "They did it. It was the White-Caps. We saw them, Helen and I."

The judge got upon his feet with an oath. He had not sworn for years until that morning. "What's this?" he said sharply.

"I ought to have told you before, but we were so frightened, and—and you went off in such a rush after Mr. Wiley was here. I never dreamed everybody wouldn't know it was the Cross-Roads; that they would *think* of any one else. And I looked for the scarecrow as soon as it was light and it was 'way off from where we saw them, and wasn't blown down at all, and Helen saw them in the field besides—saw all of them——"

He interrupted her. "What do you mean? Try to tell me about it quietly, child." He laid his hand on her shoulder.

She told him breathlessly (while he grew more and more visibly perturbed and uneasy, biting his cigar to pieces and groaning at intervals) what she and Helen had seen in the storm. When she finished he took a few quick turns about the room with his hands thrust deep in his coat pockets, and then, charging her to repeat the story to no one, left the house, and, forgetting his fatigue, rapidly crossed the fields to the point where the bizarre figures of the night had shown themselves to the two girls at the window.

The soft ground had been trampled by many feet. The boot-prints pointed to the northeast. He traced them backward to the southwest through the field, and saw where they had come from near the road, going northeast. Then, returning, he climbed the fence and followed them northward through the next field. From there, the next, beyond the road that was a continuation of Main Street, stretched to the railroad embankment. The track, raggedly defined in trampled loam and muddy furrow, bent in a direction which indicated that its terminus might be the switch where the empty cars had stood last night, waiting for the one-o'clock freight. Though the fields had been trampled down in many places by the searching parties, he felt sure of the direction taken by the Cross-Roads men, and he perceived that the searchers had mistaken the tracks he followed for those of earlier parties in the hunt. On the embankment he saw a number of men, walking west and examining the ground on each side, and a long line of people following them out from town. He stopped. He held the fate of Six-Cross-Roads in his hand and he knew it.

He knew that if he spoke, his evidence would damn the Cross-Roads, and that it meant that more than the White-Caps would be hurt, for the Cross-Roads would fight. If he had believed that the dissemination of his knowledge could have helped Harkless, he would have called to the men near him at once; but he had no hope that the young man was alive. They would not have dragged him out to their shanties wounded, or as a prisoner; such a proceeding would have courted detection, and, also, they were not that kind; they had been "looking for him" a long time, and their one idea was to kill him.

And Harkless, for all his gentleness, was the sort of man, Briscoe believed, who would have to be killed before he could be touched. Of one thing the old gentleman was sure; the editor had not been tied up and whipped while yet alive. In spite of his easy manners and geniality, there was a dignity in him that would have made him kill and be killed before the dirty fingers of a Cross-Roads "White-Cap" could have been laid upon him in chastisement. A great many good Americans of Carlow who knew him well always Mistered him as they would have Mistered only an untitled Morton or Hendricks who might have lived amongst them. He was the only man the old darky, Uncle Xenophon, had ever addressed as "Marse" since he came to Plattville, thirty years ago.

Briscoe considered it probable that a few people were wearing bandages, in the closed shanties over to the west to-day. A thought of the number they had brought against one man; a picture of the unequal struggle, of the young fellow he had liked so well, unarmed and fighting hopelessly in a trap, and a sense of the cruelty of it, made the hot anger surge up in his breast, and he started on again. Then he stopped once more. Though long retired from faithful service on the bench, he had been all his life a serious exponent of the law, and what he went to tell meant lawlessness that no one could hope to check. He knew the temper of the people; their long suffering was at an end, and they would go over at last and wipe out the Cross-Roads. It depended on him. If the mob could be held off over to-day, if men's minds could cool over night, the law could strike and the innocent and the hotheaded be spared from suffering. He would wait; he would lay his information before the sheriff; and Horner would go quietly with a strong posse, for he would need a strong one. He began to retrace his steps.

The men on the embankment were walking slowly, bending far over, their eyes fixed on the ground. Suddenly one of them stood erect and tossed his arms in the air and shouted loudly. Other men ran to him, and another far down the track repeated the shout and the gesture to another far in his rear; this man took it up, and shouted and waved to a fourth man, and so they passed the signal back to town. There came, almost immediately three long, loud whistles from a mill near the station, and the embankment grew black with people pouring out from town, while the searchers came running from the fields and woods and underbrush on both sides of the railway.

Briscoe paused for the last time; then he began to walk slowly toward the embankment.

The track lay level and straight, not dimming in the middle distances, the rails converging to points, both northwest and southeast, in the clean-washed air, like examples of perspective in a child's drawing-book. About seventy miles to the west and north lay Rouen; and, in the same direction, nearly six miles from where the signal was given, the track was crossed by a road leading directly south to Six-Cross-Roads.

The embankment had been newly ballasted with sand. What had been discovered was a broad brown stain on the south slope near the top. There were smaller stains above and below; none beyond it to left or right; and there were deep boot-prints in the sand. Men were examining the place excitedly, talking and gesticulating. It was Lige Willetts who had found it. His horse was tethered to a fence near by, at the end of a lane through a cornfield. Jared Wiley, the deputy, was talking to a group near the stain, explaining.

"You see them two must have knowed about the one-o'clock freight, and that it was to stop here to take on the empty lumber cars. I don't know how they knowed it, but they did. It was this way: when they dropped from the window, they beat through the storm, straight for this side-track. At the same time Mr. Harkless leaves Briscoes' goin' west. It begins to rain. He cuts across to the railroad to have a sure footing, and strikin' for the deepo for shelter—near place as any except Briscoes' where he'd said good-night already and prob'ly don't wish to go back, 'fear of givin' trouble or keepin' 'em up—anybody can understand that. He comes along, and gets to where we are precisely at the time *they* do, them comin' from town, him strikin' for it. They run right into each other. That's what happened. They re-*cog*-nized him and raised up on him and let him have it. What they done it with, I don't know; we took everything in that line off of 'em; prob'ly used railroad iron; and what they done with him afterwards we don't know; but we will by night. They'll sweat it out of 'em up at Rouen when they get 'em."

"I reckon maybe some of us might help," remarked Mr. Watts, reflectively.

Jim Bardlock swore a violent oath. "That's the talk!" he shouted. "Ef I ain't the first man of this crowd to set my foot in Roowun, an' first to beat in that jail door, an' take 'em out an' hang 'em by the neck till they're dead, dead, dead, I'm not Town Marshal of Plattville, County of Carlow, State of Indiana, and the Lord have mercy on our souls!"

Tom Martin looked at the brown stain and quickly turned away; then he went back slowly to the village. On the way he passed Warren Smith.

"Is it so?" asked the lawyer.

Martin answered with a dry throat. He looked out dimly over the sunlit fields, and swallowed once or twice. "Yes, it's so. There's a good deal of it there. Little more than a boy he was." The old fellow passed his seamy hand over his eyes without concealment. "Peter ain't very bright, sometimes, it seems to me," he added, brokenly; "overlook Bodeffer and Fisbee and me and all of us old husks, and— and—" he gulped suddenly, then finished—"and act the fool and take a boy that's the best we had. I wish the Almighty would take Peter off the gate; he ain't fit fer it."

When the attorney reached the spot where the crowd was thickest, way was made for him. The old colored man, Xenophon, approached at the same time, leaning on a hickory stick and bent very far over, one hand resting on his hip as if to ease a rusty joint. The negro's age was an incentive to fable; from his appearance he might have known the prophets, and he wore that hoary look of unearthly wisdom many decades of superstitious experience sometimes give to members of his race. His face, so tortured with wrinkles that it might have been made of innumerable black threads woven together, was a living mask of the mystery of his blood. Harkless had once said that Uncle Xenophon had visited heaven before Swedenborg and hell before Dante. To-day, as he slowly limped over the ties, his eyes were bright and dry under the solemn lids, and, though his heavy nostrils were unusually distended in the effort for regular breathing, the deeply puckered lips beneath them were set firmly.

He stopped and looked at the faces before him. When he spoke his voice was gentle, and though the tremulousness of age harped on the vocal strings, it was rigidly controlled. "Kin some kine gelmun," he asked, "please t' be so good ez t' show de ole main whuh de W'ite-Caips is done shoot Marse Hawkliss?"

"Here was where it happened, Uncle Zen," answered Wiley, leaning him forward. "Here is the stain."

Xenophon bent over the spot on the sand, making little odd noises in his throat. Then he painfully resumed his former position. "Dass his blood," he said, in the same gentle, quavering tone. "Dass my bes' frien' whut lay on de groun' whuh yo staind, gelmun."

There was a pause, and no one spoke.

"Dass whuh day laid 'im an' dass whuh he lie," the old negro continued. "Dey shot 'im in de fiels. Dey ain' shot 'im hear-yondeh dey drugged 'im, but dis whuh he lie." He bent over again, then knelt, groaningly, and placed his hand on the stain, one would have said, as a man might place his hand over a heart to see if it still beat. He was motionless, with the air of hearkening.

"Marse, honey, is you gone?" He raised his voice as if calling, "Is you gone, suh?—Marse?"

He looked up at the circle about him, and, still kneeling, not taking his hand from the sand, seeming to wait for a sign, to listen for a voice, he said: "Whafo' you gelmun think de good Lawd summon Marse Hawkliss? Kaze he de mos' fittes'? You know dat man he ketch me in de cole night, wintuh 'to' lais', stealin' 'is wood. You know whut he done t'de ole thief? Tek an' bull' up big fiah een ole Zen' shainty; say, 'He'p yo'se'f an' welcome. Reckon you hongry, too, ain' you, Xenophon?' Tek an' feed me. Tek an' tek keer o' me ev' since. Ah pump de baith full in de mawin'; mek 'is bed; pull de weeds out'n of de front walk—dass all. He tek me in. When Ah aisk 'im ain' he fraid keep ole thief he say, jesso: 'Dass all my fault, Xenophon; ought look you up long 'go; ought know long 'go you be cole dese baid nights. Reckon Ahm de thievenest one us two, Xenophon, keepin' all dis wood stock' up when you got none,' he say, jesso. Tek me in; say he *lahk* a thief. Pay me sala'y. Feed me. Dass de main whut de Caips gone shot lais' night." He raised his head sharply, and the mystery in his gloomy eyes intensified as they opened wide and stared at the sky, unseeingly.

"Ise bawn wid a cawl!" he exclaimed, loudly. His twisted frame was braced to an extreme tension. "Ise bawn wid a cawl! De blood anssuh!"

"It wasn't the Cross-Roads, Uncle Xenophon," said Warren Smith, laying his hand on the old man's shoulder.

Xenophon rose to his feet. He stretched a long, bony arm straight to the west, where the Cross-Roads lay; stood rigid and silent, like a seer; then spoke:

"De men whut shot Marse Hawkliss lies yondeh, hidin' f'um de light o' day. An' *him*"—he swerved his whole rigid body till the arm pointed northwest—"he lies yondeh. You won't find him heah. Dey fought 'im een de fiel's an' dey druggen 'im heah. Dis whim dey lay 'im down. Ise bawn wid a cawl!"

There were exclamations from the listeners, for Xenophon spoke as one having authority. Suddenly he turned and pointed his outstretched hand full at Judge Briscoe.

"An' dass de main," he cried, "dass de main kin tell you Ah speak de trufe."

Before he was answered, Eph Watts looked at Briscoe keenly and then turned to Lige Willetts and whispered: "Get on your horse, ride in, and ring the court-house bell like the devil. Do as I say!"

Tears stood in the judge's eyes. "It is so," he said, solemnly. "He speaks the truth. I didn't mean to tell it to-day, but somehow—" He paused. "The hounds!" he cried. "They deserve it! My daughter saw them crossing the fields in the night—saw them climb the fence, hoods, gowns, and all, a big crowd of them. She and the lady who is visiting us saw them, saw them plainly. The lady saw them several times, clear as day, by the flashes of lightning—the scoundrels were coming this way. They must have been dragging him with them then. He couldn't have had a show for his life amongst them. Do what you like—maybe they've got him at the Cross-Roads. If there's a chance of it—dead or alive—bring him back!"

A voice rang out above the clamor that followed the judge's speech.

"'Bring him back!' God could, maybe, but He won't. Who's travelling my way? I go west!" Hartley Bowlder had ridden his sorrel up the embankment, and the horse stood between the rails. There was an angry roar from the crowd; the prosecutor pleaded and threatened unheeded; and as for the deputy sheriff, he declared his intention of taking with him all who wished to go as his posse. Eph Watts succeeded in making himself heard above the tumult.

"The Square!" he shouted. "Start from the Square. We want everybody, and we'll need them. We want every one in Carlow to be implicated in this posse."

"They will be!" shouted a farmer. "Don't you worry about that."

"We want to get into some sort of shape," cried Eph.

"Shape, hell!" said Hartley Bowlder.

There was a hiss and clang and rattle behind him, and a steam whistle shrieked. The crowd divided, and Hartley's sorrel jumped just in time as the westbound accommodation rushed through on its way to Rouen. From the rear platform leaned the sheriff, Horner, waving his hands frantically as he flew by, but no one understood—or cared—what he said, or, in the general excitement, even wondered why he was leaving the scene of his duty at such a time. When the train had dwindled to a dot and disappeared, and the noise of its rush grew faint, the court-house bell was heard ringing, and the mob was piling pell-mell into the village to form on the Square. The judge stood alone on the embankment.

"That settles it," he said aloud, gloomily, watching the last figures. He took off his hat and pushed back the thick, white hair from his forehead. "Nothing to do but wait. Might as well go home for that. Blast it!" he exclaimed, impatiently. "I don't want to go there. It's too hard on the little girl. If she hadn't come till next week she'd never have known John Harkless."

CHAPTER XI

JOHN BROWN'S BODY

All morning horsemen had been galloping through Six-Cross-Roads, sometimes singly, oftener in company. At one-o'clock the last posse passed through on its return to the county-seat, and after that there was a long, complete silence, while the miry corners were undisturbed by a single hoof-beat. No unkempt colt nickered from his musty stall; the sparse young corn that was used to rasp and chuckle greenly stood rigid in the fields. Up the Plattville pike despairingly cackled one old hen, with her wabbling sailor run, smit with a superstitious horror of nothing, in the stillness; she hid herself in the shadow underneath a rickety barn, and her shrieking ceased.

Only on the Wimby farm were there signs of life. The old lady who had sent Harkless roses sat by the window all morning and wiped her eyes, watching the horsemen ride by; sometimes they would hail her and tell her there was nothing yet. About two-o'clock, her husband rattled up in a buckboard, and got out the late, and more authentic, Mr. Wimby's shot-gun, which he carefully cleaned and oiled, in spite of its hammerless and quite useless condition, sitting, meanwhile, by the window opposite his wife, and often looking up from his work to shake his weak fist at his neighbors' domiciles and creak decrepit curses and denunciations.

But the Cross-Roads was ready. It knew what was coming now. Frightened, desperate, sullen, it was ready.

The afternoon wore on, and lengthening shadows fell upon a peaceful—one would have said, a sleeping—country. The sun-dried pike, already dusty, stretched its serene length between green borders flecked with purple and yellow and white weedflowers; and the tree shadows were not shade, but warm blue and lavender glows in the general pervasion of still, bright light, the sky curving its deep, unburnished, penetrable blue over all, with no single drift of fleece upon it to be reflected in the creek that wound along past willow and sycamore. A woodpecker's telegraphy broke the quiet like a volley of pistol shots.

But far eastward on the pike there slowly developed a soft, white haze. It grew denser and larger. Gradually it rolled nearer. Dimly behind it could be discerned a darker, moving nucleus that extended far back upon the road. A heavy tremor began to stir the air—faint manifold sounds, a waxing, increasing, multitudinous rumor.

The pike ascended a long, slight slope leading west up to the Cross-Roads. From a thicket of iron-weed at the foot of this slope was thrust the hard, lean visage of an undersized girl of fourteen. Her fierce eyes examined the approaching cloud of dust intently. A redness rose under the burnt yellow skin and colored the wizened cheeks.

They were coming.

She stepped quickly out of the tangle, and darted up the road, running with the speed of a fleet little terrier, not opening her lips, not calling out, but holding her two thin hands high above her head. That was all. But Birnam wood was come to Dunsinane at last, and the messenger sped. Out of the weeds in the corners of the snake fence, in the upper part of the rise, silently lifted the heads of men whose sallowness became a sickish white as the child flew by.

The mob was carefully organized. They had taken their time and had prepared everything deliberately, knowing that nothing could stop them. No one had any thought of concealment; it was all as open as the light of day, all done in the broad sunshine. Nothing had been determined as to what was to be done at the Cross-Roads more definite than that the place was to be wiped out. That was comprehensive enough; the details were quite certain to occur. They were all on foot, marching in fairly regular ranks. In front walked Mr. Watts, the man Harkless had abhorred in a public spirit and befriended in private—to-day he was a hero and a leader, marching to avenge his professional oppressor and personal brother. Cool, unruffled, and, to outward vision, unarmed, marching the miles in his brown frock coat and generous linen, his carefully creased trousers neatly turned up out of the dust, he led the way. On one side of him were the two Bowlders, on the other was Lige Willetts, Mr. Watts preserving peace between the two young men with perfect tact and sang-froid.

They kept good order and a similitude of quiet for so many, except far to the rear, where old Wilkerson was bringing up the tail of the procession, dragging a wretched yellow dog by a slip-noose fastened around the poor cur's protesting neck, the knot carefully arranged under his right ear. In spite of every command and protest, Wilkerson had marched the whole way uproariously singing, "John Brown's Body."

The sun was in the west when they came in sight of the Cross-Roads, and the cabins on the low slope stood out angularly against the radiance beyond. As they beheld the hated settlement, the heretofore orderly ranks showed a disposition to depart from the steady advance and rush the shanties. Willetts, the Bowlders, Parker, Ross, Schofield, and fifty others did, in fact, break away and set a sharp pace up the slope.

Watts tried to call them back. "What's the use your gettin' killed?" he shouted.

"Why not?" answered Lige, who, like the others, was increasing his speed when old "Wimby" rose up suddenly from the roadside ahead of them, and motioned them frantically to go back. "They're laid out along the fence, waitin' fer ye," he warned them. "Git out the road. Come by the fields. Per the Lord's sake, spread!" Then, as suddenly as he had appeared, he dropped down into the weeds again. Lige and those with him paused, and the whole body came to a halt while the leaders consulted. There was a sound of metallic clicking and a thin rattle of steel. From far to the rear came the voice of old Wilkerson:

"John Brown's body lies a-mouldering in the ground,
John Brown's body lies a-mouldering in the ground—"

A few near him, as they stood waiting, began to take up the burden of the song, singing in slow time like a dirge; then those further away took it up; it spread, reached the leaders; they, too, began to sing, taking off their hats as they joined in; and soon the whole concourse, solemn, earnest, and uncovered, was singing—a thunderous requiem for John Harkless.

The sun was swinging lower and the edges of the world were embroidered with gold while that deep volume of sound shook the air, the song of a stern, savage, just cause—sung, perhaps, as some of the ancestors of these men sang with Hampden before the bristling walls of a hostile city. It had iron and steel in it. The men lying on their guns in the ambuscade along the fence heard the dirge rise and grow to its mighty fulness, and they shivered. One of them, posted nearest the advance, had his rifle carefully levelled at Lige Willetts, a fair target in the road. When he heard the singing, he turned to the man next behind him and laughed harshly: "I reckon we'll see a big jamboree in hell to-night, huh?"

The huge murmur of the chorus expanded, and gathered in rhythmic strength, and swelled to power, and rolled and thundered across the plain.

"John Brown's body lies a-mouldering in the ground,
John Brown's body lies a-mouldering in the ground,
John Brown's body lies a-mouldering in the ground,
        His soul goes marching on!
Glory! Glory! Hallelujah!
Glory! Glory! Hallelujah!
Glory! Glory! Hallelujah!
        His soul goes marching on!"

A gun spat from the higher ground, and Willetts dropped where he stood, but was up again in a second, with a red line across his forehead where the ball had grazed his temple. Then the mob spread out like a fan, hundreds of men climbing the fence and beginning the advance through the fields, closing on the ambuscade from both sides. Mr. Watts, wading through the high grass in the field north of the road, perceived the barrel of a gun shining from a bush some distance in front of him, and, although in the same second no weapon was seen in his hand, discharged a revolver at the bush behind the gun. Instantly ten or twelve men leaped from their hiding-places along the fences of both fields, and, firing hurriedly and harmlessly into the scattered ranks of the oncoming mob, broke for the shelter of the houses, where their fellows were posted. Taken on the flanks and from the rear, there was but one thing for them to do to keep from being hemmed in and shot or captured. (They excessively preferred being shot.) With a wild, high, joyous yell, sounding like the bay of young hounds breaking into view of their quarry, the Plattville men followed.

The most eastward of the debilitated edifices of Six-Cross-Roads was the saloon, which bore the painted legends: on the west wall, "Last Chance"; on the east wall, "First Chance." Next to this, and separated by two or three acres of weedy vacancy from the corners where the population centred thickest, stood-if one may so predicate of a building which leaned in seven directions-the house of Mr. Robert Skillett, the proprietor of the saloon. Both buildings were shut up as tight as their state of repair permitted. As they were furthest to the east, they formed the nearest shelter, and to them the Cross-Roaders bent their flight, though they stopped not here, but disappeared behind Skillett's shanty, putting it between them and their pursuers, whose guns were beginning to speak. The fugitives had a good start, and, being the picked runners of the Cross-Roads, they crossed the open, weedy acres in safety and made for their homes. Every house had become a fort, and the defenders would have to be fought and torn out one by one. As the guns sounded, a woman in a shanty near the forge began to scream, and kept on screaming.

On came the farmers and the men of Plattville. They took the saloon at a run; battered down the crazy doors with a fence-rail, and swarmed inside like busy insects, making the place hum like a hive, but with the hotter industries of destruction. It was empty of life as a tomb, but they beat and tore and battered and broke and hammered and shattered like madmen; they reduced the tawdry interior to a mere chaos, and came pouring forth laden with trophies of ruin. And then there was a charry smell in the air, and a slender feather of smoke floated up from a second-story window.

At the same time Watts led an assault on the adjoining house—an assault which came to a sudden pause, for, from cracks in the front wall, a squirrel-rifle and a shot-gun snapped and banged, and the crowd fell back in disorder. Homer Tibbs had a hat blown away, full of buck-shot holes, while Mr. Watts solicitously examined a small aperture in the skirts of his brown coat. The house commanded the road, and the rush of the mob into the village was checked, but only for the instant.

A rickety woodshed, which formed a portion of the Skillett mansion, closely joined the "Last Chance" side of the family place of business. Scarcely had the guns of the defenders sounded, when, with a loud shout, Lige Willetts leaped from an upper window on that side of the burning saloon and landed on the woodshed, and, immediately climbing the roof of the house itself, applied a fiery brand to the time-worn clapboards. Ross Schofield dropped on the shed, close behind him, his arm lovingly enfolding a gallon jug of whiskey, which he emptied (not without evident regret) upon the clapboards as Lige fired them. Flames burst forth almost instantly, and the smoke, uniting with that now rolling out of every window of the saloon, went up to heaven in a cumbrous, gray column.

As the flames began to spread, there was a rapid fusillade from the rear of the house, and a hundred men and more, who had kept on through the fields to the north, assailed it from behind. Their shots passed clear through the flimsy partitions, and there was a horrid screeching, like a beast's howls, from within. The front door was thrown open, and a lean, fierce-eyed girl, with a case-knife in her hand, ran out in the face of the mob. At sound of the shots in the rear they had begun to advance on the house a second time, and Hartley Bowlder was the nearest man to the girl. With awful words, and shrieking inconceivably, she made straight at Hartley, and attacked him with the knife. She struck at him again and again, and, in her anguish of hate and fear, was so extraordinary a spectacle that she gained for her companions the four or five seconds they needed to escape from the house. As she hurled herself alone at the oncoming torrent, they sped from the door unnoticed, sprang over the fence, and reached the open lots to the west before they were seen by Willetts from the roof.

"Don't let 'em fool you!" he shouted. "Look to I your left! There they go! Don't let 'em get away."

The Cross-Readers were running across the field. They were Bob Skillett and his younger brother, and Mr. Skillett was badly damaged: he seemed to be holding his jaw on his face with both hands. The girl turned, and sped after them. She was over the fence almost as soon as they were, and the three ran in single file, the girl last. She was either magnificently sacrificial and fearless, or she cunningly calculated that the regulators would take no chances of killing a woman-child, for she kept between their guns and her two companions, trying to cover and shield the latter with her frail body.

"Shoot, Lige," called Watts. "If we fire from here we'll hit the girl. Shoot!"

Willetts and Ross Schofield were still standing on the roof, at the edge, out of the smoke, and both fired at the same time. The fugitives did not turn; they kept on running, and they had nearly reached the other side of the field, when suddenly, without any premonitory gesture, the elder Skillett dropped flat on his face. The Cross-Roaders stood by each other that day, for four or five men ran out of the nearest shanty into the open, lifted the prostrate figure from the ground, and began to carry it back with them. But Mr. Skillett was alive; his curses were heard above all other sounds. Lige and Schofield fired again, and one of the rescuers staggered. Nevertheless, as the two men slid down from the roof, the burdened Cross-Readers were seen to break into a run; and at that, with another yell, fiercer, wilder, more joyous than the first, the Plattville men followed.

The yell rang loudly in the ears of old Wilkerson, who had remained back in the road, and at the same instant he heard another shout behind him. Mr. Wilkerson had not shared in the attack, but, greatly preoccupied with his own histrionic affairs, was proceeding up the pike alone—except for the unhappy yellow mongrel, still dragged along by the slip-noose—and alternating, as was his natural wont, from one fence to the other; crouching behind every bush to fire an imaginary rifle at his dog, and then springing out, with triumphant bellowings, to fall prone upon the terrified animal. It was after one of these victories that a shout of warning was raised behind him, and Mr. Wilkerson, by grace of the god Bacchus, rolling out of the way in time to save his life, saw a horse dash by him—a big, black horse whose polished flanks were dripping with lather. Warren Smith was the rider. He was waving a slip of yellow paper high in the air.

He rode up the slope, and drew rein beyond the burning buildings, just ahead of those foremost in the pursuit. He threw his horse across the road to oppose their progress, rose in his stirrups, and waved the paper over his head. "Stop!" he roared, "Give me one minute. Stop!" He had a grand voice; and he was known in many parts of the State for the great bass roar with which he startled his juries. To be heard at a distance most men lift the pitch of their voices; Smith lowered his an octave or two, and the result was like an earthquake playing an organ in a catacomb.

"Stop!" he thundered. "Stop!"

In answer, one of the flying Cross-Roaders turned and sent a bullet whistling close to him. The lawyer paused long enough to bow deeply in satirical response; then, flourishing the paper, he roared again: "Stop! A mistake! I have news! Stop, I say! Homer has got them!"

To make himself heard over that tempestuous advance was a feat; for him, moreover, whose counsels had so lately been derided, to interest the pursuers at such a moment enough to make them listen—to find the word— was a greater; and by the word, and by gestures at once vehemently imperious and imploring, to stop them was still greater; but he did it. He had come at just the moment before the moment that would have been too late. They all heard him. They all knew, too, he was not trying to save the Cross-Roads as a matter of duty, because he had given that up before the mob left Plattville. Indeed, it was a question if, at the last, he had not tacitly approved; and no one feared indictments for the day's work. It would do no harm to listen to what he had to say. The work could wait; it would "keep" for five minutes. They began to gather around him, excited, flushed, perspiring, and smelling of smoke. Hartley Bowlder, won by Lige's desperation and intrepidity, was helping the latter tie up his head; no one else was hurt.

"What is it?" they clamored impatiently. "Speak quick!" There was another harmless shot from a fugitive, and then the Cross-Roaders, divining that the diversion was in their favor, secured themselves in their decrepit fastnesses and held their fire. Meanwhile, the flames crackled cheerfully in Plattville ears. No matter what the prosecutor had to say, at least the Skillett saloon and homestead were gone, and Bob Skillett and one other would be sick enough to be good for a while.

"Listen," cried Warren Smith, and, rising in his stirrups again, read the missive in his hand, a Western Union telegraph form. "Warren Smith, Plattville," was the direction. "Found both shell-men. Police familiar with both, and both wanted here. One arrested at noon in a second-hand clothes store, wearing Harkless's hat, also trying dispose torn full-dress coat known to have been worn by Harkless last night. Stains on lining believed blood. Second man found later at freight-yards in empty lumber car left Plattville 1 P.M., badly hurt, shot, and bruised. Supposed Harkless made hard fight. Hurt man taken to hospital unconscious. Will die. Hope able question him first and discover whereabouts body. Other man refuses talk so far. Check any movement Cross-Roads. This clears Skillett, *etc.* Come over on 9.15."

The telegram was signed by Homer and by Barrett, the superintendent of police at Rouen.

"It's all a mistake, boys," the lawyer said, as he handed the paper to Watts and Parker for inspection. "The ladies at the judge's were mistaken, that's all, and this proves it. It's easy enough to understand: they were frightened by the storm, and, watching a fence a quarter-mile away by flashes of lightning, any one would have been confused, and imagined all the horrors on earth. I don't deny but what I believed it for a while, and I don't deny but the Cross-Roads is pretty tough, but you've done a good deal here already, to-day, and we're saved in time from a mistake that would have turned out mighty bad. This settles it. Homer got a wire from Rouen to come over there, soon as they got track of the first man; that was when we saw him on the Rouen accommodation."

A slightly cracked voice, yet a huskily tuneful one, was lifted quaveringly on the air from the roadside, where an old man and a yellow dog sat in the dust together, the latter reprieved at the last moment, his surprised head rakishly garnished with a hasty wreath of dog-fennel daisies.

"John Brown's body lies a-mouldering in the ground,
While we go marching on!"

Three-quarters of an hour later, the inhabitants of the Cross-Roads, saved, they knew not how; guilty; knowing nothing of the fantastic pendulum of opinion, which, swung by the events of the day, had marked the fatal moment of guilt, now on others, now on them, who deserved it—these natives and refugees, conscious of atrocity, dumfounded by a miracle, thinking the world gone mad, hovered together in a dark, ragged mass at the crossing corners, while the skeleton of the rotting buggy in the slough rose behind them against the face of the west. They peered with stupified eyes through the smoky twilight.

From afar, faintly through the gloaming, came mournfully to their ears the many-voiced refrain—fainter, fainter:

"John Brown's body lies a-mouldering in the ground, John Brown's body lies a-mouldering in the ground. John Brown's body lies—-mould— . . . . . we go march . . . . on."

CHAPTER XII

JERRY THE TELLER At midnight a small brougham stopped at the gates of the city hospital in Rouen. A short distance ahead, the lamps of a cab, drawn up at the curbing, made two dull orange sparks under the electric light swinging over the street. A cigarette described a brief parabola as it was tossed from the brougham, and a short young man jumped out and entered the gates, then paused and spoke to the driver of the cab.

"Did you bring Mr. Barrett here?"

"Yes, sir," answered the driver; "him and two other gentlemen."

Lighting another cigarette, from which he drew but two inspirations before he threw it away, the young man proceeded quickly up the walk. As he ascended the short flight of steps which led to the main doors, he panted a little, in a way which suggested that (although his white waistcoat outlined an ellipse still respectable) a crescendo of portliness was playing diminuendo with his youth. And, though his walk was brisk, it was not lively. The expression of his very red face indicated that his briskness was spurred by anxiety, and a fattish groan he emitted on the top step added the impression that his comfortable body protested against the mental spur. In the hall he removed his narrow-brimmed straw hat and presented a rotund and amiable head, from the top of which his auburn hair seemed to retire with a sense of defeat; it fell back, however, not in confusion, but in perfect order, and the sparse pink mist left upon his crown gave, by a supreme effort, an effect of arrangement, so that an imaginative observer would have declared that there was a part down the middle. The gentleman's plump face bore a grave and troubled expression, and gravity and trouble were patent in all the lines of his figure and in every gesture; in the way he turned his head; in the uneasy shifting of his hat from one hand to the other and in his fanning himself with it in a nervous fashion; and in his small, blue eyes, which did not twinkle behind his rimless glasses and looked unused to not twinkling. His gravity clothed him like an ill-fitting coat; or, possibly, he might have reminded the imaginative observer, just now conjured up, of a music-box set to turning its cylinder backwards.

He spoke to an attendant, and was directed to an office, which he entered without delay. There were five men in the room, three of them engaged in conversation near the door; another, a young surgeon, was writing at a desk; the fifth drowsily nodding on a sofa. The newcomer bowed as he entered.

"Mr. Barrett?" he said inquiringly.

One of the men near the door turned about. "Yes, sir," he answered, with a stem disfavor of the applicant; a disfavor possibly a perquisite of his office. "What's wanted?"

"I think I have met you," returned the other. "My name is Meredith."

Mr. Barrett probably did not locate the meeting, but the name proved an open sesame to his geniality, for he melted at once, and saying: "Of course, of course, Mr. Meredith; did you want a talk with me?" clasped the young man's hand confidentially in his, and, with an appearance of assuring him that whatever the atrocity which had occurred in the Meredith household it should be discreetly handled and hushed up, indicated a disposition to conduct him toward a more appropriate apartment for the rehearsal of scandal. The young man accepted the hand-clasp with some resignation, but rejected the suggestion of privacy.

"A telegram from Plattville reached me half an hour ago," he said. "I should have had it sooner, but I have been in the country all day."

The two men who had been talking with the superintendent turned quickly, and stared at the speaker. He went on: "Mr. Harkless was an old—and—" He broke off, with a sudden, sharp choking, and for a moment was unable to control an emotion that seemed, for some reason, as surprising and unbefitting, in a person of his rubicund presence, as was his gravity. An astonished tear glittered in the corner of his eye. The grief of the gayer sorts of stout people appears, sometimes, to dumfound even themselves. The young man took off his glasses and wiped them slowly. "—An old and very dear friend of mine." He replaced the glasses insecurely upon his nose. "I telephoned to your headquarters, and they said you had come here."

"Yes, sir; yes, sir," the superintendent of police responded, cheerfully. "These two gentlemen are from Plattville; Mr. Smith just got in. They mighty near had big trouble down there to-day, but I guess we'll settle things for 'em up here. Let me make you acquainted with my friend, Mr. Smith, and my friend, Mr. Homer. Gentlemen, my friend, Mr. Meredith, one of our well-known citizens."

"You hear it from the police, gentlemen," added Mr. Meredith, perking up a little. "I know Dr. Gay." He nodded to the surgeon.

"I suppose you have heard some of the circumstances—those that we've given out," said Barrett.

"I read the account in the evening paper. I had heard of Harkless, of Carlow, before; but it never occurred to me that it was my friend—I had heard he was abroad—until I got this telegram from a relative of mine who happened to be down there."

"Well," said the superintendent, "your friend made a mighty good fight before he gave up. The Teller, that's the man we've got out here, he's so hacked up and shot and battered his mother wouldn't know him, if she wanted to; at least, that's what Gay, here, says. We haven't seen him, because the doctors have been at him ever since he was found, and they expect to do some more tonight, when we've had our interview with him, if he lives long enough. One of my sergeants found him in, the freight-yards about four-o'clock and sent him here in the ambulance; knew it was Teller, because he was stowed away in one of the empty cars that came from Plattville last night, and Slattery—that's his running mate, the one we caught with the coat and hat—gave in that they beat their way on that freight. I guess Slattery let this one do most of the fighting; he ain't scratched; but Mr. Harkless certainly made it hot for the Teller."

"My relative believes that Mr. Harkless is still alive," said Meredith.

Mr. Barrett permitted himself an indulgent smile. He had the air of having long ago discovered everything which anybody might wish to know, and of knowing a great deal which he held in reserve because it was necessary to suppress many facts for a purpose far beyond his auditor's comprehension, though a very simple matter to himself.

"Well, hardly, I expect," he replied, easily. "No; he's hardly alive."

"Oh, don't say that," said Meredith.

"I'm afraid Mr. Barrett has to say it," broke in Warren Smith. "We're up here to see this fellow before he dies, to try and get him to tell what disposal they made of the——"

"Ah!" Meredith shivered. "I believe I'd rather he said the other than to hear you say that."

Mr. Horner felt the need of defending a fellow-townsman, and came to the rescue, flushing painfully. "It's mighty bad, I know," said the sheriff of Carlow, the shadows of his honest, rough face falling in a solemn pattern; "I reckon we hate to say it as much as you hate to hear it; and Warren really didn't get the word out. It's stuck in our throats all day; and I don't recollect as I heard a single man say it before I left our city this morning. Our folks thought a great deal of him, Mr. Meredith; I don't believe there's any thinks more. But it's come to that now; you can't hardly see no chance left. We be'n sweating this other man, Slattery, but we can't break him down. Jest tells us to go to"—the sheriff paused, evidently deterred by the thought that swear-words were unbefitting a hospital—"to the other place, and shets his jaw up tight. The one up here is called the Teller, as Mr. Barrett says; his name's Jerry the Teller. Well, we told Slattery that Jerry had died and left a confession; tried to make him think there wasn't no hope fer him, and he might as well up and tell his share; might git off easier; warned him to look out for a mob if he didn't, maybe, and so on, but it never bothered him at all. He's nervy, all right. Told us to go—that is, he said it again—and swore the Teller was on his way to Chicago, swore he seen him git on the train. Wouldn't say another word tell he got a lawyer. So, 'soon as it was any use, we come up here—they reckon he'll come to before he dies. We'll be glad to have you go in with us," Horner said kindly. "I reckon it's all the same to Mr. Barrett."

"He will die, will he, Gay?" Meredith asked, turning to the surgeon.

"Oh, not necessarily," the young man replied, yawning slightly behind his hand, and too long accustomed to straightforward questions to be shocked at an evident wish for a direct reply. "His chances are better, because they'll hang him if he gets well. They took the ball and a good deal of shot out of his side, and there's a lot more for afterwhile, if he lasts. He's been off the table an hour, and he's still going."

"That's in his favor, isn't it?" said Meredith. "And extraordinary, too?" If young Dr. Gay perceived a slur in these interrogations he betrayed no exterior appreciation of it.

"Shot!" exclaimed Homer. "Shot! I knowed there'd be'n a pistol used, though where they got it beats me—we stripped 'em—and it wasn't Mr. Harkless's; he never carried one. But a shot-gun!"

An attendant entered and spoke to the surgeon, and Gay rose wearily, touched the drowsy young man on the shoulder, and led the way to the door. "You can come now," he said to the others; "though I doubt its being any good to you. He's delirious."

They went down a long hall and up a narrow corridor, then stepped softly into a small, quiet ward.

There was a pungent smell of chemicals in the room; the light was low, and the dimness was imbued with a thick, confused murmur, incoherent whisperings that came from a cot in the corner. It was the only cot in use in the ward, and Meredith was conscious of a terror that made him dread, to look at it, to go near it. Beside it a nurse sat silent, and upon it feebly tossed the racked body of him whom Barrett had called Jerry the Teller.

The head was a shapeless bundle, so swathed it was with bandages and cloths, and what part of the face was visible was discolored and pigmented with drugs. Stretched under the white sheet the man looked immensely tall —as Horner saw with vague misgiving—and he lay in an odd, inhuman fashion, as though he had been all broken to pieces. His attempts to move were constantly soothed by the nurse, and he as constantly renewed such attempts; and one hand, though torn and bandaged, was not to be restrained from a wandering, restless movement which Meredith felt to be pathetic. He had entered the room with a flare of hate for the thug whom he had come to see die, and who had struck down the old friend whose nearness he had never known until it was too late. But at first sight of the broken figure he felt all animosity fall away from him; only awe remained, and a growing, traitorous pity as he watched the long, white fingers of the Teller "pick at the coverlet." The man was muttering rapid fragments of words, and syllables.

118

"Somehow I feel a sense of wrong," Meredith whispered to Gay. "I feel as if I had done the fellow to death myself, as if it were all out of gear. I know, now, how Henry felt over the great Guisard. My God, how tall he looks! That doesn't seem to me like a thug's hand."

The surgeon nodded. "Of course, if there's a mistake to be made, you can count on Barrett and his sergeants to make it. I doubt if this is their man. When they found him what clothes he wore were torn and stained; but they had been good once, especially the linen."

Barrett bent over the recumbent figure. "See here. Jerry," he said, "I want to talk to you a little. Rouse up, will you? I want to talk to you as a friend."

The incoherent muttering continued.

"See here, Jerry!" repeated Barrett, more sharply. "Jerry! rouse up, will you? We don't want any fooling; understand that, Jerry!" He dropped his hand on the man's shoulder and shook him slightly. The Teller uttered a short, gasping cry.

"Let me," said Gay, and swiftly interposed. Bending over the cot, he said in a pleasant, soft voice: "It's all right, old man; it's all right. Slattery wants to know what you did with that man down at Plattville, when you got through with him. He can't remember, and he thinks there was money left on him. Slattery's head was hurt—he can't remember. He'll go shares with you, when he gets it. Slattery's going to stand by you, if he can get the money."

The Teller only tried to move his free hand to the shoulder Barrett had shaken.

"Slattery wants to know," repeated the surgeon, gently moving the hand back upon the sheet. "He'll divvy up, when he gets it. He'll stand by you, old man."

"Would you please not mind," whispered the Teller faintly, "would you please not mind if you took care not to brush against my shoulder again?"

The surgeon drew back with an exclamation; but the Teller's whisper gathered strength, and they heard him murmuring oddly to himself. Meredith moved forward.

"What's that?" he asked, with a startled gesture.

"Seems to be trying to sing, or something," said Barrett, bending over to listen. The Teller swung his arm heavily over the side of the cot, the fingers never ceasing their painful twitching, and Gay leaned down and gently moved the cloths so that the white, scarred lips were free. They moved steadily; they seemed to be framing the semblance of an old ballad that Meredith knew; the whisper grew more distinct, and it became a rich but broken voice, and they heard it singing, like the sound of some far, halting minstrelsy:

"Wave willows—murmur waters—golden sunbeams smile, Earthly music—cannot waken—lovely—Annie Lisle."

"My God!" cried Tom Meredith.

The bandaged hand waved jauntily over the Teller's head. "Ah, men," he said, almost clearly, and tried to lift himself on his arm, "I tell you it's a grand eleven we have this year! There will be little left of anything that stands against them. Did you see Jim Romley ride over his man this afternoon?"

As the voice grew clearer the sheriff stepped forward, but Tom Meredith, with a loud exclamation of grief, threw himself on his knees beside the cot and seized the wandering fingers in his own. "John!" he cried. "John! Is it *you*?"

The voice went on rapidly, not heeding him: "Ah, you needn't howl; I'd have been as much use at right as that Sophomore. Well, laugh away, you Indians! If it hadn't been for this ankle—but it seems to be my chest that's hurt—and side—not that it matters, you know; the Sophomore's just as good, or better. It's only my egotism. Yes, it must be the side—and chest—and head—all over, I believe. Not that it matters—I'll try again next year—next year I'll make it a daily, Helen said, not that I should call you Helen—I mean Miss—Miss—Fisbee—no, Sherwood—but I've always thought Helen was the prettiest name in the world—you'll forgive me?—And please tell Parker there's no more copy, and won't be—I wouldn't grind out another stick to save his immortal—yes, yes, a daily—she said-ah, I never made a good trade—no—they can't come seven miles—but I'll finish *you*, Skillett, first; I know *you*! I know nearly all of you! Now let's sing 'Annie Lisle.'" He lifted his hand as if to beat the time for a chorus.

"Oh, John, John!" cried Tom Meredith, and sobbed outright. "My boy—my boy—old friend——" The cry of the classmate was like that of a mother, for it was his old idol and hero who lay helpless and broken before him.

The brougham lamps and the apathetic sparks of the cab gleamed in front of the hospital till daylight. Two other pairs of lamps joined them in the earliest of the small hours, these subjoined to two deep-hooded phaetons, from each of which quickly descended a gentleman with a beard, an air of eminence, and a small, ominous black box. The air of eminence was justified by the haste with which Meredith had sent for them, and by their wide repute. They arrived almost simultaneously, and hastily shook hands as they made their way to the ward down the long hall and up the narrow corridor. They had a short conversation with Gay and a word with the nurse, then turned the others out of the room by a practiced innuendo of manner. They stayed a long time in the room without opening the door. Meredith paced the hall alone, sometimes stopping to speak to Warren Smith; but the two officials of peace sat together in dumb consternation and astonishment. The sleepy young man relaxed himself resignedly upon a bench in the hall had returned to the dormance from which he had been roused. The big hospital was very still. Now and then a nurse went through the hall, carrying something, and sometimes a neat young physician passed cheerfully along, looking as if he had many patients who were well enough to testify to his skill, but sick enough to pay for it. Outside, through the open front doors, the crickets chirped.

Meredith went out on the steps, and breathed the cool night air. A slender taint of drugs hung everywhere about the building, and the almost imperceptible permeation sickened him; it was deadly, he thought, and imbued with a hideous portent of suffering. That John Harkless, of all men, should lie stifled with ether, and bandaged and splintered, and smeared with horrible unguents, while they stabbed and slashed and tortured him, and made an outrage and a sin of that grand, big, dexterous body of his! Meredith shuddered. The lights in the little ward were turned up, and they seemed to shine from a chamber of horrors, while he waited, as a brother might have waited outside the Inquisition—if, indeed, a brother would have been allowed to wait outside the Inquisition.

Alas, he had found John Harkless! He had "lost track" of him as men sometimes do lose track of their best beloved, but it had always been a comfort to know that Harkless *was*—somewhere, a comfort without which he could hardly have got along. Like others he had been waiting for John to turn up—on top, of course; for people would always believe in him so, that he would be shoved ahead, no matter how much he hung back himself— but Meredith had not expected him to turn up in Indiana. He had heard vaguely that Harkless was abroad, and he had a general expectation that people would hear of him over there some day, with papers like the "Times" beseeching him to go on missions. And he found him here, in his own home, a stranger, alone and dying, receiving what ministrations were reserved for Jerry the Teller. But it was Helen Sherwood who had found him. He wondered how much those two had seen of each other, down there in Plattville. If they had liked each other, and Harkless could have lived, he thought it might have simplified some things for Helen. "Poor Helen!" he exclaimed aloud. Her telegram had a ring, even in the barren four sentences. He wondered how much they had liked each other. Perhaps she would wish to come at once. When those fellows came out of the room he would send her a word by telegraph.

When they came out—ah! he did not want them to come out; he was afraid. They were an eternity—why didn't they come? No; he hoped they would not come, just now. In a little time, in a few minutes, even, he would not dread a few words so much; but *now* he couldn't quite bear to be told he had found his friend only to lose him, the man he had always most needed, wanted, loved. Everybody had always cared for Harkless, wherever he went. That *he* had always cared for everybody was part of the reason, maybe. Meredith remembered, now, hearing a man who had spent a day in Plattville on business speak of him: "They've got a young fellow down there who'll be Governor in a few years. He's a sort of dictator; and runs the party all over that part of the State to suit his own sweet will, just by sheer personality. And there isn't a man in that district who wouldn't cheerfully lie down in the mud to let him pass over dry. It's that young Harkless, you know; owns the 'Herald,' the paper that downed McCune and smashed those imitation 'White-Caps' in Carlow County." Meredith had been momentarily struck by the coincidence of the name, but his notion of Harkless was so inseparably connected with what was (to his mind) a handsome and more spacious—certainly more illuminated—field of action, that the idea that this might be his friend never entered his head. Helen had said something once—he could not remember what—that made him think she had half suspected it, and he had laughed. He thought of the whimsical fate that had taken her to Plattville, of the reason for her going, and the old thought came to him that the world is, after all, so very small. He looked up at the twinkling stars; they were reassuring and kind. Under their benignancy no loss could befall, no fate miscarry—for in his last thought he felt his vision opened, for the moment, to perceive a fine tracery of fate.

"Ah, that would be too beautiful!" he said.

And then he shivered; for his name was spoken from within.

It was soon plain to him that he need not have feared a few words, for he did not in the least understand those with which the eminent surgeons favored him; and they at once took their departure. He did understand, however, what Horner told him. Mr. Barrett, Warren Smith, and the sleepy young man had reentered the ward; and Horner was following, but waited for Meredith. Somehow, the look of the sheriff's Sunday coat, wrinkling forlornly from his broad, bent shoulders, was both touching and solemn. He said simply: "He's conscious and not out of his head. They're gone in to take his ante-mortem statement," and they went into the room.

Harkless's eyes were bandaged. The lawyer was speaking to him, and as Horner went awkwardly toward the cot. Warren said something indicative of the sheriff's presence, and the hand on the sheet made a formless motion which Horner understood, for he took the pale fingers in his own, very gently, and then set them back. Smith turned toward Meredith, but the latter made a gesture which forbade the attorney to speak of him, and went to a corner and sat down with his head in his hands.

The sleepy young man opened a notebook and shook a stylographic pen so that the ink might flow freely. The lawyer, briefly and with unlegal agitation, administered an oath, to which Harkless responded feebly, and then there was silence.

"Now, Mr. Harkless, if you please," said Barrett, insinuatingly; "if you feel like telling us as much as you can about it?"

He answered in a low, rather indistinct voice, very deliberately, pausing before almost every word. It was easy work for the sleepy stenographer.

"I understand. I don't want to go off my head again before I finish. Of course I know why you want this. If it were only for myself I should tell you nothing, because, if I am to leave, I should like it better if no one were punished. But that's a bad community over there; they are everlastingly worrying our people; they have

122

always been a bother to us, and it's time it was stopped for good. I don't believe very much in punishment, but you can't do a great deal of reforming with the Cross-Roaders unless you catch them young—very young, before they're weaned— they wean them on whiskey, I think. I realize you needn't have sworn me for me to tell you this."

Homer and Smith had started at the mention of the Cross-Roads, but they subdued their ejaculations, while Mr. Barrett looked as if he had known it, of course. The room was still, save for the dim voice and the soft transcribings of the stylographic pen.

"I left Judge Briscoe's, and went west on the pike to a big tree. It rained, and I stepped under the tree for shelter. There was a man on the other side of the fence. It was Bob Skillett. He was carrying his gown and hood—I suppose it was that—on his arm. Then I saw two others a little farther east, in the middle of the road; and I think they had followed me from the Briscoes', or near there. They had their foolish regalia on, as all the rest had,—there was plenty of lightning to see. The two in the road were simply standing there in the rain, looking at me through the eye-holes in their hoods. I knew there were others—plenty—but I thought they were coming from behind me—the west.

"I wanted to get home—the court-house yard was good enough for me—so I started east, toward town. I passed the two gentlemen; and one fell down as I went by him, but the other fired a shot as a signal, and I got his hood off his face for it—I stopped long enough—and it was Force Johnson. I know him well. Then I ran, and they followed. A little ahead of me I saw six or eight of them spread across the road. I knew I'd have a time getting through, so I jumped the fence to cut across the fields, and I lit in a swarm of them—it had rained them just where I jumped. I set my back to the fence, but one of the fellows in the road leaned over and smashed my head in, rather—with the butt of a gun, I believe. I came out from the fence and they made a little circle around me. No one said anything. I saw they had ropes and saplings, and I didn't want that, exactly, so I went into them. I got a good many hoods off before it was over, and I can swear to quite a number besides those I told you."

He named the men, slowly and carefully. Then he went on: "I think they gave up the notion of whipping. We all got into a bunch, and they couldn't clear to shoot without hitting some of their own: and there was a lot of gouging and kicking—one fellow nearly got my left eye, and I tried to tear him apart and he screamed so that I think he was hurt. Once or twice I thought I might get away, but somebody hammered me over the head and face again, and I got dizzy; and then they all jumped away from me suddenly, and Bob Skillett stepped up—and—shot me. He waited for a good flurry of lightning, and I was slow tumbling down. Some one else fired a shot-gun, I think—I can't be sure—about the same time, from the side. I tried to get up, but I couldn't, and then they got together, for a consultation. The man I had hurt—I didn't recognize him—came and looked at me. He was nursing himself all over; and groaned; and I laughed, I—at any rate, my arm was lying stretched out on the grass, and he stamped his heel into my hand, and after a little of that I quit feeling.

"I'm not quite clear about what happened afterwards. They went away, not far, I think. There's an old shed, a cattle-shelter, near there, and I think the storm drove them under it to wait for a slack. It seemed a long time. Sometimes I was conscious, sometimes I wasn't. I thought I might be drowned, but I suppose the rain was good for me. Then I remember being in motion, being dragged and carried a long way. They took me up a steep, short slope, and set me down near the top. I knew that was the railroad embankment, and I thought they meant to lay me across the track, but it didn't occur to them, I suppose—they are not familiar with melodrama—and a long time after that I felt and heard a great banging and rattling under me and all about me, and it came to me that they had disposed of me by hoisting me into an empty freight-car. The odd part of it was that the car wasn't empty, for there were two men already in it, and I knew them by what they said to me.

"They were the two shell-men who cheated Hartley Bowlder, and they weren't vindictive; they even seemed to be trying to help me a little, though perhaps they were only stealing my clothes, and maybe they thought for them to do anything unpleasant would be superfluous; I could see that they thought I was done for, and that they had been hiding in the car when I was put there. I asked them to try to call the train men for me, but they wouldn't listen, or else I couldn't make myself understood. That's all. The rest is a blur. I haven't known anything more until those surgeons were here. Please tell me how long ago it happened. I shall not die, I think; there are a good many things I want to know about." He moved restlessly and the nurse soothed him.

Meredith rose and left the room with a noiseless step. He went out to the stars again, and looked to them to check the storm of rage and sorrow that buffeted his bosom. He understood lynching, now the thing was home to him, and his feeling was no inspiration of a fear lest the law miscarry; it was the itch to get his own hand on the rope. Horner came out presently, and whispered a long, broad, profound curse upon the men of the Cross-Roads, and Meredith's gratitude to him was keen. Barrett went away, soon after, leaving the cab for the gentlemen from Plattville. Meredith had a strange, unreasonable desire to kick Barrett, possibly for his sergeant's sake. Warren Smith sat in the ward with the nurse and Gay, and the room was very quiet. It was a long vigil.

They were only waiting.

At five o'clock he was still alive—just that, Smith came out to say. Meredith sent his driver with a telegram to Helen which would give Plattville the news that Harkless was found and was not yet gone from them. Homer took the cab and left for the station; there was a train, and there were things for him to do in Carlow. At noon Meredith sent a second telegram to Helen, as barren of detail as the first: he was alive—was a little improved. This telegram did not reach her, for she was on the way to Rouen, and half of the population of Carlow—at least, so it appeared to the unhappy conductor of the accommodation—was with her.

They seemed to feel that they could camp in the hospital halls and corridors, and they were an incalculable worry to the authorities. More came on every train, and nearly all brought flowers, and jelly, and chickens for preparing broth, and they insisted that the two latter delicacies be fed to the patient at once. Meredith was possessed by an unaccountable responsibility for them all, and invited a great many to stay at his own house. They were still in ignorance of the truth about the Cross-Roads, and some of them spent the day (it was Sunday) in planning an assault upon the Rouen jail for the purpose of lynching Slattery in case Harkless's condition did not improve at once. Those who had heard his statement kept close mouths until the story appeared in full in the Rouen papers on Monday morning; but by that time every member of the Cross-Roads White-Caps was lodged in the Rouen jail with Slattery. Homer and a heavily armed posse rode over to the muddy corners on Sunday night, and the sheriff discovered that he might have taken the Skilletts and Johnsons single-handed and unarmed. Their nerve was gone; they were shaken and afraid; and, to employ a figure somewhat inappropriate to their sullen, glad surrender, they fell upon his neck in their relief at finding the law touching them. They had no wish to hear "John Brown's Body" again. They wanted to get inside of a strong jail, and to throw themselves on the mercy of the court as soon as possible. And those whom Harkless had not recognized delayed not to give themselves up; they did not desire to remain in Six-Cross-Roads. Bob Skillett, Force Johnson, and one or two others needed the care of a physician badly, and one man was suffering from a severely wrenched back. Homer had a train stopped at a crossing, so that his prisoners need not be taken through Plattville, and he brought them all safely to Rouen. Had there chanced any one to ride through the deserted Cross-Roads the next morning, passing the trampled fields and the charred ruins of the two shanties to the east, and listening to the lamentations of the women and children, he would have declared that at last the old score had been paid, and that Six-Cross-Roads was wiped out.

The Carlow folks were deeply impressed with the two eminent surgeons, of whom some of them had heard, and on Tuesday, the bulletins marking considerable encouragement, most of them decided to temporarily risk the editor of the "Herald" to such capable hands, and they returned quietly to their homes; only a few were delayed in reaching Carlow by travelling to the first station in the opposite direction before they succeeded in planting themselves on the proper train.

Meanwhile, the object of their solicitude tossed and burned on his bed of pain. He was delirious most of the time, and, in the intervals of half-consciousness, found that his desire to live, very strong at first, had disappeared; he did not care much about anything except rest—he wanted peace. In his wanderings he was almost always back in his college days, beholding them in an unhappy, distorted fashion. He would lie asprawl on the sward with the others, listening to the Seniors singing on the steps, and, all at once, the old, kindly faces would expand enormously and press over him with hideous mouthings, and an ugly Senior in cap and gown would stamp him and grind a spiked heel into his hand; then they would toss him high into air that was all flames, and he would fall and fall through the raging heat, seeing the cool earth far beneath him, but never able to get down to it again. And then he was driven miles and miles by dusky figures, through a rain of boiling water; and at other times the whole universe was a vast, hot brass bell, and it gave off a huge, continuous roar and hum, while he was a mere point of consciousness floating in the exact centre of the heat and sound waves, and he listened, listened for years, to the awful, brazen hum from which there could be no escape; at the same time it seemed to him that he was only a Freshman on the slippery roof of the tower, trying to steal the clapper of the chapel bell.

Finally he came to what he would have considered a lucid interval, had it not appeared that Helen Sherwood was whispering to Tom Meredith at the foot of his bed. This he knew to be a fictitious presentation of his fever, for was she not by this time away and away for foreign lands? And, also, Tom Meredith was a slim young thing, and not the middle-aged youth with an undeniable stomach and a baldish head, who, by the grotesque necromancy of his hallucinations, assumed a preposterous likeness to his old friend. He waved his hand to the figures and they vanished like figments of a dream; but all the same the vision had been realistic enough for the lady to look exquisitely pretty. No one could help wishing to stay in a world which contained as charming a picture as that.

And then, too quickly, the moment of clearness passed; and he was troubled about the "Herald," beseeching those near him to put copies of the paper in his hands, threatening angrily to believe they were deceiving him, that his paper had suspended, if the three issues of the week were not instantly produced. What did they mean by keeping the truth from him? He knew the "Herald" had not come out. Who was there to get it out in his absence? He raised himself on his elbow and struggled to be up; and they had hard work to quiet him.

But the next night Meredith waited near his bedside, haggard and dishevelled. Harkless had been lying in a long stupor; suddenly he spoke, quite loudly, and the young surgeon, Gay, who leaned over him, remembered the words and the tone all his life.

"Away and away—across the waters," said John Harkless. "She was here— once— in June."

"What is it, John?" whispered Meredith, huskily. "You're easier, aren't you?"

And John smiled a little, as if, for an instant, his swathed eyes penetrated the bandages, and saw and knew his old friend again.

That same night a friend of Rodney McCune's sent a telegram from Rouen: "He is dying. His paper is dead. Your name goes before convention in September."

126

CHAPTER XIII

JAMES FISBEE

On Monday morning three men sat in council in the "Herald" office; that is, if staring out of dingy windows in a demented silence may be called sitting in council; that was what Mr. Fisbee and Parker and Ross Schofield were doing. By almost desperate exertions, these three and Bud Tipworthy had managed to place before the public the issues of the paper for the previous week, unaided by their chief, or, rather, aided by long accounts of his condition and the manner of his mishap; and, in truth, three copies were at that moment in the possession of Dr. Gay, accompanied by a note from Parker warning the surgeon to exhibit them to his patient only as a last resort, as the foreman feared the perusal of them might cause a relapse.

By indiscriminate turns, acting as editors, reporters, and typesetters— and particularly space-writers—the three men had worried out three issues, and part of the fourth (to appear the next morning) was set up; but they had come to the end of their string, and there were various horrid gaps yet to fill in spite of a too generous spreading of advertisements. Bud Tipworthy had been sent out to besiege Miss Tibbs, all of whose recent buds of rhyme had been hot-housed into inky blossom during the week, and after a long absence the youth returned with a somewhat abrupt quatrain, entitled "The Parisians of Old," which she had produced while he waited— only four lines, according to the measure they meted, which was not regardful of art—less than a drop in the bucket, or, to preserve the figure, a single posy where they needed a bouquet. Bud went down the rickety outside stairs, and sat on the lowest step, whistling "Wait till the Clouds Roll by, Jenny"; Ross Schofield descended to set up the quatrain, and Fisbee and Parker were left to silence and troubled meditation.

They were seated on opposite sides of Harkless's desk. Sheets of blank scratch-paper lay before them, and they relaxed not their knit brows. Now and then, one of them, after gazing vacantly about the room for ten or fifteen minutes, would attack the sheet before him with fiercest energy; then the energy would taper off, and the paragraph halt, the writer peruse it dubiously, then angrily tear off the sheet and hurl it to the floor. All around them lay these snowballs of defeated journalism.

Mr. Parker was a long, loose, gaunt gentleman, with a peremptory forehead and a capable jaw, but on the present occasion his capability was baffled and swamped in the attempt to steer the craft of his talent up an unaccustomed channel without a pilot. "I don't see as it's any use, Fisbee," he said, morosely, after a series of efforts that littered the floor in every direction. "I'm a born compositor, and I can't shift my trade. I stood the pace fairly for a week, but I'll have to give up; I'm run plumb dry. I only hope they won't show him our Saturday with your three columns of 'A Word of the Lotus Motive,' reprinted from February. I begin to sympathize with the boss, because I know what he felt when I ballyragged him for copy. Yes, sir, I know how it is to be an editor in a dead town now."

"We must remember, too," said his companion, thoughtfully, "there is the Thursday issue of this week to be prepared, almost at once."

"*Don't*! Please don't mention that, Fisbee!" Parker tilted far back in his chair with his feet anchored under the desk, preserving a precarious balance. "I ain't as grateful for my promotion to joint Editor-in-Chief as I might be. I'm a middling poor man for the hour, I guess," he remarked, painfully following the peregrinations of a fly on his companion's sleeve.

Mr. Fisbee twisted up another sheet, and employed his eyes in following the course of a crack in the plaster, a slender black aperture which staggered across the dusty ceiling and down the dustier wall to disappear behind a still dustier map of Carlow County. "That's the trouble!" exclaimed Parker, observing the other's preoccupation. "Soon as you get to writing a line or two that seems kind of promising, you begin to take a morbid interest in that blamed crack. It's busted up enough copy for me, the last eight days, to have filled her up twenty times over. I don't know as I ever care to see that crack again. I turned my back on it, but there wasn't any use in that, because if a fly lights on you I watch him like a brother, and if there ain't any fly I've caught a mania for tapping my teeth with a pencil, that is just as good."

To these two gentlemen, thus disengaged, reentered (after a much longer absence than Miss Selina's quatrain justified) Mr. Ross Schofield, a healthy glow of exertion lending pleasant color to his earnest visage, and an almost visible laurel of success crowning his brows. In addition to this imaginary ornament, he was horned with pencils over both ears, and held some scribbled sheets in his hand.

"I done a good deal down there," he announced cheerfully, drawing up a chair to the desk. "I thought up a heap of things I've heard lately, and they'll fill up mighty well. That there poem of Miss Seliny's was a kind of an inspiration to me, and I tried one myself, and it didn't come hard at all. When I got started once, it jest seemed to flow from me. I didn't set none of it up," he added modestly, but with evident consciousness of having unearthed genius in himself and an elate foreknowledge of the treat in store for his companions. "I thought I'd ort to see how you liked it first." He offered the papers to Mr. Parker, but the foreman shook his head.

"You read it, Ross," I said. "I don't believe I feel hearty enough to-day. Read the items first—we can bear the waiting."

"What waiting?" inquired Mr. Schofield.

"For the poem," replied Parker, grimly.

With a vague but not fleeting smile, Ross settled the sheets in order, and exhibited tokens of that pleasant nevousness incident to appearing before a critical audience,

128

armed with literature whose merits should delight them out of the critical attitude. "I run across a great scheme down there," he volunteered amiably, by way of preface; "I described everything in full, in as many words as I could think up; it's mighty filling, and it'll please the public, too; it gives 'em a lot more information than they us'ally git. I reckon there's two sticks of jest them extry words alone."

"Go on," said the foreman, rather ominously.

Ross began to read, a matter necessitating a puckered brow and at times an amount of hesitancy and ruminating, as his results had already cooled a little, and he found his hand difficult to decipher. "Here's the first," he said:

"'The large and handsome, fawn-colored, two years and one-half year old Jersey of Frederick Bibshaw Jones, Esquire——'"

The foreman interrupted him: "Every reader of the 'Herald' will be glad to know that Jersey's age and color! But go on."

"'—Frederick Bibshaw Jones, Esquire,'" pursued his assistant, with some discomfiture, "'—Esquire, our popular and well-dressed fellow-citizen—— '"

"You're right; Bib Jones is a heavy swell," said Parker in a breaking voice.

"'—Citizen, can be daily seen wandering from the far end of his pasture-lot to the other far end of it.'"

"'His!'" exclaimed Parker. "'*His* pasture-lot?' The Jersey's?"

"No," returned the other, meekly, "Bib Jones's."

"Oh," said Parker. "Is that the end of that item? It is! You want to get out of Plattville, my friend; it's too small for you; you go to Rouen and you'll be city editor of the 'Journal' inside of a week. Let's have another."

Mr. Schofield looked up blankly; however, he felt that there was enough live, legitimate news in his other items to redeem the somewhat tame quality of the first, and so, after having crossed out several of the extra words which had met so poor a reception, he proceeded:

"'Whit Upton's pigs broke out last Wednesday and rooted up a fine patch of garden truck. Hard luck, Whit.'

"'Jerusalem Hawkins took a drive yesterday afternoon. He had the bay to his side-bar. Jee's buggy has been recently washed. Congratulations, Jee.'"

"There's thrilling information!" shouted the foreman. "That'll touch the gentle reader to the marrow. The boss had to use some pretty rotten copy himself, but he never got as low as that. But we'll use it; oh, we'll use it! If we don't get her out he'll have a set-back, but if they show her to him it'll kill him. If it doesn't, and he gets well, he'll kill us. But we'll use it, Ross. Don't read any more to us, though; I feel weaker than I did, and I wasn't strong before. Go down and set it all up."

Mr. Schofield rejoined with an injured air, and yet hopefully: "I'd like to see what you think of the poetry—it seemed all right to me, but I reckon you ain't ever the best judge of your own work. Shall I read it?" The foreman only glanced at him in silence, and the young man took this for assent. "I haven't made up any name for it yet."

"'O, the orphan boy stood on the hill,
The wind blew cold and very chill—'"

Glancing at his auditors, he was a trifle abashed to observe a glaze upon the eyes of Mr. Parker, while a purple tide rose above his neck-band and unnaturally distended his throat and temples. With a placative little laugh, Mr. Schofield remarked: "I git the swing to her all right, I reckon, but somehow it doesn't sound so kind of good as when I was writing it." There was no response, and he went on hurriedly:

"'But there he saw the little rill—'"

The poet paused to say, with another amiable laugh: "It's sort of hard to git out of them ill, hill, chill rhymes once you strike 'em. It runs on like this:

"'—Little rill
That curved and spattered around the hill.'

"I guess that's all right, to use 'hill' twice; don't you reckon so?

"'And the orphan he stood there until
The wind and all gave him a chill;
And he sickened—'"

That day Ross read no more, for the tall printer, seemingly incapable of coherent speech, kicked the desk impotently, threw his arms above his head, and, his companions confidently looking to see him foam at the mouth, lost his balance and toppled over backward, his extensive legs waving wildly in the air as he struck the floor. Mr. Schofield fled.

Parker made no effort to rise, but lay glaring at the ceiling, breathing hard. He remained in that position for a long time, until finally the glaze wore away from his eyes and a more rational expression settled over his features. Mr. Fisbee addressed him timidly: "You don't think we could reduce the size of the sheet?"

130

"It would kill him," answered his prostrate companion. "We've got to fill her solid some way, though I give up; I don't know how. How that man has worked! It was genius. He just floated around the county and soaked in items, and he wrote editorials that people read. One thing's certain: we can't do it. We're ruining his paper for him, and when he gets able to read, it'll hurt him bad. Mighty few knew how much pride he had in it. Has it struck you that now would be a precious good time for it to occur to Rod McCune to come out of his hole? Suppose we go by the board, what's to stop him? What's to stop him, anyway? Who knows where the boss put those copies and affidavits, and if we did know, would we know the best way to use 'em? If we did, what's to keep the 'Herald' alive until McCune lifts his head? And if we don't stop him, the 'Carlow County Herald' is finished. Something's got to be done!'"

No one realized this more poignantly than Mr. Fisbee, but no one was less capable of doing something of his own initiation. And although the Tuesday issue was forthcoming, embarrassingly pale in spots—most spots—Mr. Martin remarked rather publicly that the items were not what you might call stirring, and that the unpatented pages put him in mind of Jones's field in winter with a dozen chunks of coal dropped in the snow. And his observations on the later issues of the week (issues which were put forth with a suggestion of spasm, and possibly to the permanent injury of Mr. Parker's health, he looked so thin) were too cruelly unkind to be repeated here. Indeed, Mr. Fisbee, Parker, the luckless Mr. Schofield, and the young Tipworthy may be not untruthfully likened to a band of devoted mariners lost in the cold and glaring regions of a journalistic Greenland: limitless plains of empty white paper extending about them as far as the eye could reach, while life depended upon their making these terrible voids productive; and they shrank appalled from the task, knowing no means to fertilize the barrens; having no talent to bring the still snows into harvests, and already feeling-in the chill of Mr. Martin's remarks—a touch of the frost that might wither them.

It was Fisbee who caught the first glimpse of a relief expedition clipping the rough seas on its lively way to rescue them, and, although his first glimpse of the jaunty pennant of the relieving vessels was over the shoulder of an iceberg, nothing was surer than that the craft was flying to them with all good and joyous speed. The iceberg just mentioned assumed—by no melting process, one may be sure—the form of a long letter, first postmarked at Rouen, and its latter substance was as follows:

"Henry and I have always believed you as selfish, James Fisbee, as you are self-ingrossed and incapable. She has told us of your 'renunciation'; of your 'forbidding' her to remain with you; how you 'commanded,' after you had 'begged' her, to return to us, and how her conscience told her she should stay and share your life in spite of our long care of her, but that she yielded to your 'wishes' and our entreaty. What have you ever done for her and what have you to offer her? She is our daughter, and needless to say we shall still take care of her, for no one believes you capable of it, even in that miserable place, and, of course, in time she will return to her better wisdom, her home, and her duty. I need scarcely say we have given up the happy months we had planned to spend in Dresden. Henry and I can only stay at home to pray that her preposterous mania will wear itself out in short order, as she will find herself unfitted for the ridiculous task which she insists upon attempting against the earnest wishes of us who have been more than father and mother to her. Of course, she has talked volumes of her affection for us, and of her gratitude, which we do not want—we only want her to stay with us. Please, please try to make her come back to us—we cannot bear it long. If you are a man you will send her to us soon. Her excuse for not returning on the day we wired our intention to go abroad at once (and I may as well tell you now that our intention to go was formed in order to bring affairs to a crisis and to draw her away from your influence—we always dreaded her visit to you and held it off for years)—her excuse was that your best friend, and, as I understand it, your patron, had been injured in some brawl in that Christian country of yours—a charming place to take a girl like her—and she would not leave you in your 'distress' until more was known of the man's injuries. And now she insists—and you will know it from her by the next mail—on returning to Plattville, forsooth, because she has been reading your newspaper, and she says she knows you are in difficulties over it, and it is her moral obligation—as by some wild reasoning of her own she considers herself responsible for your ruffling patron's having been alone when he was shot—to go down and help. I suppose he made love to her, as all the young men she meets always do, sooner or later, but I have no fear of any rustic entanglements tor her; she has never been really interested, save in one affair. We are quite powerless—we have done everything; but we cannot alter her determination to edit your paper for you. Naturally, she knows nothing whatever about such work, but she says, with the air of triumphantly quelching all such argument, that she has talked a great deal to Mr. Macauley of the 'Journal.' Mr. Macauley is the affair I have alluded to; he is what she has meant when she has said, at different times, that she was interested in journalism. But she is very business-like now. She has bought a typewriter and purchased a great number of soft pencils and erasers at an art shop; I am only surprised that she does not intend to edit your miserable paper in water-colors. She is coming at once. For mercy's sake don't telegraph her not to; your forbiddings work the wrong way. Our only hope is that she will find the conditions so utterly discouraging at the very start that she will give it up and come home. If you are a man you will help to make them so. She has promised to stay with that country girl with whom she contracted such an incomprehensible friendship at Miss Jennings's.

"Oh, James, pray for grace to be a man once in your life and send her back to us! Be a man—try to be a man! Remember the angel you killed! Remember all we have done for you and what a return you have made, and be a man for the first time. Try and be a man!

"Your unhappy sister-in-law,

"MARTHA SHERWOOD."

Mr. Fisbee read the letter with a great, rising delight which no sense of duty could down; indeed, he perceived that his sense of duty had ceased to conflict with the one strong hope of his life, just as he perceived that to be a man, according to Martha

Sherwood, was, in part, to assist Martha Sherwood to have her way in things; and, for the rest, to be the sort of man she persuaded herself she would be were she not a woman. This he had never been able to be.

By some whimsy of fate, or by a failure of Karma (or, perhaps, by some triumph of Kismetic retribution), James Fisbee was born in one of the most business-like and artless cities of a practical and modern country, of money-getting, money-saving parents, and he was born a dreamer of the past. He grew up a student of basilican lore, of choir-screens, of Persian frescoes, and an ardent lounger in the somewhat musty precincts of Chaldea and Byzantium and Babylon. Early Christian Symbolism, a dispute over the site of a Greek temple, the derivation of the lotus column, the restoration of a Gothic buttress—these were the absorbing questions of his youth, with now and then a lighter moment spent in analytical consideration of the extra-mural decorations of St. Mark's. The world buzzed along after its own fashion, not disturbing him, and his absorptions permitted only a faint consciousness of the despair of his relatives regarding his mind. Arrived at middle-age, and a little more, he found himself alone in the world (though, for that matter, he had always been alone and never of the world), and there was plenty of money for him with various bankers who appeared to know about looking after it. Returning to the town of his nativity after sundry expeditions in Syria— upon which he had been accompanied by dusky gentlemen with pickaxes and curly, long-barrelled muskets— he met, and was married by, a lady who was ambitious, and who saw in him (probably as a fulfilment of another Kismetic punishment) a power of learning and a destined success. Not long after the birth of their only child, a daughter, he was "called to fill the chair" of archaeology in a newly founded university; one of the kind which a State and a millionaire combine to purchase ready-made. This one was handed down off the shelf in a more or less chaotic condition, and for a period of years betrayed considerable doubt as to its own intentions, undecided whether they were classical or technical; and in the settlement of that doubt lay the secret of the past of the one man in Plattville so unhappy as to possess a past. From that settlement and his own preceding action resulted his downfall, his disgrace with his wife's relatives, the loss of his wife, the rage, surprise, and anguish of her sister, Martha, and Martha's husband, Henry Sherwood, and the separation from his little daughter, which was by far to him the hardest to bear. For Fisbee, in his own way, and without consulting anybody—it never occurred to him, and he was supposed often to forget that he had a wife and child—had informally turned over to the university all the money which the banks had kindly taken care of, and had given it to equip an expedition which never expedited. A new president of the institution was installed; he talked to the trustees; they met, and elected to become modern and practical and technical; they abolished the course in fine arts, which abolished Fisbee's connection with them, and they then employed his money to erect a building for the mechanical engineering department. Fisbee was left with nothing. His wife and her kinsfolk exhibited no brilliancy in holding a totally irresponsible man down to responsibilities, and they made a tragedy of a not surprising fiasco. Mrs. Fisbee had lived in her ambitions, and she died of heartbreak over the discovery of what manner of man she had married. But, before she died, she wisely provided for her daughter.

Fisbee told Parker the story after his own queer fashion.

"You see, Mr. Parker," he said, as they sat together in the dust and litter of the "Herald" office, on Sunday afternoon, "you see, I admit that my sister-in-law has always withheld her approbation from me, and possibly her disapproval is well founded—I shall say probably. My wife had also a considerable sum, and this she turned over to me at the time of our marriage, though I had no wish regarding it one way or the other. When I gave my money to the university with which I had the honor to be connected, I added to it the fund I had received from her, as I was the recipient of a comfortable salary as a lecturer in the institution and had no fear of not living well, and I was greatly interested in providing that the expedition should be perfectly equipped. Expeditions of the magnitude of that which I had planned are expensive, I should, perhaps, inform you, and this one was to carry on investigations regarding several important points, very elaborately; and I am still convinced it would have settled conclusively many vital questions concerning the derivation of the Babylonian column, as: whether the lotus column may be without prejudice said to—but at the present moment I will not enter into that. I fear I had no great experience in money matters, for the transaction had been almost entirely verbal, and there was nothing to bind the trustees to carry out my plans for the expedition. They were very sympathetic, but what could they do? they begged leave to inquire. Such an institution cannot give back money once donated, and it was clearly out of character for a school of technology and engineering to send savants to investigate the lotus column."

"I see," Mr. Parker observed, genially. He listened with the most ingratiating attention, knowing that he had a rich sensation to set before Plattville as a dish before a king, for Fisbee's was no confidential communication. The old man might have told a part of his history long ago, but it had never occurred to him to talk about his affairs—things had a habit of not occurring to Fisbee—and the efforts of the gossips to draw him out always passed over his serene and absent head.

"It was a blow to my wife," the old man continued, sadly, "and I cannot deny that her reproaches were as vehement as her disappointment was sincere." He hurried over this portion of his narrative with a vaguely troubled look, but the intelligent Parker read poor Mrs. Fisbee's state of mind between the sentences. "She never seemed to regard me in the same light again," the archaeologist went on. "She did not conceal from me that she was surprised and that she could not look upon me as a practical man; indeed, I may say, she appeared to regard me with marked antipathy. She sent for her sister, and begged her to take our daughter and keep her from me, as she did not consider me practical enough-I will substitute for her more embittered expressions—to provide for a child and instruct it in the world's ways. My sister-in-law, who was childless, consented to adopt the little one, on the conditions that I renounced all claim, and that the child legally assumed her name and should be in all respects as her own daughter, and that I consented to see her but once a year, in Rouen, at my brother-in-law's home.

134

"I should have refused, but I—my wife—that is—she was—very pressing— in her last hours, and they all seemed to feel that I ought to make amends—all except the little girl herself, I should say, for she possessed, even as an infant, an exceptional affection for her father. I had nothing; my salary was gone, and I was discomfited by the combined actions of the trustees and my relatives, so—I—I gave her up to them, and my wife passed away in a more cheerful frame of mind, I think. That is about all. One of the instructors obtained the position here for me, which I—I finally— lost, and I went to See the little girl every New Year's day. This year she declared her intention of visiting *me*, but she was persuaded by friends who were conversant with the circumstances to stay with them, where I could be with her almost as much as at my apartment at Mr. Tibbs's. She had long since declared her intention of some day returning to live with me, and when she came she was strenuous in insisting that the day had come." The old man's voice broke suddenly as he observed: "She has—a very—beautiful—character, Mr. Parker."

The foreman nodded with warm confirmation. "I believe you, sir. Yes, sir; I saw her, and I guess she looks it. You take that kind of a lady usually, and catch her in a crowd like the one show-day, and she can't help doing the Grand Duchess, giving the tenants a treat—but not her; she didn't seem to *separate* herself from 'em, some way."

"She is a fine lady," said the other simply. "I did not accept her renunciation, though I acknowledge I forbade it with a very poignant envy. I could not be the cause of her giving up for my sake her state of ease and luxury—for my relatives are more than well-to-do, and they made it plain she must choose between them and me, with the design, I think, of making it more difficult to choose me. And, also, it seemed to me, as it did to her, that she owed them nearly everything, but she declared I had lived alone so long that she owed me everything, also. She is a— beautiful—character, Mr. Parker."

"Well," said Parker, after a pause, "the town will be upside down over this; and folks will be mighty glad to have it explained about your being out there so much, and at the deepo, and all this and that. Everybody in the place has been wondering what in—that is—" he finished in some confusion—"that is—what I started to say was that it won't be so bad as it might be, having a lady in the office here. I don't cuss to speak of, and Ross can lay off on his till the boss comes back. Besides, it's our only chance. If she can't make the 'Herald' hum, we go to the wall."

The old man did not seem to hear him. "I forbade the renunciation she wished to make for my sake," he said, gently, "but I accept it now for the sake of our stricken friend—for Mr. Harkless."

"And for the Carlow 'Herald,'" completed the foreman.

The morning following that upon which this conversation took place, the two gentlemen stood together on the station platform, awaiting the arrival of the express from Rouen. It was a wet gray day; the wide country lay dripping under formless wraps of thin mist, and a warm, drizzling rain blackened the weather-beaten shingles of the station; made clear-reflecting puddles of the unevenly worn planks of the platform, and dampened the packing-cases that never went anywhere too thoroughly for occupation by the station-lounger, and ran in a little crystal stream off Fisbee's brown cotton umbrella and down Mr. Parker's back. The 'bus driver, Mr. Bennett, the proprietor of two attendant "cut-unders," and three or four other worthies whom business, or the lack of it, called to that locality, availed themselves of the shelter of the waiting-room, but the gentlemen of the "Herald" were too agitated to be confined, save by the limits of the horizon. They had reached the station half an hour before train time, and consumed the interval in pacing the platform under the cotton umbrella, addressing each other only in monosyllables. Those in the waiting-room gossiped eagerly, and for the thousandth time, about the late events, and the tremendous news concerning Fisbee. Judd Bennett looked out through the rainy doorway at the latter with reverence and a fine pride of townsmanship, declaring it to be his belief that Fisbee and Parker were waiting for her at the present moment. It was a lady, and a bird of a lady, too, else why should Cale Parker be wearing a coat, and be otherwise dooded and fixed up beyond any wedding? Judd and his friends were somewhat excited over Parker.

Fisbee was clad in his best shabby black, which lent an air of state to the occasion, but Mr. Parker—Caleb Parker, whose heart, during his five years of residence in Plattville, had been steel-proof against all the feminine blandishments of the town, whose long, lank face had shown beneath as long, and lanker, locks of proverbially uncombed hair, he who had for weeks conspicuously affected a single, string-patched suspender, who never, even upon the Sabbath day, wore a collar or blacked his shoes— what aesthetic leaven had entered his soul that he donned not a coat alone but also a waistcoat with checks?—and, more than *that*, a gleaming celluloid collar?—and, more than that, a brilliant blue tie? What had this iron youth to do with a rising excitement at train time and brilliant blue ties?

Also, it might have been inquired if this parade of fashion had no connection with the simultaneous action of Mr. Ross Schofield; for Ross was at this hour engaged in decorating the battered chairs in the "Herald" editorial room with blue satin ribbon, the purchase of which at the Dry Goods Emporium had been directed by a sudden inspiration of his superior of the composing force. It was Ross's intention to garnish each chair with an elaborately tied bow, but, as he was no sailor and understood only the intricacies of a hard-knot, he confined himself to that species of ornamentation, leaving, however, very long ends of ribbon hanging down after the manner of the pendants of rosettes.

It scarcely needs the statement that his labors were in honor of the new editor-in-chief of the Carlow "Herald." The advent and the purposes of this personage were, as yet, known certainly to only those of the "Herald" and to the Briscoes. It had been arranged, however, that Minnie and her father were not to come to the station, for the journalistic crisis was immoderately pressing; the "Herald" was to appear on the morrow, and the new editor wished to plunge directly, and without the briefest distraction, into the paper's difficulties, now accumulated into a veritable sea of

136

troubles. The editor was to be delivered to the Briscoes at eventide and returned by them again at dewy morn; and this was to be the daily programme. It had been further—and most earnestly—stipulated that when the wounded proprietor of the ailing journal should be informed of the addition to his forces, he was not to know, or to have the slenderest hint of, the sex or identity of the person in charge during his absence. It was inevitable that Plattville (already gaping to the uttermost) would buzz voluminously over it before night, but Judge Briscoe volunteered to prevent the buzz from reaching Rouen. He undertook to interview whatever citizens should visit Harkless, or write to him—when his illness permitted visits and letters—and forewarn them of the incumbent's desires. To-day, the judge stayed at home with his daughter, who trilled about the house for happiness, and, in their place, the "Herald" deputation of two had repaired to the station to act as a reception committee.

Far away the whistle of the express was heard, muffled to sweetness in the damp, and the drivers, whip in hand, came out upon the platform, and the loafers issued, also, to stand under the eaves and lean their backs against the drier boards, preparing to eye the travellers with languid raillery.

Mr. Parker, very nervous himself, felt the old man's elbow trembling against his own as the great engine, reeking in the mist, and sending great clouds of white vapor up to the sky, rushed by them, and came to a standstill beyond the platform.

Fisbee and the foreman made haste to the nearest vestibule, and were gazing blankly at its barred approaches when they heard a tremulous laugh behind them and an exclamation.

"Upstairs and downstairs and in my lady's chamber! Just behind you, dear."

Turning quickly, Parker beheld a blushing and smiling little vision, a vision with light-brown hair, a vision enveloped in a light-brown rain-cloak and with brown gloves, from which the handles of a big brown travelling bag were let fall, as the vision disappeared under the cotton umbrella, while the smitten Judd Bennett reeled gasping against the station.

"Dearest," the girl cried to the old man, "you were looking for me between the devil and deep sea—the parlor-car and the smoker. I've given up cigars, and I've begun to study economy, so I didn't come on either."

There was but this one passenger for Plattville; two enormous trunks thundered out of the baggage car onto the truck, and it was the work of no more than a minute for Judd to hale them to the top of the omnibus (he well wished to wear them next his heart, but their dimensions forbade the thought), and immediately he cracked his whip and drove off furiously through the mud to deposit his freight at the Briscoes'. Parker, Mr. Fisbee, and the new editor-in-chief set forth, directly after, in one of the waiting cut-unders, the foreman in front with the driver, and holding the big brown bag on his knees in much the same manner he would have held an alien, yet respected, infant.

CHAPTER XIV

A RESCUE

The drizzle and mist blew in under the top of the cut-under as they drove rapidly into town, and bright little drops sparkled on the fair hair above the new editor's forehead and on the long lashes above the new editor's cheeks.

She shook these transient gems off lightly, as she paused in the doorway of the office at the top of the rickety stairway. Mr. Schofield had just added the last touch to his decorations and managed to slide into his coat as the party came up the stairs, and now, perspiring, proud, embarrassed, he assumed an attitude at once deprecatory of his endeavors and pointedly expectant of commendation for the results. (He was a modest youth and a conscious; after his first sight of her, as she stood in the doorway, it was several days before he could lift his distressed eyes under her glance, or, indeed, dare to avail himself of more than a hasty and fluttering stare at her when her back was turned.) As she entered the room, he sidled along the wall and laughed sheepishly at nothing.

Every chair in the room was ornamented with one of his blue rosettes, tied carefully (and firmly) to the middle slat of each chair-back. There had been several yards of ribbon left over, and there was a hard knot of glossy satin on each of the ink-stands and on the door-knobs; a blue band, passing around the stovepipe, imparted an antique rakishness suggestive of the charioteer; and a number of streamers, suspended from a hook in the ceiling, encouraged a supposition that the employees of the "Herald" contemplated the intricate festivities of May Day. It needed no genius to infer that these garnitures had not embellished the editorial chamber during Mr. Harkless's activity, but, on the contrary, had been put in place that very morning. Mr. Fisbee had not known of the decorations, and, as his glance fell upon them, a faint look of pain passed over his brow; but the girl examined the room with a dancing eye, and there were both tears and laughter in her heart.

"How beautiful!" she cried. "How beautiful!" She crossed the room and gave her hand to Ross. "It is Mr. Schofield, isn't it? The ribbons are delightful. I didn't know Mr. Harkless's room was so pretty."

Ross looked out of the window and laughed as he took her hand (which he shook with a long up and down motion), but he was set at better ease by her apparent unrecognition of the fact that the decorations were for her. "Oh, it ain't much, I reckon," he replied, and continued to look out of the window and laugh.

She went to the desk and removed her gloves and laid her rain-coat over a chair near by. "Is this Mr. Harkless's chair?" she asked, and, Fisbee answering that it was, she looked gravely at it for a moment, passed her hand gently over the back of it, and then, throwing the rain-cloak over another chair, said cheerily:

138

"Do you know, I think the first thing for us to do will be to dust everything very carefully."

"You remember I was confident she would know precisely where to begin?" was Fisbee's earnest whisper in the willing ear of the long foreman. "Not an instant's indecision, was there?"

"No, siree!" replied the other; and, as he went down to the press-room to hunt for a feather-duster which he thought might be found there, he collared Bud Tipworthy, who, not admitted to the conclave of his superiors, was whistling on the rainy stairway. "You hustle and find that dust brush we used to have, Bud," said Parker. And presently, as they rummaged in the nooks and crannies about the machinery, he melted to his small assistant. "The paper is saved, Buddie—saved by an angel in light brown. You can tell it by the look of her."

"Gee!" said Bud.

Mr. Schofield had come, blushing, to join them. "Say, Cale, did you notice the color of her eyes?"

"Yes; they're gray."

"I thought so, too, show day, and at Kedge Halloway's lecture; but, say, Cale, they're kind of changeable. When she come in upstairs with you and Fisbee, they were jest as blue!—near matched the color of our ribbons."

"Gee!" repeated Mr. Tipworthy.

When the editorial chamber had been made so Beat that it almost glowed— though it could never be expected to shine as did Fisbee and Caleb Parker and Ross Schofield that morning—the editor took her seat at the desk and looked over the few items the gentlemen had already compiled for her perusal. Mr. Parker explained many technicalities peculiar to the Carlow "Herald," translated some phrases of the printing-room, and enabled her to grasp the amount of matter needed to fill the morrow's issue.

When Parker finished, the three incompetents sat watching the little figure with the expression of hopeful and trusting terriers. She knit her brow for a second—but she did not betray an instant's indecision.

"I think we should have regular market reports," she announced, thoughtfully. "I am sure Mr. Harkless would approve. Don't you think he would?" She turned to Parker.

"Market reports!" Mr. Fisbee exclaimed. "I should never have thought of market reports, nor, do I imagine, would either of my—my associates. A woman to conceive the idea of market reports!"

The editor blushed. "Why, who would, dear, if not a woman, or a speculator, and I'm not a speculator; and neither are you, and that's the reason you didn't think of them. So, Mr. Parker, as there is so much pressure, and if you don't mind continuing to act as reporter as well as compositor until after to-morrow, and if it isn't too wet— you must take an umbrella—would it be too much bother if you went around to all the shops—*stores*, I mean—to all the grocers', and the butchers', and that leather place we passed, the tannery?—and if there's one of those places where they bring cows, would it be too much to ask you to stop there?—and at the flour-mill, if it isn't too far?—and at the dry-goods store? And you must take a blank-book and sharpened pencil, And will you price everything, please, and jot down how much things are?"

Orders received, the impetuous Parker was departing on the instant, when she stopped him with a little cry: "But you haven't any umbrella!" And she forced her own, a slender wand, upon him; it bore a cunningly wrought handle and its fabric was of glistening silk. The foreman, unable to decline it, thanked her awkwardly, and, as she turned to speak to Fisbee, bolted out of the door and ran down the steps without unfolding the umbrella; and as he made for Mr. Martin's emporium, he buttoned it securely under his long "Prince Albert," determined that not a drop of water should touch and ruin so delicate a thing. Thus he carried it, triumphantly dry, through the course of his reportings of that day.

When he had gone the editor laid her hand on Fisbee's arm. "Dear," she said, "do you think you would take cold if you went over to the hotel and made a note of all the arrivals for the last week—and the departures, too? I noticed that Mr. Harkless always filled two or three—sticks, isn't it?—with them and things about them, and somehow it 'read' very nicely. You must ask the landlord all about them; and, if there aren't any, we can take up the same amount of space lamenting the dull times, just as he used to. You see I've read the 'Herald' faithfully; isn't it a good thing I always subscribed for it?" She patted Fisbee's cheek, and laughed gaily into his mild, vague old eyes.

"It won't be this scramble to 'fill up' much longer. I have plans, gentlemen," she cried, "and before long we will print news. And we must buy 'plate matter' instead of 'patent insides'; and I had a talk with the Associated Press people in Rouen—but that's for afterwhile. And I went to the hospital this morning before I left. They wouldn't let me see him again, but they told me all about him, and he's better; and I got Tom to go to the jail—he was so mystified, he doesn't know what I wanted it for —and he saw some of those beasts, and I can do a column of description besides an editorial about them, and I will be fierce enough to suit Carlow, you may believe that. And I've been talking to Senator Burns—that is, listening to Senator Burns, which is much stupider—and I think I can do an article on national politics. I'm not very well up on local issues yet, but I—" She broke off suddenly. "There! I think we can get out to-morrow's number without any trouble. By the time you get back from the hotel, father, I'll have half my stuff written—'written up,' I mean. Take your big umbrella and go, dear, and please ask at the express office if my typewriter has come."

She laughed again with sheer delight, like a child, and ran to the corner and got the cotton umbrella and placed it in the old man's hand. As he reached the door, she called after him: "Wait!" and went to him and knelt before him, and, with the humblest, proudest grace in the world, turned up his trousers to keep them from the mud. Ross Schofield had never considered Mr. Fisbee a particularly sacred sort of person, but he did from that moment. The old man made some timid protest, at his daughter's action, But she answered; "The great ladies used to buckle the Chevalier Bayard's spurs for him, and you're a great deal nicer than the Chev—— *You haven't any rubbers*! I don't believe *any* of you have any rubbers!" And not until both Fisbee and Mr. Schofield had promised to purchase overshoes at once, and in the meantime not to step in any puddles, would she let her father depart upon his errand. He crossed the Square with the strangest, jauntiest step ever seen in Plattville. Solomon Tibbs had a warm argument with Miss Selina as to his identity. Miss Selina maintaining that the figure under the big umbrella—only the legs and coat-tails were visible to them—was that of a stranger, probably an Englishman.

In the "Herald" office the editor turned, smiling, to the paper's remaining vassal. "Mr. Schofield, I heard some talk in Rouen of an oil company that had been formed to prospect for kerosene in Carlow County. Do you know anything about it?"

Ross, surfeited with honor, terror, and possessed by a sweet distress at finding himself tete-a-tete with the lady, looked at the wall and replied:

"Oh, it's that Eph Watts's foolishness."

"Do you know if they have begun to dig for it yet?"

"Ma'am?" said Ross.

"Have they begun the diggings yet?"

"No, ma'am; I think not. They've got a contrapshun fixed up about three mile south. I don't reckon they've begun yet, hardly; they're gittin' the machinery in place. I heard Eph say they'd begin to bore—*dig*, I mean, ma'am, I meant to say dig——" He stopped, utterly confused and unhappy; and she understood his manly purpose, and knew him for a gentleman whom she liked.

"You mustn't be too much surprised," she said; "but in spite of my ignorance about such things, I mean to devote a good deal of space to the oil company; it may come to be of great importance to Carlow. We won't go into it in to-morrow's paper, beyond an item or so; but do you think you could possibly find Mr. Watts and ask him for some information as to their progress, and if it would be too much trouble for him to call here some time to-morrow afternoon, or the day after? I want him to give me an interview if he will. Tell him, please, he will very greatly oblige us."

"Oh, he'll come all right," answered her companion, quickly. "I'll take Tibbs's buggy and go down there right off. Eph won't lose no time gittin' *here*!" And with this encouraging assurance he was flying forth, when he, like the others, was detained by her solicitous care. She was a born mother. He protested that in the buggy he would be perfectly sheltered; besides, there wasn't another umbrella about the place; he *liked* to get wet, anyway; had always loved rain. The end of it was that he went away in a sort of tremor, wearing her rain-cloak over his shoulders, which garment, as it covered its owner completely when she wore it, hung almost to his knees. He darted around a corner; and there, breathing deeply, tenderly removed it; then, borrowing paper and cord at a neighboring store, wrapped it neatly, and stole back to the printing-office on the ground floor of the "Herald" building, and left the package in charge of Bud Tipworthy, mysteriously charging him to care for it as for his own life, and not to open it, but if the lady so much as set one foot out of doors before his return, to hand it to her with the message: "He borrowed another off J. Hankins."

Left alone, the lady went to the desk and stood for a time looking gravely at Harkless's chair. She touched it gently, as she had touched it once before that morning, and then she spoke to it as if he were sitting there, and as she would not have spoken, had he been sitting there.

"You didn't want gratitude, did you?" she whispered, with sad lips.

Soon she smiled at the blue ribbons, patted the chair gaily on the back, and, seizing upon pencil and pad, dashed into her work with rare energy. She bent low over the desk, her pencil moving rapidly, and, except for a momentary interruption from Mr. Tipworthy, she seemed not to pause for breath; certainly her pencil did not. She had covered many sheets when her father returned; and, as he came in softly, not to disturb her, she was so deeply engrossed she did not hear him; nor did she look up when Parker entered, but pursued the formulation of her fast-flying ideas with the same single purpose and abandon; so the two men sat and waited while their chieftainess wrote absorbedly. At last she glanced up and made a little startled exclamation at seeing them there, and then gave them cheery greeting. Each placed several scribbled sheets before her, and she, having first assured herself that Fisbee had bought his overshoes, and having expressed a fear that Mr. Parker had found her umbrella too small, as he looked damp (and indeed he *was* damp), cried praises on their notes and offered the reporters great applause.

"It is all so splendid!" she cried. "How could you do it so quickly? And in the rain, too! This is exactly what we need. I've done most of the things I mentioned, I think, and made a draught of some plans for hereafter. And about that man's coming out for Congress, I must tell you it is my greatest hope that he will. We can let it go until he does, and then——But doesn't it seem to you that it would be a good notion for the 'Herald' to have a woman's page—'For Feminine Readers,' or, 'Of Interest to Women'—once a week?"

142

"A woman's page!" exclaimed Fisbee. "I could never have thought of that, could you, Mr. Parker?"

"And now," she continued, "I think that when I've gone over what I've written and beat it into better shape I shall be ready for something to eat. Isn't it almost time for luncheon?"

This simple, and surely natural, inquiry had a singular, devastating effect upon her hearers. They looked upon each other with fallen jaws and complete stupefaction. The old man began to grow pale, and Parker glared about him with a wild eye. Fortunately, the editor was too busy at her work to notice their agitation; she applied herself to making alterations here and there, sometimes frowningly crossing out whole lines and even paragraphs, sometimes smiling and beaming at the writing; and, as she bent earnestly over the paper, against the darkness of the rainy day, the glamour about her fair hair was like a light in the room. To the minds of her two companions, this lustre was a gentle but unbearable accusation; and each dreaded the moment when her Work should be finished, with a great dread. There was a small "store-room" adjoining the office, and presently Mr. Parker, sweating at the brow, walked in there. The old man gave him a look of despairing reproach, but in a moment the foreman's voice was heard: "Oh, Mr. Fisbee, can you step here a second?"

"Yes, indeed!" was Fisbee's reply; and he fled guiltily into the "store-room," and Parker closed the door. They stood knee-deep in the clutter and lumber, facing each other abjectly.

"Well, we're both done, anyway, Mr. Fisbee," remarked the foreman.

"Indubitably, Mr. Parker," the old man answered; "it is too true."

"Never to think a blame thing about dinner for her!" Parker continued, remorsefully. "And her a lady that can turn off copy like a rotary snowplough in a Dakota blizzard! Did you see the sheets she's piled up on that desk?"

"There is no cafe—nothing—in Plattville, that could prepare food worthy of her," groaned Fisbee. "Nothing!"

"And we never thought of it. Never made a single arrangement. Never struck us she didn't live on keeping us dry and being good, I guess."

"How can I go there and tell her that?"

"Lord!"

"She cannot go to the hotel——"

"Well, I guess not! It ain't fit for her. Lum's table is hard enough on a strong man. Landis doesn't know a good cake from a Fiji missionary pudding. I don't expect pie is much her style, and, besides, the Palace Hotel pies—well!—the boss was a mighty uncomplaining man, but I used to notice his articles on field drainage got kind of sour and low-spirited when they'd been having more than the regular allowance of pie for dinner. She can't go there anyway; it's no use; it's after two o'clock, and the dining-room shuts off at one. I wonder what kind of cake she likes best."

"I don't know," said the perplexed Fisbee. "If we ask her—"

"If we could sort of get it out of her diplomatically, we could telegraph to Rouen for a good one."

"Ha!" said the other, brightening up. "You try it, Mr. Parker. I fear I have not much skill in diplomacy, but if you——"

The compositor's mouth drooped at the corners, and he interrupted gloomily: "But it wouldn't get here till to-morrow."

"True; it would not."

They fell into a despondent reverie, with their chins in their bosoms. There came a cheerful voice from the next room, but to them it brought no cheer; in their ears it sounded weak from the need of food and faint with piteous reproach.

"Father, aren't you coming to have luncheon with me?"

"Mr. Parker, what are we to do?" whispered the old man, hoarsely.

"Is it too far to take her to Briscoes'?"

"In the rain?"

"Take her with you to Tibbs's."

"Their noon meal is long since over; and their larder is not—is not— extensive."

"Father!" called the girl. She was stirring; they could hear her moving about the room.

"You've got to go in and tell her," said the foreman, desperately, and together they stumbled into the room. A small table at one end of it was laid with a snowy cloth and there was a fragrance of tea, and, amidst various dainties, one caught a glimpse of cold chicken and lettuce leaves. Fisbee stopped, dumfounded, but the foreman, after stammeringly declining an invitation to partake, alleging that his own meal

144

awaited, sped down to the printing-room, and seized upon Bud Tipworthy with a heavy hand.

"Where did all that come from, up there?"

"Leave go me! *What* 'all that'?"

"All that tea and chicken and salad and wafers—all kinds of things; sardines, for all I know!"

"They come in Briscoes' buckboard while you was gone. Briscoes sent 'em in a basket; I took 'em up and she set the basket under the table. You'd seen it if you'd 'a' looked. *Quit* that!" And it was unjust to cuff the perfectly innocent and mystified Bud, and worse not to tell him what the punishment was for.

Before the day was over, system had been introduced, and the "Herald" was running on it: and all that warm, rainy afternoon, the editor and Fisbee worked in the editorial rooms, Parker and Bud and Mr. Schofield (after his return with the items and a courteous message from Ephraim Watts) bent over the forms downstairs, and Uncle Xenophon was cleaning the store-room and scrubbing the floor.

An extraordinary number of errands took the various members of the printing force up to see the editor-in-chief, literally to see the editor-in-chief; it was hard to believe that the presence had not flown—hard to keep believing, without the repeated testimony of sight, that the dingy room upstairs was actually the setting for their jewel; and a jewel they swore she was. The printers came down chuckling and gurgling after each interview; it was partly the thought that she belonged to the "Herald," *their* paper. Once Ross, as he cut down one of the temporarily distended advertisements, looked up and caught the foreman giggling to himself.

"What in the name of common-sense you laughin' at, Cale?" he asked.

"What are *you* laughing at?" rejoined the other.

"I dunno!"

The day wore on, wet and dreary outside, but all within the "Herald's" bosom was snug and busy and murmurous with the healthy thrum of life and prosperity renewed. Toward six o'clock, system accomplished, the new guiding-spirit was deliberating on a policy as Harkless would conceive a policy, were he there, when Minnie Briscoe ran joyously up the stairs, plunged into the room, waterproofed and radiant, and caught her friend in her eager arms, and put an end to policy for that day.

But policy and labor did not end at twilight every day; there were evenings, as in the time of Harkless, when lamps shone from the upper windows of the "Herald" building. For the little editor worked hard, and sometimes she worked late; she always worked early. She made some mistakes at first, and one or two blunders which she took more seriously than any one else did. But she found a remedy for all such results of her inexperience, and she developed experience. She set at her task with the energy of her youthfulness and no limit to her ambition, and she felt that Harkless had prepared the way for a wide expansion of the paper's interests; wider than he knew. She had a belief that there were possibilities for a country newspaper, and she brought a fresh point of view to operate in a situation where Harkless had fallen, perhaps, too much in the rut; and she watched every chance with a keen eye and looked ahead of her with clear foresight. What she waited and yearned for and dreaded, was the time when a copy of the new "Herald" should be placed in the trembling hands of the man who lay in the Rouen hospital. Then, she felt, if he, unaware of her identity, should place everything in her hands unreservedly, that would be a tribute to her work—and how hard she would labor to deserve it! After a time, she began to realize that, as his representative and the editor of the "Herald," she had become a factor in district politics. It took her breath—but with a gasp of delight, for there was something she wanted to do.

Above all, she brought a light heart to her work. One evening in the latter part of that first week of the new regime, Parker perceived Bud Tipworthy standing in the doorway of the printing-room, beckoning him silently to come without.

"What's the matter, Buddie?"

"Listen. She's singin' over her work."

Parker stepped outside. On the pavement, people had stopped to listen; they stood in the shadow, looking up with parted lips at the open, lighted Windows, whence came a clear, soft, reaching voice, lifted in song; now it swelled louder, unconsciously; now its volume was more slender and it melted liquidly into the night; again, it trembled and rose and dwelt in the ear, strong and pure; and, hearing it, you sighed with unknown longings. It was the "Angels' Serenade."

Bud Tipworthy's sister, Cynthia, was with him, and Parker saw that she turned from the window and that she was crying, quietly; she put her hand on the boy's shoulder and patted it with a forlorn gesture which, to the foreman's eye, was as graceful as it was sad. He moved closer to Bud and his big hand fell on Cynthia's brother's other shoulder, as he realized that red hair could look pretty sometimes; and he wondered why the editor's singing made Cynthy cry; and at the same time he decided to be mighty good to Bud henceforth. The spell of night and song was on him; that and something more; for it is a strange, inexplicable fact that the most practical chief ever known to the "Herald" had a singularly sentimental influence over her subordinates, from the moment of her arrival. Under Harkless's domination there had been no more steadfast bachelors in Carlow than Ross Schofield and Caleb Parker, and, like timorous youths in a graveyard, daring and mocking the ghosts in order to assuage their own fears, they had so jibed and jeered at the married state that there was talk of urging the minister to preach at them; but now let it be recorded that at the moment Caleb laid his hand on Bud's other shoulder, his associate, Mr. Schofield, was enjoying a walk in the far end of town with a widow, and it is not to be doubted that Mr. Tipworthy's heart, also, was no longer in his possession, though, as it was after eight o'clock, the damsel of his desire had probably long since retired to her couch.

For some faint light on the cause of these spells, we must turn to a comment made by the invaluable Mr. Martin some time afterward. Referring to the lady to whose voice he was now listening in silence (which shows how great the enthralling of her voice was), he said: "When you saw her, or heard her, or managed to be around, any, where she was, why, if you couldn't git up no hope of marryin' *her*, you wanted to marry *somebody*."

Mr. Lige Willetts, riding idly by, drew rein in front of the lighted windows, and listened with the others. Presently he leaned from his horse and whispered to a man near him:

"I know that song."

"Do you?" whispered the other.

"Yes; he and I heard her sing it, the night he was shot."

"So!"

"Yes, sir. It's by Beethoven."

"Is it?"

"It's a seraphic song," continued Lige.

"No!" exclaimed his friend; then, shaking his head, he sighed: "Well, it's mighty sweet."

The song was suddenly woven into laughter in the unseen chamber, and the lights in the windows went out, and a small lady and a tall lady and a thin old man, all three laughing and talking happily, came down and drove off in the Briscoe buckboard. The little crowd dispersed quietly; Lige Willetts plucked to his horse and cantered away to overtake the buckboard; William Todd took his courage between his teeth, and, the song ringing in his ears, made a desperate resolve to call upon Miss Bardlock that evening, in spite of its being a week day, and Caleb Parker gently and stammeringly asked Cynthia if she would wait till he shut up the shop, and let him walk home with her and Bud.

Soon the Square was quiet as before, and there was naught but peace under the big stars of July.

That day the news had come that Harkless, after weeks of alternate improvement and relapse, hazardously lingering in the borderland of shadows, had passed the crucial point and was convalescent. His recovery was assured. But from their first word of him, from the message that he was found and was alive, none of the people of Carlow had really doubted it. They are simple country people, and they know that God is good.

CHAPTER XV

NETTLES

Two men who have been comrades and classmates at the Alma Mater of John Harkless and Tom Meredith; two who have belonged to the same dub and roomed in the same entry; who have pooled their clothes and money in a common stock for either to draw on; who have shared the fortunes of athletic war, triumphing together, sometimes with an intense triumphancy; two men who were once boys getting hazed together, hazing in no unkindly fashion in their turn, always helping each other to stuff brains the night before an examination and to blow away the suffocating statistics like foam the night after; singing, wrestling, dancing, laughing, succeeding together, through the four kindest years of life; two such brave companions, meeting in the after years, are touchingly tender and caressive of each other, but the tenderness takes the shy, United States form of insulting epithets, and the caresses are blows. If John Harkless had been in health, uninjured and prosperous, Tom Meredith could no more have thrown himself on his knees beside him and called him "old friend" than he could have danced on the slack-wire.

One day they thought the patient sleeping; the nurse fanned him softly, and Meredith had stolen in and was sitting by the cot. One of Harkless's eyes had been freed of the bandage, and, when Tom came in, it was closed; but, by and by, Meredith became aware that the unbandaged eye had opened and that it was suffused with a pathetic moisture; yet it twinkled with a comprehending light, and John knew that it was his old Tom Meredith who was sitting beside him, with the air of having sat there very often before. But this bald, middle-aged young man, not without elegance, yet a prosperous burgher for all that—was *this* the slim, rollicking broth of a boy whose thick auburn hair used to make one streak of flame as he spun around the bases on a home run? Without doubt it was the stupendous fact, wrought by the alchemy of seven years.

For, though seven years be a mere breath in the memories of the old, it is a long transfiguration to him whose first youth is passing, and who finds unsolicited additions accruing to some parts of his being and strange deprivations in others, and upon whom the unhappy realization begins to be borne in, that his is no particular case, and that he of all the world is not to be spared, but, like his forbears, must inevitably wriggle in the disguising crucible of time. And, though men accept it with apparently patient humor, the first realization that people do grow old, and that they do it before they have had time to be young, is apt to come like a shock.

Perhaps not even in the interminable months of Carlow had Harkless realized the length of seven years so keenly as he did when he beheld his old friend at his bedside. How men may be warped apart in seven years, especially in the seven years between twenty-three and thirty! At the latter age you may return to the inseparable of seven years before and speak not the same language; you find no heartiness to carry on with each other after half an hour. Not so these classmates, who had known each other to the bone.

Ah, yes, it was Tom Meredith, the same lad, in spite of his masquerade of flesh; and Helen was right: Tom had not forgotten.

"It's the old horse-thief!" John murmured, tremulously.

"You go plumb to thunder," answered Meredith between gulps.

When he was well enough, they had long talks; and at other times Harkless lay by the window, and breathed deep of the fresh air, while Meredith attended to his correspondence for him, and read the papers to him. But there was one phenomenon of literature the convalescent insisted upon observing for himself, and which he went over again and again, to the detriment of his single unswathed eye, and this was the Carlow "Herald."

The first letter he had read to him was one from Fisbee stating that the crippled forces left in charge had found themselves almost distraught in their efforts to carry on the paper (as their chief might conclude for himself on perusal of the issues of the first fortnight of his absence), and they had made bold to avail themselves of the services of a young relative of the writer's from a distant city—a capable journalist, who had no other employment for the present, and who had accepted the responsibilities of the "Herald" temporarily. There followed a note from Parker, announcing that Mr. Fisbee's relative was a bird, and was the kind to make the "Herald" hum. They hoped Mr. Harkless would approve of their bespeaking the new hand on the sheet; the paper must have suspended otherwise. Harkless, almost overcome by his surprise that Fisbee possessed a relative, dictated a hearty and grateful indorsement of their action, and, soon after, received a typewritten rejoinder, somewhat complicated in the reading, because of the numerous type errors and their corrections. The missive was signed "H. Fisbee," in a strapping masculine hand that suggested six feet of enterprise and muscle spattering ink on its shirt sleeves.

John groaned and fretted over the writhings of the "Herald's" headless fortnight, but, perusing the issues produced under the domination of H. Fisbee, he started now and then, and chuckled at some shrewd felicities of management, or stared, puzzled, over an oddity, but came to a feeling of vast relief; and, when the question of H. Fisbee's salary was settled and the tenancy assured, he sank into a repose of mind. H. Fisbee might be an eccentric fellow, but he knew his business, and, apparently, he knew something of other business as well, for he wrote at length concerning the Carlow oil fields, urging Harkless to take shares in Mr. Watts's company while the stock was very low, two wells having been sunk without satisfactory results. H. Fisbee explained with exceeding technicality his reasons for believing that the third well would strike oil.

But with his ease of mind regarding the "Herald," Harkless found himself possessed by apathy. He fretted no longer to get back to Plattville. With the prospect of return it seemed an emptiness glared at him from hollow sockets, and the thought of the dreary routine he must follow when he went back gave him the same faint nausea he had felt the evening after the circus. And, though it was partly the long sweat of

150

anguish which had benumbed him, his apathy was pierced, at times, by a bodily horror of the scene of his struggle. At night he faced the grotesque masks of the Cross-Roads men and the brutal odds again; over and over he felt the blows, and clapped his hand to where the close fire of Bob Skillett's pistol burned his body.

And, except for the release from pain, he rejoiced less and less in his recovery. He remembered a tedious sickness of his childhood and how beautiful he had thought the world, when he began to get well, how electric the open air blowing in at the window, how green the smile of earth, and how glorious to live and see the open day again. He had none of that feeling now. No pretty vision came again near his bed, and he beheld his convalescence as a mistake. He had come to a jumping-off place in his life—why had they not let him jump? What was there left but the weary plod, plod, and dust of years?

He could have gone back to Carlow in better spirit if it had not been for the few dazzling hours of companionship which had transformed it to a paradise, but, gone, left a desert. She, by the sight of her, had made him wish to live, and now, that he saw her no more, she made him wish to die. How little she had cared for him, since she told him she did not care, when he had not meant to ask her. He was weary, and at last he longed to find the line of least resistance and follow it; he had done hard things for a long time, but now he wanted to do something easy. Under the new genius—who was already urging that the paper should be made a daily—the "Herald" could get along without him; and the "White-Caps" would bother Carlow no longer; and he thought that Kedge Halloway, an honest man, if a dull one, was sure to be renominated for Congress at the district convention which was to meet at Plattville in September—these were his responsibilities, and they did not fret him. Everything was all right. There was only one thought which thrilled him: his impression that she had come to the hospital to see him was not a delusion; she had really been there—as a humane, Christian person, he said to himself. One day he told Meredith of his vision, and Tom explained that it was no conjuration of fever.

"But I thought she'd gone abroad," said Harkless, staring.

"They had planned to," answered his friend. "They gave it up for some reason. Uncle Henry decided that he wasn't strong enough for the trip, or something."

"Then—is she—is she here?"

"No; Helen is never here in summer. When she came back from Plattville, she went north, somewhere, to join people she had promised, I think." Meredith had as yet no inkling or suspicion that his adopted cousin had returned to Plattville. What he told Harkless was what his aunt had told him, and he accepted it as the truth.

Mrs. Sherwood (for she was both Mr. and Mrs. Sherwood) had always considered Fisbee an enigmatic rascal, and she regarded Helen's defection to him in the light of a family scandal to be hushed up, as well as a scalding pain to be borne. Some day the unkind girl-errant would "return to her wisdom and her duty"; meanwhile, the less known about it the better.

Meredith talked very little to Harkless of his cousin, beyond lightly commenting on the pleasure and oddity of their meeting, and telling him of her friendly anxiety about his recovery; he said she had perfect confidence from the first that he would recover. Harkless had said a word or two in his delirium and a word or two out of it, and these, with once a sudden brow of suffering, and a difference Meredith felt in Helen's manner when they stood together by the sick man's bedside, had given the young man a strong impression, partly intuitive, that in spite of the short time the two had known each other, something had happened between them at Plattville, and he ventured a guess which was not far from the truth. Altogether, the thing was fairly plain—a sad lover is not so hard to read—and Meredith was sorry, for they were the two people he liked best on earth.

The young man carried his gay presence daily to the hospital, where Harkless now lay in a pleasant room of his own, and he tried to keep his friend cheery, which was an easy matter on the surface, for the journalist turned ever a mask of jokes upon him; but it was not hard for one who liked him as Meredith did to see through to the melancholy underneath. After his one reference to Helen, John was entirely silent of her, and Meredith came to feel that both would be embarrassed if occasion should rise and even her name again be mentioned between them.

He did not speak of his family connection with Mr. Fisbee to the invalid, for, although the connection was distant, the old man was, in a way, the family skeleton, and Meredith had a strong sense of the decency of reserve in such a matter. There was one thing Fisbee's shame had made the old man unable not to suppress when he told Parker his story; the wraith of a torrid palate had pursued him from his youth, and the days of drink and despair from which Harkless had saved him were not the first in his life. Meredith wondered as much as did Harkless where Fisbee had picked up the journalistic "young relative" who signed his extremely business-like missives in such a thundering hand. It was evident that the old man was grateful to his patron, but it did not occur to Meredith that Fisbee's daughter might have an even stronger sense of gratitude, one so strong that she could give all her young strength to work for the man who had been good to her father.

There came a day in August when Meredith took the convalescent from the hospital in a victoria, and installed him in his own home. Harkless's clothes hung on his big frame limply; however, there was a drift of light in his eyes as they drove slowly through the pretty streets of Rouen. The bandages and splints and drugs and swathings were all gone now, and his sole task was to gather strength. The thin face was sallow no longer; it was the color of evening shadows; indeed he lay among the cushions seemingly no more than a gaunt shadow of the late afternoon, looking old and gray and weary. They rolled along abusing each other, John sometimes gratefully threatening his friend with violence.

The victoria passed a stone house with wide lawns and an inhospitable air of wealth and importunate rank; over the sward two peacocks swung, ambulating like caravals in a green sea; and one expected a fine lady to come smiling and glittering from the door. Oddly enough, though he had never seen the place before, it struck Harkless with a sense of familiarity. "Who lives there?" he asked abruptly.

"Who lives there? On the left? Why that—that is the Sherwood place," Meredith answered, in a tone which sounded as if he were not quite sure of it, but inclined to think his information correct. Harkless relapsed into silence.

Meredith's home was a few blocks further up the same street; a capacious house in the Western fashion of the Seventies. In front, on the lawn, there was a fountain with a leaping play of water; maples and shrubbery were everywhere; and here and there stood a stiff sentinel of Lombardy poplar. It was all cool and incongruous and comfortable; and, on the porch, sheltered from publicity by a multitude of palms and flowering plants, a white-jacketed negro appeared with a noble smile and a more important tray, whereon tinkled bedewed glasses and a crystal pitcher, against whose sides the ice clinked sweetly. There was a complement of straws.

When they had helped him to an easy chair on the porch, Harkless whistled luxuriously. "Ah, my bachelor!" he exclaimed, as he selected a straw.

"'Who would fardels bear?'" rejoined Mr. Meredith. Then came to the other a recollection of an auburn-haired ball player on whom the third strike had once been called while his eyes wandered tenderly to the grandstand, where the prettiest girl of that commencement week was sitting.

"Have you forgot the 'Indian Princess'?" he asked.

"You're a dull old person," Tom laughed. "Haven't you discovered that 'tis they who forget us? And why shouldn't they? Do *we* remember well?— anybody except just us two, I mean, of course."

"I've a notion we do, sometimes."

The other set his glass on the tray, and lit his cigarette. "Yes; when we're unsuccessful. Then I think we do."

"That may be true."

"Of course it is. If a lady wishes to make an impression on me that is worth making, let her let me make none on her."

"You think it is always our vanity?"

"Analyze it as your revered Thomas does and you shall reach the same conclusion. Let a girl reject you and—" Meredith broke off, cursing himself inwardly, and, rising, cried gaily: "What profiteth it a man if he gain the whole wisdom in regard to women and loseth not his own heart? And neither of us is lacking a heart—though it may be; one can't tell, one's self; one has to find out about that from some girl. At least, I'm rather sure of mine; it's difficult to give a tobacco-heart away; it's drugged on the market. I'm going to bring out the dogs; I'm spending the summer at home just to give them daily exercise."

This explanation of his continued presence in Rouen struck John as quite as plausible as Meredith's more seriously alleged reasons for not joining his mother and sister, at Winter Harbor. (He possessed a mother, and, as he explained, he had also sisters to satiety, in point of numbers.) Harkless knew that Tom had stayed to look after him; and he thought there never was so poor a peg as himself whereon to hang the warm mantle of such a friendship. He knew that other mantles of affection and kindliness hung on that self-same peg, for he had been moved by the letters and visits from Carlow people, and he had heard the story of their descent upon the hospital, and of the march on the Cross-Roads. Many a good fellow, too, had come to see him during his better days—from Judge Briscoe, openly tender and solicitous, to the embarrassed William Todd, who fiddled at his hat and explained that, being as he was in town on business (a palpable fiction) he thought he'd look in to see if "they was any word would wish to be sent down to our city." The good will the sick man had from every one touched him, and made him feel unworthy, and he could see nothing he had done to deserve it. Mr. Meredith could (and would not— openly, at least) have explained to him that it made not a great deal of difference what he did; it was what people thought he was.

His host helped him upstairs after dinner, and showed him the room prepared for his occupancy. Harkless sank, sighing with weakness, into a deep chair, and Meredith went to a window-seat and stretched himself out for a smoke and chat.

"Doesn't it beat your time," he said, cheerily, "to think of what's become of all the old boys? They turn up so differently from what we expected, when they turn up at all. We sized them up all right so far as character goes, I fancy, but we couldn't size up the chances of life. Take poor old Pickle Haines: who'd have dreamed Pickle would shoot himself over a bankruptcy? I dare say that wasn't all of it—might have been cherchez la femme, don't you think? What do you make of Pickle's case, John?"

There was no answer. Harkless's chair was directly in front of the mantel-piece, and upon the carved wooden shelf, amongst tobacco-jars and little curios, cotillion favors and the like, there were scattered a number of photographs. One of these was that of a girl who looked straight out at you from a filigree frame; there was hardly a corner of the room where you could have stood without her clear, serious eyes seeming to rest upon yours.

"Cherchez la femme?" repeated Tom, puffing unconsciously. "Pickle was a good fellow, but he had the deuce of an eye for a girl. Do you remember—" He stopped short, and saw the man and the photograph looking at each other. Too late, he unhappily remembered that he had meant, and forgotten, to take that photograph out of the room before he brought Harkless in. Now he would have to leave it; and Helen Sherwood was not the sort of girl, even in a flat presentment, to be continually thrown in the face of a man who had lost her. And it always went hard, Tom reflected, with men who stretched vain hands to Helen, only to lose her. But there was one, he thought, whose outstretched hands might not prove so vain. Why couldn't she have cared for John Harkless? Deuce take the girl, did she want to marry an emperor? He looked at Harkless, and pitied him with an almost tearful compassion. A feverish color dwelt in the convalescent's cheek; the apathy that had dulled his eyes was there no longer; instead, they burned with a steady fire. The image returned his unwavering gaze with inscrutable kindness.

"You heard that Pickle shot himself, didn't you?" Meredith asked. There was no answer; John did not hear him.

"Do you know that poor Jeny Haines killed himself, last March?" Tom said sharply.

There was only silence in the room. Meredith got up and rattled some tongs in the empty fireplace, but the other did not move or notice him in any way.

Meredith set the tongs down, and went quietly out of the room, leaving his friend to that mysterious interview.

When he came back, after a remorseful cigarette in the yard, Harkless was still sitting, motionless, looking up at the photograph above the mantel-piece.

They drove abroad every day, at first in the victoria, and, as Harkless's strength began to come back, in a knock-about cart of Tom's, a light trail of blue smoke floating back wherever the two friends passed. And though the country editor grew stronger in the pleasant, open city, Meredith felt that his apathy and listlessness only deepened, and he suspected that, in Harkless's own room, where the photograph reigned, the languor departed for the time, making way for a destructive fire. Judge Briscoe, paying a second visit to Rouen, told Tom, in an aside, that their friend did not seem to be the same man. He was altered and aged beyond belief, the old gentleman whispered sadly.

Meredith decided that his guest needed enlivening—something to take him out of himself; he must be stirred up to rub against people once more. And therefore, one night he made a little company for him: two or three apparently betrothed very young couples, for whom it was rather dull, after they had looked their fill of Harkless (it appeared that every one was curious to see him); and three or four married young couples, for whom the entertainment seemed rather diverting in an absent-minded way (they had the air of remembering that they had forgotten the baby); and three or four bachelors, who seemed contented in any place where they were allowed to smoke; and one widower, whose manner indicated that any occasion whatever was gay enough for him; and four or five young women, who (Meredith explained to John) were of their host's age, and had been "left over" out of the set he grew up with; and for these the modest party took on a hilarious and chipper character. "It is these girls that have let the men go by because they didn't see any good enough; they're the jolly souls!" the one widower remarked, confidentially. "They've been at it a long while, and they know how, and they're light-hearted as robins. They have more fun than people who have responsibilities."

All of these lively demoiselles fluttered about Harkless with commiserative pleasantries, and, in spite of his protestations, made him recline in the biggest and deepest chair on the porch, where they surfeited him with kindness and grouped about him with extra cushions and tenderness for a man who had been injured. No one mentioned the fact that he had been hurt; it was not spoken of, though they wished mightily he would tell them the story they had read luridly in the public prints. They were very good to him. One of them, in particular, a handsome, dark, kind-eyed girl, constituted herself at once his cicerone in Rouen gossip and his waiting-maid. She sat by him, and saw that his needs (and his not-needs, too) were supplied and oversupplied; she could not let him move, and anticipated his least wish, though he was now amply able to help himself; and she fanned him as if he were a dying consumptive.

They sat on Meredith's big porch in the late twilight and ate a substantial refection, and when this was finished, a buzz of nonsense rose from all quarters, except the remote corners where the youthful affianced ones had defensively stationed themselves behind a rampart of plants. They, having eaten, had naught to do, and were only waiting a decent hour for departure. Laughing voices passed up and down the street, and mingled with the rhythmic plashing of Meredith's fountain, and, beyond the shrubberies and fence, one caught glimpses of the light dresses of women moving to and fro, and of people sitting bareheaded on neighboring lawns to enjoy the twilight. Now and then would pass, with pipe and dog, the beflanneled figure of an undergraduate, home for vacation, or a trio of youths in knickerbockers, or a band of young girls, or both trio and band together; and from a cross street, near by, came the calls and laughter of romping children and the pulsating whirr of a lawn-mower: This sound Harkless remarked as a ceaseless accompaniment to life in Rouen; even in the middle of the night there was always some unfortunate, cutting grass.

When the daylight was all gone, and the stars had crept out, strolling negroes patrolled the sidewalks, thrumming mandolins and guitars, and others came and went, singing, making the night Venetian. The untrained, joyous voices, chording eerily in their sweet, racial minors, came on the air, sometimes from far away. But there swung out a chorus from fresh, Aryan throats, in the house south of Meredith's:

'Where, oh where, are the grave old Seniors?
Safe, now, in the wide, wide world!"

156

"Doesn't that thrill you, boy?" said Meredith, joining the group about Harkless's chair. "Those fellows are Sophomores, class of heaven knows what. *Aren't* you feeling a fossil. Father Abraham?"

A banjo chattered on the lawn to the north, and soon a mixed chorus of girls and boys sang from there:

"O, 'Arriet, I'm waiting, waiting alone out 'ere."

Then a piano across the street sounded the dearthful harmonies of Chopin's Funeral March.

"You may take your choice," remarked Meredith, flicking a spark over the rail in the ash of his cigar, "Chopping or Chevalier."

"Chopin, my friend," said the lady who had attached herself to Harkless. She tapped Tom's shoulder with her fan and smiled, graciously corrective.

"Thank you, Miss Hinsdale," he answered, gratefully. "And as I, perhaps, had better say, since otherwise there might be a pause and I am the host, we have a wide selection. In addition to what is provided at present, I predict that within the next ten minutes a talented girl who lives two doors south will favor us with the Pilgrims' Chorus, piano arrangement, break down in the middle, and drift, into 'Rastus on Parade,' while a double quartette of middle-aged colored gentlemen under our Jim will make choral offering in our own back yard."

"My dear Tom," exclaimed Miss Hinsdale, "you forget Wetherford Swift!"

"I could stand it all," put forth the widower, "if it were not for Wetherford Swift."

"When is Miss Sherwood coming home?" asked one of the ladies. "Why does she stay away and leave him to his sufferings?"

"Us to his sufferings," substituted a bachelor. "He is just beginning; listen."

Through all the other sounds of music, there penetrated from an unseen source, a sawish, scraped, vibration of catgut, pathetic, insistent, painstaking, and painful beyond belief.

"He is in a terrible way to-night," said the widower.

Miss Hinsdale laughed. "Worse every night. The violinist is young Wetherford Swift," she explained to Harkless. "He is very much in love, and it doesn't agree with him. He used to be such a pleasant boy, but last winter he went quite mad over

Helen Sherwood, Mr. Meredith's cousin, our beauty, you know—I am so sorry she isn't here; you'd be interested in meeting her, I'm sure—and he took up the violin."

"It is said that his family took up chloroform at the same time," said the widower.

"His music is a barometer," continued the lady, "and by it the neighborhood nightly observes whether Miss Sherwood has been nice to him or not."

"It is always exceedingly plaintive," explained another.

"Except once," rejoined Miss Hinsdale. "He played jigs when she came home from somewhere or other, in June."

"It was Tosti's 'Let Me Die,' the very next evening," remarked the widower.

"Ah," said one of the bachelors, "but his joy was sadder for us than his misery. Hear him now."

"I think he means it for 'What's this dull town to me,'" observed another, with some rancor. "I would willingly make the town sufficiently exciting for him—"

"If there were not an ordinance against the hurling of missiles," finished the widower.

The piano executing the funeral march ceased to execute, discomfited by the persistent and overpowering violin; the banjo and the coster-songs were given over; even the collegians' music was defeated; and the neighborhood was forced to listen to the dauntless fiddle, but not without protest, for there came an indignant, spoken chorus from the quarter whence the college songs had issued: "Ya-a-ay! Wetherford, put it away! *She'll* come back!" The violin played on.

"We all know each other here, you see, Mr. Harkless," Miss Hinsdale smiled benignantly.

"They didn't bother Mr. Wetherford Swift," said the widower. "Not that time. Do you hear him?—'Could ye come back to me, Douglas'?"

"Oh, but it isn't absence that is killing him and his friends," cried one of the young women. "It is Brainard Macauley."

"That is a mistake," said Tom Meredith, as easily as he could. "There goes Jim's double quartette. Listen, and you will hear them try to——"

But the lady who had mentioned Brainard Macauley cried indignantly: "You try to change the subject the moment it threatens to be interesting. They were together

158

everywhere until the day she went away; they danced and 'sat out' together through the whole of one country-club party; they drove every afternoon; they took long walks, and he was at the Sherwoods' every evening of her last week in town. 'That is a mistake!'"

"I'm afraid it looks rather bleak for Wetherford," said the widower. "I went up to the 'Journal' office on business, one day, and there sat Miss Sherwood in Macauley's inner temple, chatting with a reporter, while Brainard finished some work."

"Helen is eccentric," said the former speaker, "but she's not quite that eccentric, unless they were engaged. It is well understood that they will announce it in the fall."

Miss Hinsdale kindly explained to Harkless that Brainard Macauley was the editor of the "Rouen Morning Journal"—"a very distinguished young man, not over twenty-eight, and perfectly wonderful." Already a power to be accounted with in national politics, he was "really a tremendous success," and sure to go far; "one of those delicate-looking men, who are yet so strong you know they won't let the lightning hurt you." It really looked as if Helen Sherwood (whom Harkless really ought to meet) had actually been caught in the toils at tet, those toils wherein so many luckless youths had lain enmeshed for her sake. He must meet Mr. Macauley, too, the most interesting man in Rouen. After her little portrait of him, didn't Mr. Harkless agree that it looked really pretty dull for Miss Sherwood's other lovers?

Mr. Harkless smiled, and agreed that it did indeed. She felt a thrill of compassion for him, and her subsequent description of the pathos of his smile was luminous. She said it was natural that a man who had been through so much suffering from those horrible "White-Cappers" should have a smile that struck into your heart like a knife.

Despite all that Meredith could do, and after his notorious effort to shift the subject he could do very little, the light prattle ran on about Helen Sherwood and Brainard Macauley. Tom abused himself for his wild notion of cheering his visitor with these people who had no talk, and who, if they drifted out of commonplace froth, had no medium to float them unless they sailed the currents, of local personality, and he mentally upbraided them for a set of gossiping ninnies. They conducted a conversation (if it could be dignified by a name) of which no stranger could possibly partake, and which, by a hideous coincidence, was making his friend writhe, figuratively speaking, for Harkless sat like a fixed shadow. He uttered scarcely a word the whole evening, though Meredith knew that his guests would talk about him enthusiastically, the next day, none the less. The journalist's silence was enforced by the topics; but what expression and manner the light allowed them to see was friendly and receptive, as though he listened to brilliant suggestions. He had a nice courtesy, and Miss Hinsdale felt continually that she was cleverer than usual this evening, and no one took his silence to be churlish, though they all innocently wondered why he did not talk more; however, it was probable that a man who had been so interestingly and terribly shot would be rather silent for a time afterward.

That night, when Harkless had gone to bed Meredith sat late by his own window calling himself names. He became aware of a rhomboidal patch of yellow light on a wall of foliage without, and saw that it came from his friend's window. After dubious consideration, he knocked softly on the door.

"Come."

He went in. Harkless was in bed, and laughed faintly as Meredith entered. "I—I'm fearing you'll have to let me settle your gas bill, Tom. I'm not like I used to be, quite. I find—since—since that business, I can't sleep without a light. I rather get the—the horrors in the dark."

Incoherently, Meredith made a compassionate exclamation and turned to go, and, as he left the room, his eye fell upon the mantel-piece. The position of the photographs had been altered, and the picture of the girl who looked straight out at you was gone. The mere rim of it was visible behind the image of an old gentleman with a sardonic mouth.

An hour later, Tom came back, and spoke through the closed door. "Boy, don't you think you can get to sleep now?"

"Yes, Tom. It's all right. You get to bed. Nothing troubles me."

Meredith spent the next day in great tribulation and perplexity; he felt that something had to be done, but what to do he did not know. He still believed that a "stirring-up" was what Harkless needed—not the species of "stirring-up" that had taken place last night, but a diversion which would divert. As they sat at dinner, a suggestion came to him and he determined to follow it. He was called to the telephone, and a voice strange to his ear murmured in a tone of polite deference: "A lady wishes to know if Mr. Meredith and his visitor intend being present at the country-club this evening."

He had received the same inquiry from Miss Hinsdale on her departure the previous evening, and had answered vaguely; hence he now rejoined:

"You are quite an expert ventriloquist, but you do not deceive me."

"I beg your pardon, sir," creaked the small articulation.

"This is Miss Hinsdale, isn't it?"

"No, sir. The lady wishes to know if you will kindly answer her question."

"Tell her, yes." He hung up the receiver, and returned to the table. "Some of Clara Hinsdale's play," he explained. "You made a devastating impression on her, boy; you were wise enough not to talk any, and she foolishly thought you were as

160

interesting as you looked. We're going out to a country-club dance. It's given for the devotees who stay here all summer and swear Rouen is always cool; and nobody dances but me and the very young ones. It won't be so bad; you can smoke anywhere, and there are little tables. We'll go."

"Thank you, Tom, you're so good to think of it, but——"

"But what?"

"Would you mind going alone? I find it very pleasant sitting on your veranda, or I'll get a book."

"Very well, if you don't want to go, I don't. I haven't had a dance for three months and I'm still addicted to it. But of course——"

"I think I'd like to go." Harkless acquiesced at once, with a cheerful voice and a lifeless eye, and the good Tom felt unaccountably mean in persisting.

They drove out into the country through mists like lakes, and found themselves part of a procession of twinkling carriage-lights, and cigar sparks shining above open vehicles, winding along the levels like a canoe fête on the water. In the entrance hall of the club-house they encountered Miss Hinsdale, very handsome, large, and dark, elaborately beaming and bending toward them warmly.

"Who do you think is here?" she said.

"Gomez?" ventured Meredith.

"Helen Sherwood!" she cried. "Go and present Mr. Harkless before Brainard Macauley takes her away to some corner."

CHAPTER XVI

PRETTY MARQUISE

The two friends walked through a sort of opera-bouffe to find her; music playing, a swaying crowd, bright lights, bright eyes, pretty women, a glimpse of dancers footing it over a polished floor in a room beyond—a hundred colors flashing and changing, as the groups shifted, before the eye could take in the composition of the picture. A sudden thrill of exhilaration rioted in John's pulses, and he trembled like a child before the gay disclosure of a Christmas tree. Meredith swore to himself that he would not have known him for the man of five minutes agone. Two small, bright red spots glowed in his cheeks; he held himself erect with head thrown back and shoulders squared, and the idolizing Tom thought he looked as a king ought to look at the acme of power and dominion. Miss Hinsdale's word in the hallway was the geniuses touch: a bent, gray man of years—a word—and behold the Great John Harkless, the youth of elder days ripened to his prime of wisdom and strength! People made way for them and whispered as they passed. It had been years since John Harkless had been in the midst of a crowd of butterfly people; everything seemed unreal, or like a ball in a play; presently the curtain would fall and close the lights and laughter from his view, leaving only the echo of music. It was like a kaleidoscope for color: the bouquets of crimson or white or pink or purple; the profusion of pretty dresses, the brilliant, tender fabrics, and the handsome, foreshortened faces thrown back over white shoulders in laughter; glossy raven hair and fair tresses moving in quick salutations; and the whole gay shimmer of festal tints and rich artificialities set off against the brave green of out-doors, for the walls were solidly adorned with forest branches, with, here and there amongst them, a blood-red droop of beech leaves, stabbed in autumn's first skirmish with summer. The night was cool, and the air full of flower smells, while harp, violin, and 'cello sent a waltz-throb through it all.

They looked rapidly through several rooms and failed to find her indoors, and they went outside, not exchanging a word, and though Harkless was a little lame, Tom barely kept up with his long stride. On the verandas there were fairy lamps and colored incandescents over little tables, where people sat chatting. She was not there. Beyond was a terrace, where a myriad of Oriental lanterns outlined themselves clearly in fantastically shaped planes of scarlet and orange and green against the blue darkness. Many couples and groups were scattered over the terrace, and the young men paused on the steps, looking swiftly from group to group. She was not there.

"We haven't looked in the dancing-room," said Tom, looking at his companion rather sorrowfully. John turned quickly and they reentered the house.

He had parted from her in the blackness of storm with only the flicker of lightning to show her to him, but it was in a blaze of lights that he saw her again. The dance was just ended, and she stood in a wide doorway, half surrounded by pretty girls and young men, who were greeting her. He had one full look at her. She was leaning to

162

them all, her arms full of flowers, and she seemed the radiant centre of all the light and gaiety of the place. Even Meredith stopped short and exclaimed upon her; for one never got used to her; and he remembered that whenever he saw her after absence the sense of her beauty rushed over him anew. And he believed the feeling on this occasion was keener than ever before, for she was prettier than he had ever seen her.

"No wonder!" he cried; but Harkless did not understand. As they pressed forward, Meredith perceived that they were only two more radii of a circle of youths, sprung from every direction as the waltz ended, bearing down upon the common focus to secure the next dance. Harkless saw nothing but that she stood there before him. He feared a little that every one might notice how he was trembling, and he was glad of the many voices that kept them from hearing his heart knock against his ribs. She saw him coming toward her, and nodded to him pleasantly, in just the fashion in which she was bowing to half a dozen others, and at that a pang of hot pain went through him like an arrow—an arrow poisoned with cordial, casual friendliness.

She extended her hand to him and gave him a smile that chilled him—it, was so conventionally courteous and poised so nicely in the manner of society. He went hot and cold fast enough then, for not less pleasantly in that manner did she exclaim: "I am very glad to see you, Mr. Harkless, so extremely glad! And so delighted to find you looking strong again! Do tell me about all our friends in Plattville. I should like to have a little chat with you some time. So good of you to find me in this melee."

And with that she turned from the poor fellow to Meredith. "How do you do. Cousin Tom? I've saved the next dance for you." Then she distributed words here and there and everywhere, amongst the circle about her—pretty Marquise with a vengeance! "No, Mr. Swift, I shall not make a card; you must come at the beginning of a dance if you want one. I cannot promise the next; it is quite impossible. No, I did not go as far north as Mackinac. How do you do, Mr. Burlingame?—Yes, quite an age;—no, not the next, I am afraid; nor the next;—I'm not keeping a card. Good evening, Mr. Baird. No, not the next. Oh, *thank* you, Miss Hinsdale!—No, Mr. Swift, it is quite impossible—I'm so sorry. Cousin, the music is commencing; this is ours."

As she took Meredith's arm, she handed her flowers to a gentleman beside her with the slightest glance at the recipient; and the gesture and look made her partner heartsick for his friend; it was so easy and natural and with the air of habit, and had so much of the manner with which a woman hands things to a man who partakes of her inner confidences. Tom knew that Harkless divined the gesture, as well as the identity of the gentleman. They started away, but she paused, and turned to the latter. "Mr. Macauley, you must meet Mr. Harkless. We leave him in your care, and you must see that he meets all the pretty girls—you are used to being nice to distinguished strangers, you know."

Tom put his arm about her, and whirled her away, and Harkless felt as if a soft hand had dealt him blow after blow in the face. Was this lady of little baffling forms and small cold graces the girl who had been his kind comrade, the girl who stood with him by the blue tent-pole, she who had run to him to save his life, she who walked at his side along the pike? The contrast of these homely scenes made him laugh grimly. Was this she who had wept before him—was it she who had been redolent of kindness so fragrantly natural and true—was it she who said she "loved all these people very much, in spite of having known them only two days"?

He cried out upon himself for a fool. What was he in her eyes but a man who had needed to be told that she did not love him! Had he not better— and more courteously to her—have avoided the meeting which was necessarily an embarrassment to her? But no; he must rush like a Mohawk till he found her and forced her to rebuff him, to veil her kindness in little manners, to remind him that he put himself in the character of a rejected importunate. She had punished him enough, perhaps a little too cruelly enough, in leaving him with the man to whom she handed bouquets as a matter of course. And this man was one whose success had long been a trumpet at his ear, blaring loudly of his own failure in the same career.

It had been several years since he first heard of the young editor of the Rouen "Journal," and nowadays almost everybody knew about Brainard Macauley. Outwardly, he was of no unusual type: an American of affairs; slight, easy, yet alert; relaxed, yet sharp; neat, regular, strong; a quizzical eye, a business chin, an ambitious head with soft, straight hair outlining a square brow; and though he was "of a type," he was not commonplace, and one knew at once that he would make a rattling fight to arrive where he was going.

It appeared that he had heard of Harkless, as well as the Carlow editor of him. They had a few moments of shop, and he talked to Harkless as a brother craftsman, without the offense of graciousness, and spoke of his pleasure in the meeting and of his relief at Harkless's recovery, for, aside from the mere human feeling, the party needed him in Carlow—even if he did not always prove himself "quite a vehement partisan." Macauley laughed. "But I'm not doing my duty," he said presently; "I was to present you to the pretty ones only, I believe. Will you designate your preferred fashion of beauty? We serve all styles."

"Thank you," the other answered, hurriedly. "I met a number last night— quite a number, indeed." He had seen them only in dim lights, however, and except Miss Hinsdale and the widower, had not the faintest recognition of any of them, and he cut them all, except those two, one after the other, before the evening was over; and this was a strange thing for a politician to do; but he did it with such an innocent eye that they remembered the dark porch and forgave him.

"Shall we watch the dancing, then?" asked Macauley. Harkless was already watching part of it.

"If you will. I have not seen this sort for more than five years."

"It is always a treat, I think, and a constant proof that the older school of English caricaturists didn't overdraw."

"Yes; one realizes they couldn't."

Harkless remembered Tom Meredith's fine accomplishment of dancing; he had been the most famous dancer of college days, and it was in the dancer that John best saw his old friend again as he had known him, the light lad of the active toe. Other couples flickered about the one John watched, couples that plodded, couples that bobbed, couples that galloped, couples that slid, but the cousins alone passed across the glistening reflections as lightly as October leaves blown over the forest floor. In the midst of people who danced with fixed, glassy eyes, or who frowned with determination to do their duty or to die, and seemed to expect the latter, or who were pale with the apprehension of collision, or who made visible their anxiety to breathe through the nose and look pleased at the same time, these two floated and smiled easily upon life. Three or four steep steps made the portly and cigarette-smoking Meredith pant like an old man, but a dance was a cooling draught to him. As for the little Marquise—when she danced, she danced away with all those luckless hearts that were not hers already. The orchestra launched the jubilant measures of the deux-temps with a torrent of vivacity, and the girl's rhythmic flight answered like a sail taking the breeze.

There was one heart she had long since won which answered her every movement. Flushed, rapturous, eyes sparkling, cheeks aglow, the small head weaving through the throng like a golden shuttle—ah, did she know how adorable she was! Was Tom right: is it the attainable unattainable to one man and given to some other that leaves a deeper mark upon him than success? At all events the unattainable was now like a hot sting in the heart, but yet a sting more precious than a balm. The voice of Brainard Macauley broke in:

"A white brow and a long lash, a flushing cheek and a soft eye, a voice that laughs and breaks and ripples in the middle of a word, a girl you could put in your hat, Mr. Harkless—and there you have a strong man prone! But I congratulate you on the manner your subordinates operate the 'Herald' during your absence. I understand you are making it a daily."

Macauley was staring at him quizzically, and Harkless, puzzled, but without resentment of the other's whimsey, could only decide that the editor of the Rouen "Journal" was an exceedingly odd young man. All at once he found Meredith and the girl herself beside him; they had stopped before the dance was finished. He had the impulse to guard himself from new blows as a boy throws up his elbow to ward a buffet, and, although he could not ward with his elbow, for his heart was on his sleeve—where he began to believe that Macauley had seen it—he remembered that he could smile with as much intentional mechanism as any wornout rounder of afternoons. He stepped aside for her, and she saw what she had known but had not seen before, for the thickness of the crowd, and this was that he limped and leaned upon his stick.

"Do let me thank you," he said, with a louder echo of her manner of greeting him, a little earlier. "It has been such a pleasure to watch you dance. It is really charming to meet you here. If I return to Plattville I shall surely remember to tell Miss Briscoe."

At this she surprised him with a sudden, clear look in the eyes, so reproachful, so deep, so sad, that he started. She took her flowers from Macauley, who had the air of understanding the significance of such ceremonies very well, and saying, "Shan't we all go out on the terrace?" placed her arm in Harkless's, and conducted him (and not the others) to the most secluded corner of the terrace, a nook illumined by one Japanese lantern; to which spot it was his belief that he led her. She sank into a chair, with the look of the girl who had stood by the blue tent-pole. He could only stare at her, amazed by her abrupt change to this dazzling, if reproachful, kindness, confused by his good fortune.

"*If* you go back to Plattville!'" she said in a low voice. "What do you mean?"

"I don't know. I've been dull lately, and I thought I might go somewhere else." Caught in a witchery no lack of possession could dispel, and which the prospect of loss made only stronger while it lasted, he took little thought of what he said; little thought of anything but of the gladness it was to be with her again.

"'Somewhere else?' Where?"

"Anywhere."

"Have you no sense of responsibility? What is to become of your paper?"

"The 'Herald'? Oh, it will potter along, I think."

"But what has become of it in your absence, already? Has it not deteriorated very much?"

"No," he said; "it's better than it ever was before."

"What!" she cried, with a little gasp.

"You're so astounded at my modesty?"

"But please tell me what you mean," she said quickly. "What happened to it?"

"Isn't the 'Herald' rather a dull subject? I'll tell you how well Judge Briscoe looked when he came to see me; or, rather, tell me of your summer in the north."

166

"No," she answered earnestly. "Don't you remember my telling you that I am interested in newspaper work?"

"I have even heard so from others," he said, with an instant of dryness.

"Please tell me about the 'Herald'?"

"It is very simple. Your friend, Mr. Fisbee, found a substitute, a relative six feet high with his coat off, a traction engine for energy and a limited mail for speed. He writes me letters on a type writer suffering from an impediment in its speech; and in brief, he is an enterprising idiot with a mania for work-baskets."

Her face was in the shadow.

"You say the—idiot—is enterprising?" she inquired.

"Far more enterprising and far less idiot than I. They are looking for oil down there, and when he came he knew less about oil than a kindergarten babe, and spoke of 'boring for kerosene' in his first letter to me; but he knows it all now, and writes long and convincing geological arguments. If a well comes in, he is prepared to get out an extra! Perhaps you may understand what that means in Plattville, with the 'Herald's' numerous forces. I owe him everything, even the shares in the oil company, which he has persuaded me to take. And he is going to dare to make the 'Herald' a daily. Do you remember asking me why I had never done that? It seemed rather a venture to try to compete with the Rouen papers in offering State and foreign news, but this young Gulliver has tacked onto the Associated Press, and means to print a quarto—that's eight pages, you know—once a week, Saturday, and a double sheet, four pages, on other mornings. The daily venture begins next Monday."

"Will it succeed?"

"Oh, no!" he laughed.

"You think not?" Her interest in this dull business struck him as astonishing, and yet in character with her as he had known her in Plattville. Then he wondered unhappily if she thought that talking of the "Herald" and learning things about the working of a country newspaper would help her to understand Brainard Macauley.

"Why have you let him go on with it?" she asked. "I suppose you have encouraged him?"

"Oh, yes, I encouraged him. The creature's recklessness fascinated me. A dare-devil like that is always charming.'"

"You think there is no chance for the creature's succeeding with the daily?"

"None," he replied indifferently.

"You mentioned work-baskets, I think?"

He laughed again. "I believe him to be the original wooden-nutmeg man. Once a week he produces a 'Woman's Page,' wherein he presents to the Carlow female public three methods for making currant jelly, three receipts for the concoction of salads, and directs the ladies how to manufacture a pretty work-basket out of odd scraps in twenty minutes. The astonishing part of it is that he has not yet been mobbed by the women who have followed his directions."

"So you think the daily is a mistake and that your enterprising idiot should be mobbed? Why?" She seemed to be taking him very seriously.

"I think he may be—for his 'Woman's Page.'"

"It is all wrong, you think?"

"What could a Yankee six-footer cousin of old Fisbee's know about currant jelly and work-baskets?"

"You know about currant jelly and work-baskets yourself?"

"Heaven defend the right, I do not!"

"You are sure he is six feet?"

"You should see his signature; that leaves no doubt. And, also, his ability denotes his stature."

"You believe that ability is in proportion to height, do you not?" There was a dangerous luring in her tone.

His memory recalled to him that he was treading on undermined ground, so he hastened to say: "In inverse proportion."

"Then your substitute is a failure. I see," she said, slowly.

What muffled illumination there was in their nook fell upon his face; her back was toward it, so that she was only an outline to him, and he would have been startled and touched to the quick, could he have known that her lip quivered and her eyes filled with tears as she spoke the last words. He was happy as he had not been since his short June day; it was enough to be with her again. Nothing, not even Brainard Macauley, could dull his delight. And, besides, for a few minutes he had forgotten Brainard Macauley. What more could man ask than to sit in the gloom with her, to

168

know that he was near her again for a little while, and to talk about anything—if he talked at all? Nonsense and idle exaggeration about young Fisbee would do as well as another thing.

"The young gentleman is an exception," he returned. "I told you I owed everything to him; my gratitude will not allow me to admit that his ability is less than his stature. He suggested my purchase of a quantity of Mr. Watts's oil stock when it was knocked flat on its back by two wells turning out dry; but if Mr. Watts's third well comes in, and young Fisbee has convinced me that it will, and if my Midas's extra booms the stock and the boom develops, I shall oppose the income tax. Poor old Plattville will be full of strangers and speculators, and the 'Herald' will advocate vast improvements to impress the investor's eye. Stagnation and picturesqueness will flee together; it is the history of the Indiana town. Already the 'Herald' is clamoring with Schofields' Henry—you remember the bell-ringer?—for Main Street to be asphalted. It will all come. The only trouble with young Fisbee is that he has too much ability."

"And yet the daily will not succeed?"

"No. That's too big a jump, unless my young man's expressions on the tariff command a wide sale amongst curio-hunters."

"Then he is quite a fool about political matters?"

"Far from it; he is highly ingenious. His editorials are often the subtlest cups of flattery I ever sipped, many of them showing assiduous study of old files to master the method and notions of his eagle-eyed predecessor. But the tariff seems to have got him. He is a very masculine person, except for this one feminine quality, for, if I may say it without ungallantry, there is a legend that no woman has ever understood the tariff. Young Fisbee must be an extremely travelled person, because the custom-house people have made an impression upon him which no few encounters with them could explain, and he conceives the tariff to be a law which discommodes a lady who has been purchasing gloves in Paris. He thinks smuggling the great evil of the present tariff system; it is such a temptation, so insidious a break-down of moral fibre. His views must edify Carlow."

She gave a quick, stifled cry. "Oh! there isn't a word of truth in what you say! Not a word! I did not think you could be so cruel!"

He bent forward, peering at her in astonishment.

"Cruel!"

"You know it is a hateful distortion—an exaggeration!" she exclaimed passionately. "No man living could have so little sense as you say he has. The tariff is perfectly plain to any child. When you were in Plattville you weren't like this—I didn't know you were unkind!"

"I—I don't understand, please——"

"Miss Hinsdale has been talking—raving—to me about you! You may not know it—though I suppose you do—but you made a conquest last night. It seems a little hard on the poor young man who is at work for you in Plattville, doing his best for you, plodding on through the hot days, and doing all he knows how, while you sit listening to music in the evenings with Clara Hinsdale, and make a mock of his work and his trying to please you——"

"But I didn't mention him to Miss Hinsdale. In fact, I didn't mention *anything* to Miss Hinsdale. What have I done? The young man is making his living by his work—and my living, too, for that matter. It only seems to me that his tariff editorials are rather humorous."

She laughed suddenly—ringingly. "Of course they are! How should I know? Immensely humorous! And the good creature knows nothing beyond smuggling and the custom-house and chalk marks? Why, even *I*—ha, ha, ha!—even *I*—should have known better than that. What a little fool your enterprising idiot must be!—with his work-baskets and currant jelly and his trying to make the 'Herald' a daily!—It will be a ludicrous failure, of course. No doubt he thought he was being quite wise, and was pleased over his tariff editorials—his funny, funny editorials—his best—to please you! Ha, ha, ha! How immensely funny!"

"Do you know him?" he asked abruptly.

"I have not the honor of the gentleman's acquaintance. Ah," she rejoined bitterly, "I see what you mean; it is the old accusation, is it? I am a woman, and I 'sound the personal note.' I could not resent a cruelty for the sake of a man I do not know. But let it go. My resentment is personal, after all, since it is against a man I do know—*you!*"

He leaned toward her because he could not help it. "I'd rather have resentment from you than nothing."

"Then I will give you nothing," she answered quickly.

"You flout me!" he cried. "That is better than resentment."

"I hate you most, I think," she said with a tremulousness he did not perceive, "when you say you do not care to go back to Plattville."

"Did I say it?"

170

"It is in every word, and it is true; you don't care to go back there."

"Yes, it is true; I don't."

"You want to leave the place where you do good; to leave those people who love you, who were ready to die to avenge your hurt!" she exclaimed vehemently. "Oh, I say that is shameful!"

"Yes, I know," he returned gravely. "I am ashamed."

"Don't say that!" she cried. "Don't say you are ashamed of it. Do you suppose I do not understand the dreariness it has been for you? Don't you know that I see it is a horror to you, that it brings back your struggle with those beasts in the dark, and revivifies all your suffering, merely to think of it?" Her turns and sudden contradictions left him tangled in a maze; he could not follow, but must sit helpless to keep pace with her, while the sheer happiness of being with her tingled through his veins. She rose and took a step aside, then spoke again: "Well, since you want to leave Carlow, you shall; since you do not wish to return, you need not.— Are you laughing at me?" She leaned toward him, and looked at him steadily, with her face close to his. He was not laughing; his eyes shone with a deep fire; in that nearness he hardly comprehended what she said. "Thank you for not laughing," she whispered, and leaned back from him. "I suppose you think my promises are quite wild, and they are. I do not know what I was talking about, or what I meant, any better than you do. You may understand some day. It is all—I mean that it hurts one to hear you say you do not care for Carlow." She turned away. "Come."

"Where?"

"It is my turn to conclude the interview. You remember, the last time it was you who—" She broke off, shuddering, and covered her face with her hands. "Ah, that!" she exclaimed. "I did not think—I did not mean to speak of that miserable, miserable night. And *I* to be harsh with you for not caring to go back to Carlow!"

"Your harshness," he laughed. "A waft of eider."

"We must go," she said. He did not move, but sat staring at her like a thirsty man drinking. With an impulsive and pretty gesture she reached out her hand to him. Her little, white glove trembled in the night before his eyes, and his heart leaped to meet its sudden sweet generosity; his thin fingers closed over it as he rose, and then that hand he had likened to a white butterfly lay warm and light and quiet in his own. And as they had so often stood together in their short day and their two nights of the moon, so now again they stood with a serenading silence between them. A plaintive waltz-refrain from the house ran through the blue woof of starlit air as a sad-colored thread through the tapestry of night; they heard the mellow croon of the 'cello and the silver plaints of violins, the chiming harp, and the triangle bells, all woven into a minor strain of dance-music that beat gently upon their ears with such suggestion of the past, that, as by some witchcraft of hearing, they listened to music made for lovers dancing, and lovers listening, a hundred years ago.

"I care for only one thing in this world," he said, tremulously. "Have I lost it? I didn't mean to ask you, that last night, although you answered. Have I no chance? Is it still the same? Do I come too late?"

The butterfly fluttered in his hand and then away.

She drew back and looked at him a moment.

"There is one thing you must always understand," she said gently, "and that is that a woman can be grateful. I give you all the gratitude there is in me, and I think I have a great deal; it is all yours. Will you always remember that?"

"Gratitude? What can there—"

"You do not understand now, but some day you will. I ask you to remember that my every act and thought which bore reference to you—and there have been many— came from the purest gratitude. Although you do not see it now, will you promise to believe it?"

"Yes," he said simply.

"For the rest—" She paused. "For the rest—I do not love you."

He bowed his head and did not lift it.

"Do you understand?" she asked.

"I understand," he answered, quietly.

She looked at him long, and then, suddenly, her hand to her heart, gave a little, pitying, tender cry and moved toward him. At this he raised his head and smiled sadly. "No; don't you mind," he said. "It's all right. I was such a cad the other time I needed to be told; I was so entirely silly about it, I couldn't face the others to tell them good-night, and I left you out there to go in to them alone. I didn't realize, for my manners were all gone. I'd lived in a kind of stupor, I think, for a long time; then being with you was like a dream, and the sudden waking was too much for me. I've been ashamed often, since, in thinking of it—and I was well punished for not taking you in. I thought only of myself, and I behaved like a whining, unbalanced boy. But I had whined from the moment I met you, because I was sickly with egoism and loneliness and self-pity. I'm keeping you from the dancing. Won't you let me take you back to the house?"

172

A commanding and querulous contralto voice was heard behind them, and a dim, majestic figure appeared under the Japanese lantern.

"Helen?"

The girl turned quickly. "Yes, mamma."

"May I ask you to return to the club-house for supper with me? Your father has been very much worried about you. We have all been looking for you."

"Mamma, this is Mr. Harkless."

"How do you do?" The lady murmured this much so far under her breath that the words might have been mistaken for anything else—most plausibly, perhaps, for, "Who cares if it is?"—nor further did she acknowledge John's profound inclination. Frigidity and complaint of ill-usage made a glamour in every fold of her expensive garments; she was large and troubled and severe. A second figure emerged from behind her and bowed with the suave dignity that belonged to Brainard Macauley. "Mr. Macauley has asked to sit at our table," Mrs. Sherwood said to Helen. "May I beg you to come at once? Your father is holding places for us."

"Certainly," she answered. "I will follow you with Mr. Harkless."

"I think Mr. Harkless will excuse you," said the elder lady. "He has an engagement. Mr. Meredith has been looking everywhere for him to take Miss Hinsdale out to supper."

"Good-night, Miss Sherwood," said John in a cheerful voice. "I thank you for sitting out the dance with me."

"Good-night," she said, and gave him her hand. "I'm so sorry I shan't see you again; I am only in Rouen for this evening, or I should ask you to come to see me. I am leaving to-morrow morning. Good-night.—Yes, mamma."

The three figures went toward the bright lights of the club-house. She was leaning on Macauley's arm and chatting gaily, smiling up at him brightly. John watched her till she was lost in the throng on the veranda. There, in the lights, where waiters were arranging little tables, every one was talking and moving about, noisily, good-humored and happy. There was a flourish of violins, and then the orchestra swung into a rampant march that pranced like uncurbed cavalry; it stirred the blood of old men with militant bugle calls and blast of horns; it might have heralded the chariot of a flamboyant war god rioting out of sunrise, plumed with youth. Some quite young men on the veranda made as if they were restive horses champing at the bit and heading a procession, and, from a group near by, loud laughter pealed.

John Harkless lifted to his face the hand that had held hers; there was the faint perfume of her glove. He kissed his own hand. Then he put that hand and the other to his forehead, and sank into her chair.

"Let me get back," he said. "Let me get back to Plattville, where I belong."

Tom Meredith came calling him. "Harkless? John Harkless?"

"Here I am, Tom."

"Come along, boy. What on earth are you doing out here all alone? I thought you were with—I thought some people were with you. You're bored to death, I know; but come along and be bored some more, because I promised to bring you in for supper. Then we'll go home. They've saved a place for you by Miss Hinsdale."

"Very well, lad," answered Harkless, and put his hand on the other's shoulder. "Thank you."

The next day he could not leave his bed; his wounds were feverish and his weakness had returned. Meredith was shaken with remorse because he had let him wander around in the damp night air with no one to look after him.

CHAPTER XVII

HELEN'S TOAST

Judge Briscoe was sitting out under the afternoon sky with his chair tilted back and his feet propped against the steps. His coat was off, and Minnie sat near at hand sewing a button on the garment for him, and she wore that dreamy glaze that comes over women's eyes when they sew for other people.

From the interior of the house rose and fell the murmur of a number of voices engaged in a conversation, which, for a time, seemed to consist of dejected monosyllables; but presently the judge and Minnie heard Helen's voice, clear, soft, and trembling a little with excitement. She talked only two or three minutes, but what she said stirred up a great commotion. All the voices burst forth at once in ejaculations—almost shouts; but presently they were again subdued and still, except for the single soft one, which held forth more quietly, but with a deeper agitation, than any of the others.

"You needn't try to bamboozle me," said the judge in a covert tone to his daughter, and with a glance at the parlor window, whence now issued the rumble of Warren Smith's basso. "I tell you that girl would follow John Harkless to Jericho."

Minnie shook her head mysteriously, and bit a thread with a vague frown.

"Well, why not?" asked the judge crossly.

"Why wouldn't she have him, then?"

"Well, who knows he's asked her yet?"

Minnie screamed derisively at the density of man, "What made him run off that way, the night he was hurt? Why didn't he come back in the house with her?"

"Pshaw!"

"Don't you suppose a woman understands?"

"Meaning that you know more about it than I do, I presume," grunted the old gentleman.

"Yes, father," she replied, smiling benignantly upon him.

"Did she tell you?" he asked abruptly.

"No, no. I guess the truth is that women don't know more than men so much as they see more; they understand more without having to read about it."

"That's the way of it, is it?" he laughed. "Well, it don't make any difference, she'll have him some time."

"No, father; it's only gratitude."

"Gratitude!" The judge snorted scornfully. "Girls don't do as much as she's done for him out of gratitude. *Look* what she's doing; not only running the 'Herald' for him, but making it a daily, and a good daily at that. First time I saw her I knew right away she was the smartest girl I ever laid eyes on;—I expect she must have got it from her mother. Gratitude! Pooh! Look how she's studied his interests, and watched like a cat for chances for him in everything. Didn't she get him into Eph Watts's company? She talked to Watts and the other fellows, day after day, and drove around their leased land with 'em, and studied it up, and got on the inside, and made him buy. Now, if they strike it—and she's sure they will, and *I'*m sure she knows when to have faith in a thing—why, they'll sell out to the Standard, and they can all quit work for the rest of their lives if they want to; and Harkless gets as much as any without lifting a finger, all because he had a little money—mighty little, too—laid up in bank and a girl that saw where to put it. She did that for him, didn't she?"

"Don't you see what fun it's been for her?" returned Minnie. "She's been having the best time she ever had; I never knew any one half so happy."

"Yes; she went up and saw him at that party, and she knows he's still thinking about her. I shouldn't be surprised if he asked her then, and that's what makes her so gay."

"Well, she couldn't have said 'yes,' because he went back to his bed the next day, and he's been there most of the time since."

"Pshaw! He wasn't over his injuries, and he was weak and got malaria."

"Well, she couldn't be so happy while he's sick, if she cared very much about him."

"He's not very sick. She's happy because she's working for him, and she knows his illness isn't serious. He'll be a well man when she says the word. He's love-sick, that's what he is; I never saw a man so taken down with it in my life."

"Then it isn't malaria?" Minnie said, with a smile of some superiority.

"You're just like your poor mother," the old gentleman answered, growing rather red. "She never could learn to argue. What I say is that Helen cares about him, whether she says she does or not, whether she acts like it or not—or whether she thinks she does or not," he added irascibly. "Do you know what she's doing for him to-day?"

176

"Not exactly."

"Well, when they were talking together at that party, he said something that made her think he was anxious to get away from Plattville—you're not to repeat this, child; she told me, relying on my discretion."

"Well?"

"Do you know why she's got these men to come here to-day to meet her— Warren Smith and Landis and Homer, and Boswell and young Keating of Amo, and Tom Martin and those two fellows from Gaines County?"

"Something about politics, isn't it?"

"'Something about politics!'" he echoed. "I should say it is! Wait till it's done, and this evening I'll tell you—if you can keep a secret."

Minnie set her work-basket on the steps. "Oh, I guess I can keep a secret," she said. "But it won't make any difference."

"You mean you've said it, and you'll stick to it that it's gratitude till their wedding day."

"She knows he gave her father something to do, and helped him in other ways, when no one else did."

"I know all about that. She reproaches herself for having neglected Fisbee while a stranger took care of him, and saved him from starving—and worse. She's unreasonable about it; she didn't know he was in want till long after. That's just like Fisbee, to tell her, afterwards. He didn't tell her how low he got; but he hinted at it to her, and I guess she understood; I gathered that much from him. Of course she's grateful, but gratefulness don't account for everything."

"Yes it does."

"Well, I never expected to have the last word with a woman."

"Well, you needn't," said Minnie.

"I don't. I never do," he retorted. She did not answer, but hummed a little tune and looked up at the tree-tops.

Warren Smith appeared in the doorway. "Judge," he said, "will you step inside? We need you."

Briscoe nodded and rose at once. As he reached the door, Minnie said in a piercing whisper:

"It's hard to be sure about her, but I'm right; it's gratitude."

"There," he replied, chuckling, "I thought I shouldn't have the last word." Minnie began to sing, and the judge, after standing in the doorway till he was again summoned from within, slowly retired.

Briscoe had persisted in his own explanation of Helen's gaiety; nevertheless he did not question his daughter's assumption that the young lady was enjoying her career in Carlow. She was free as a bird to go and come, and her duties and pleasures ran together in a happy excitement. Her hands were full of work, but she sought and increased new tasks, and performed them also. She came to Carlow as unused to the soil as was Harkless on his arrival, and her educational equipment for the work was far less than his; her experience, nothing. But both were native to the State; and the genius of the American is adaptability, and both were sprung from pioneers whose means of life depended on that quality.

There are, here and there, excrescent individuals who, through stock decadence, or their inability to comprehend republican conditions, are not assimilated by the body of the country; but many of these are imports, while some are exports. Our foreign-born agitators now and then find themselves removed by the police to institutions of routine, while the romantic innocents who set up crests in the face of an unimpressionable democracy are apt to be lured by their own curious ambitions, or those of their women-folk, to spend a great part of their time in or about the villas of Albion, thus paid for its perfidy; and, although the anarchists and the bubble-hunters make a noise, it is enormously out of proportion to their number, which is relatively very small, and neither the imported nor the exported article can be taken as characteristic of our country. For the American is one who soon fits any place, or into any shaped hole in America, where you can set him down. It may be that without going so far as to suggest the halls of the great and good and rich, one might mention a number of houses of entertainment for man and beast in this country, in which Mr. Martin of the Plattville Dry Goods Emporium would find himself little at ease. But even in the extreme case, if Mr. Martin were given his choice of being burned to death, or drowned, or of spending a month at the most stupendously embellished tavern located in our possessions, and supposing him to have chosen the third alternate, it is probable that he would have grown almost accustomed to his surroundings before he died; and if he survived the month, we may even fancy him really enjoying moments of conversation with the night-clerks.

As Mr. Parker observed, Miss Sherwood did not do the Grand Duchess, giving the Carlow tenants a treat. She felt no duchess symptoms within herself, and though, of course, she had various manners tucked away to wear as one suits garments to occasions—and it was a Rouen "party-gown" wherewith she chose to abash poor John Harkless at their meeting—here in Carlow, she was a woman of affairs, lively, shrewd, engaging, capable; she was herself (at least she was that side of herself).

178

And it should be explained that Harkless had based his calumny regarding the tariff on a paragraph or two that crept inadvertently into an otherwise statesmanlike article, and that "H. Fisbee" understood the tariff as well as any woman who ever lived. But the tariff inspired no more articles from that pen.

Rodney McCune had lifted his head, and those who had followed his stricken enemy felt that the cause was lost, without the leader. The old ring that the "Herald" had crushed was a ring once more, and the heelers had rallied—"the boys were in line again." The work had been done quietly, and Halloway was already beaten, and beaten badly. John Harkless lay sick, and Rodney McCune would sit in Congress, for the nomination meant election. But one day the Harkless forces, demoralized, broken, almost hopeless, woke up to find that they had a leader. Many of them were content with the belief that this was a young lawyer named Keating, who had risen up in Amo; but Mr. Keating himself had a different impression.

Helen was a little nervous, and very much excited, over the political conference at Judge Briscoe's. She planned it with careful diplomacy, and arranged the details with a fine sense of the dramatic. There was a suggestion she desired to have made in this meeting, which she wished should emanate from the Amo and Gaines County people, instead of proceeding from Carlow—for she thought it better to make the outsiders believe her idea an inspiration of their own—so she made a little comedy and provided for Briscoe's entrance at an effective moment. The judge was a substantial influence, strong in the councils of his party when he chose to be; and though of late years he had contented himself with voting at the polls, every one knew what weight he carried when he saw fit to bestir himself.

When he entered the parlor, he found the politicians in a state of subdued excitement. Helen sat by the window, blushing, and talking eagerly to old Fisbee. One of the gentlemen from Gaines County was walking about the room exclaiming, "A glorious conception! A glorious conception!" addressing the bric-a-brac, apparently. (He thought the conception his own.) Mr. Martin was tugging at his beard and whispering to Landis and Homer, and the two Amo men were consulting in a corner, but as the judge came in, one of them turned and said loudly, "That's the man."

"What man am I, Keating?" asked Briscoe, cheerily.

"We better explain, I guess," answered the other; and turning to his compatriot: "You tell him, Boswell."

"Well—it's this way—" said Boswell, and came at once to an awkward pause, turning aside sheepishly and unable to proceed.

"So that's the way of it, is it?" said the old gentleman.

Helen laughed cheerfully, and looked about her with a courageous and encouraging eye. "It is embarrassing," she said. "Judge Briscoe, we are contemplating 'a piece of the blackest treachery and chicanery.' We are going to give Mr. Halloway the—the go-by!" The embarrassment fell away, and everybody began to talk at once.

"Hold on a minute," said the judge; "let's get at it straight. What do you want with me?"

"I'll tell you," volunteered Keating. "You see, the boys are getting in line again for this convention. They are the old file that used to rule the roost before the 'Herald' got too strong for them, and they rely on Mr. Harkless's being sick to beat Kedge Halloway with that Gaines County man, McCune. Now, none of us here want Rod McCune I guess. We had trouble enough once with him and his heelers, and now that Mr. Harkless is down, they've taken advantage of it to raise a revolution: Rod McCune for Congress! He's a dirty-hearted swindler—I hope Miss Sherwood will pardon the strong expression—and everybody thought the 'Herald' had driven him out of politics, though it never told how it did it; but he's up on top again. Now, the question is to beat him. We hold the committees, but the boys have been fighting the committees—call 'em the 'Harkless Ring,' and never understood that the 'Herald' would have turned us down in a second if it thought we weren't straight. Well, we saw a week ago that Kedge Halloway was going to lose to McCune; we figured it out pretty exactly, and there ain't a ray of hope for Kedge. We wrote to Mr. Harkless about it, and asked him to come down—if he'd been on the ground last Monday and had begun to work, I don't say but what his personal influence might have saved Halloway—but a friend of his, where he's staying, answered the letter: said Mr. Harkless was down with a relapse and was very fretful; and he'd taken the liberty of reading the letter and temporarily suppressing it under doctor's orders; they were afraid he'd come, sick as he was, from a sense of duty, and asked us to withdraw the letter, and referred us to Mr. Harkless's representative on the 'Herald.' So we applied here to Miss Sherwood, and that's why we had this meeting. Now, Halloway is honest—everybody knows that—and I don't say but what he's been the best available material Mr. Harkless had to send to Washington; but he ain't any too bright——"

Mr. Martin interrupted the speaker. "I reckon, maybe, you never heard that lecture of his on the Past, Present, and Future'?"

"Besides that," Keating continued, "Halloway has had it long enough, and he's got enough glory out of it, and, except for getting beat by Rod McCune, I believe he'd almost as soon give it up. Well, we discussed all this and that, and couldn't come to any conclusion. We didn't want to keep on with a losing fight if there was any way to put up a winner, though of course we all recognized that Mr. Harkless would want us to support Kedge to the death, and that's what he'd do if he was on the ground. But Miss Sherwood mentioned that she'd had one note since his last illness began, and he'd entrusted her and her associates on the paper with the entire policy, and she would take the responsibility for anything we determined on. Mr. Smith said the only thing to do was to give up Halloway and get a man that could beat McCune;

Kedge would recognize it himself, that that was the only thing to do, and he could retire gracefully. Miss Sherwood said she was still more or less a stranger, and asked what man we could find who was strong enough to do it by popularity alone and who was also a man we wanted; somebody that had worked a good deal, but had never had any office. It was to such a man she could promise the 'Herald's' support, as for a time the paper was being operated almost independently, it might be said, of Mr. Harkless. Well, I expect it came to all of us at the same time, but it was Mr. Bence here that said it first."

Mr. Bence was the gentleman who had walked about saying "A glorious conception," and he now thrust one hand into his breast and extended the other in a wide gesture, and looked as impressive as a very young man with white eyebrows can look.

"The name of Harkless," he said abruptly, "the name of Harkless will sweep the convention like the fire of a Western prairie; the name of Harkless will thunder over their astonished heads and strike a peal of joy bells in every home in the district; it will re-echo in the corridors of posterity and teem with prosperity like a mighty river. The name of Harkless will reverberate in that convention hall, and they shall sit ashamed."

"Harkless!" exclaimed the judge. "Why didn't some one think of that long ago?"

"Then you approve?" asked Keating.

"Yes, I think I do!"

The Amo man shook hands with him. "We'll swim out," he exclaimed. "It will be the same everywhere. A lot of the old crowd themselves will be swept along with us when we make our nomination. People feel that that Cross-Roads business ought never to have been allowed to happen, and they'd like to make it up to him some way. There are just two difficulties, Halloway and Mr. Harkless himself. It's a sure thing that he wouldn't come out against Kedge and that he'd refuse to let his name be used against him. Therefore, we've got to keep it quiet from him; the whole thing has to be worked quietly. The McCune folks were quiet until they thought they were sure; we've got to be quieter still. Well, we've made out a plan."

"And a plan that will operate," added Mr. Bence. "For the name of Harkless shall—" Mr. Keating interrupted him energetically:

"We explain it to all the Halloway delegates, you see, and to all the shaky McCune people, and interview all the undecided ones. The McCune crowd may see them afterwards, but they can't fix men in this district against John Harkless. All we've got to do is to pass the word. It's all kept quiet, you understand. We go into the convention, and the names of Halloway and McCune are placed before it. Then will come a speech naming Harkless—and you want to stuff your ears with cotton! On the first ballot Harkless gets the scattering vote that was going to nominate McCune if we'd let things run, and Halloway is given every vote he'd have got if he'd run against McCune alone; it's as a compliment; it will help him see how things were, afterwards; and on the second ballot his vote goes to Harkless. There won't be any hitch if we get down to work right off; it's a mighty short campaign, but we've got big chances. Of course, it can't be helped that Halloway has to be kept in the dark; he won't spend any money, anyway."

"It looks a little underhanded at first glance," said Warren Smith; "but, as Miss Sherwood said, you've got to be a little underhanded sometimes, especially when you're dealing with as scrupulous a man as John Harkless. But it's a perfectly honest deal, and it will be all right with him when he finds it's all over and he's nominated."

"It's a plain case," added Boswell. "We want him, and we've got to have him."

"There's one danger," Mr. Keating continued. "Kedge Halloway is honest, but I believe he's selfish enough to disturb his best friend's deathbed for his own ends, and it's not unlikely that he will get nervous towards the last and be telegraphing Harkless to have himself carried on a cot to the convention to save him. That wouldn't do at all, of course, and Miss Sherwood thinks maybe there'd be less danger if we set the convention a little ahead of the day appointed. It's dangerous, because it shortens our time; but we can fix it for three days before the day we'd settled on, and that will bring it to September 7th. What we want of you, judge, is to go to the convention as a delegate, and make the nominating speech for Mr. Harkless. Will you do it?"

"Do it?" cried the old man, and he struck the table a resounding blow with his big fist. "Do it? I'd walk from here to Rouen and back again to do it!"

They were all on their feet at this, and they pressed forward to shake Briscoe's hand, congratulating him and each other as though they were already victorious. Mr. Martin bent over Helen and asked her if she minded shaking hands with a man who had voted for Shem at the first election in the Ark.

"I thought I'd rightly ort to thank you for finishin' off Kedge Halloway," he added. "I made up my mind I'd never vote for him again, the night he killed that intellectual insect of his."

"Intellectual insect, Mr. Martin?" she asked, puzzled.

He sighed. "The recollection never quits ha'ntin' me. I reckon I haven't had a restful night since June. Maybe you don't remember his lecture."

"Oh, but I do," she laughed; "and I remember the story of the fly, vividly."

182

"I never was jest what you might exactly call gushin' over Kedge," Mr. Martin drawled. "He doesn't strike me as havin' many ideas, precisely—he had kind of a symptom of one once, that he caught from Harkless, but it didn't take; it sloshed around in his mind and never really come out on him. I always thought his brain was sort of syrupy. Harkless thought there was fruit in it, and I reckon there is; but some way it never seems to jell."

"Go on," said Helen gayly. "I want to hear him abused. It helps me to feel less mean about the way we are treating him."

"Yes; I'm slickin' over my conscience, too. I feel awnrier about it because he done me a good turn once, in the Hayes and Wheeler campaign. I went to a meetin' to hear him speak, and he got sick and couldn't."

Warren Smith addressed the company. "Well, is this all for the present?" he asked. "Is everything settled?"

"Wait a minute," said Keating. "I'd like to hear from the 'Herald' about its policy, if Miss Sherwood will tell us."

"Yes, indeed," she answered. "It will be very simple. Don't you think there is only one course to pursue? We will advocate no one very energetically, but we will print as much of the truth about Mr. McCune as we can, with delicacy and honor, in this case, but, as I understand it, the work is almost all to be done amongst the delegates. We shall not mention our plan at all—but—but, when the convention is over, and he is nominated, we will get out an extra; and I am so confident of your success that I'll tell you now that the extra will be ready the night before the convention. We will contrive that Mr. Harkless shall not receive his copy of the paper containing the notice of the change of date, and I think the chance of his seeing it in any Rouen paper may be avoided. That is all, I think."

"Thank you," said Keating. "That is certainly the course to follow." Every one nodded, or acquiesced in words; and Keating and Bence came over to Helen and engaged her in conversation. The others began to look about for their hats, vaguely preparing to leave.

"Wait a minute," said the judge. "There's no train due just now." And Minnie appeared in the doorway with a big pitcher of crab-apple cider, rich and amber-hued, sparkling, cold, and redolent of the sweet-smelling orchard where it was born. Behind Miss Briscoe came Mildy Upton with glasses and a fat, shaking, four-storied jelly-cake on a second tray. The judge passed his cigars around, and the gentlemen took them blithely, then hesitatingly held them in their fingers and glanced at the ladies, uncertain of permission.

"Let me get you some matches," Helen said, quickly, and found a box on the table and handed it to Keating. Every one sat beaming, and fragrant veils of smoke soon draped the room.

"Why do you call her 'Miss Sherwood'?" Boswell whispered in Keating's ear.

"That's her name."

"Ain't she the daughter of that old fellow over there by the window? Ain't her name Fisbee?"

"No; she's his daughter, but her legal name's Sherwood; she's an adop——"

"Great Scott! I know all about that. I'd like to know if there's a man, woman, or child in this part of the country that doesn't. I guess it won't be Fisbee or Sherwood either very long. She can easy get a new name, *that* lady! And if she took a fancy to Boswell, why, I'm a bach——"

"I expect she won't take a fancy to Boswell very early," said Keating. "They say it will be Harkless."

"Go 'way," returned Mr. Boswell. "What do you want to say that for? Can't you bear for anybody to be happy a minute or two, now and then?"

Warren Smith approached Helen and inquired if it would be asking too much if they petitioned her for some music; so she went to the piano, and sang some darky songs for them, with a quaint suggestion of the dialect—two or three old-fashioned negro melodies of Foster's, followed by some rollicking modern imitations with the movement and spirit of a tinshop falling down a flight of stairs. Her audience listened in delight from the first; but the latter songs quite overcame them with pleasure and admiration, and before she finished, every head in the room was jogging from side to side, and forward and back, in time to the music, while every foot shuffled the measures on the carpet.

When the gentlemen from out of town discovered that it was time to leave if they meant to catch their train, Helen called to them to wait, and they gathered about her.

"Just one second," she said, and she poured all the glasses full to the brim; then, standing in the centre of the circle they made around her, she said:

"Before you go, shan't we pledge each other to our success in this good, home-grown Indiana cider, that leaves our heads clear and our arms strong? If you will—then—" She began to blush furiously and her voice trembled, but she lifted the glass high over her head and cried bravely, "Here's to 'Our Candidate'!"

184

The big men, towering over her, threw back their heads and quaffed the gentle liquor to the last drop. Then they sent up the first shout of the campaign, and cheered John Harkless till the rafters rang.

"My friends," said Mr. Keating, as he and Boswell and the men from Gaines drove away in Judd Bennett's omnibus, "my friends, here is where I begin the warmest hustling I ever did. I want Harkless, everybody wants him——"

"It is a glorious idea," said Mr. Bence. "The name of Harkless——"

Keating drowned the oratory. "But that isn't all. That little girl wants him to go to Congress, and that settles it. He goes."

That evening Minnie and her father were strolling up and down the front walk together, between the flowered borders.

"Do you give up?" asked the judge.

"Give up what? No!" returned his daughter.

"She hasn't told you?"

"Not yet; she and Mr. Fisbee left for the office right after those men went."

"Haven't you discovered what the 'something about politics' she's doing for him is? Did you understand what she meant by 'Our Candidate'?"

"Not exactly."

"Did you see her blush when she proposed that toast?"

"Yes. So would anybody—with all those men, and their eyes hanging out on their cheeks!"

"Pooh! She got up the whole show. Do you know why?"

"I only know it's politics."

"Politics!" He glanced over his shoulder, and then, leaning toward her, he said, in a low tone: "I'll tell you in confidence, Minnie; she's sending him to Congress!"

"Ah!" she cried triumphantly. "If she loved him she wouldn't do *that*, would she?"

185

"Minnie!" Briscoe turned upon her sternly. "I don't want to hear any more talk like that. It's the way with some papers to jibe at our great institutions, and you've been reading them; that's the trouble with you. The only criticism any one has any business making against Congress is that it's too good for some of the men we send there. Congress is our great virtue, understand; the congressmen are our fault."

"I didn't mean anything like that," protested the girl. "I haven't been reading any papers except the 'Herald.' I meant why should she send him away if she cared about him?"

"She'll go with him."

"They couldn't both go. What would become of the 'Herald'?"

"They'd fix that easy enough; there are plenty of smart young fellows in Rouen they could get to run it while they are in Washington."

"Mr. Harkless is sure to be elected, is he?"

"He is, if he's nominated."

"Can't he get the nomination?"

"Get it! Nobody ever happened to think of him for it till it came into *her* head; and the only thing I look to see standing in the way of it is Harkless himself; but I expect we can leave it to her to manage, and I guess she will. She's got more diplomacy than Blaine. Kedge Halloway is up the spout all right, but they want to keep it quiet; that's why she had them come here instead of the office."

"She wouldn't marry him a minute sooner because he went to Congress," said Minnie thoughtfully.

"You're giving up," he exclaimed. "You know I'm right."

"Wait and see. It might—No, you're wrong as wrong can be! I wish you weren't. Don't you see? You're blind. She *couldn't* do all these things for him if she loved him. That's the very proof itself. I suppose you— well, you can't understand."

"I'll tell you one thing," he returned. "If she doesn't, the rest of it won't amount to a rip with John Harkless."

"Yes, it will. Nobody could help liking to find himself as big a man as he'll be when he comes back here. Besides, don't you see, it's her way of making it up to him for not liking him as much as he wants. *You* give up, don't you?"

"No," he cried, with feeble violence, "I don't. She'll find out some things about herself when she sees him again."

Minnie shook her head.

There was a sound of wheels; the buckboard drew up at the gate, and Helen, returning from her evening's labor, jumped out lightly, and ran around to pat the horses' heads. "Thank you so much, Mr. Willetts," she said to the driver. "I know you will handle the two delegates you are to look after as well as you do the judge's team; and you ought to, you know, because the delegates are men. You dears!" She stroked the sleek necks of the colts and handed them bunches of grass.

Briscoe came out, and let the friendly animals nose his shoulder as he looked gravely down on the piquant face beside him in the dusk. "Young lady," he said, "go East. Wait till we get on to Washington, and sit in the gallery, and see John Harkless rise up in his place, and hear the Speaker say: 'The Gentleman from Indiana!' I know the chills would go up and down my spine, and I guess you'd feel pretty well paid for your day's work. I guess we all would."

"Aren't you tired, Helen?" asked Minnie, coming to her in the darkness and clasping her waist.

"Tired? No; I'm happy. Did you ever see the stars so bright?"

CHAPTER XVIII

THE TREACHERY OF H. FISBEE

An Indiana town may lie asleep a long time, but there always comes a day when it wakes up; and Plattville had wakened in August when the "Herald" became a daily and Eph Watts struck oil. It was then that history began to be made. The "Herald" printed News, and the paper was sold every morning at stands in all the towns in that section of the State. Its circulation tripled. Parker talked of new presses; two men were added to his staff, and a reporter was brought from Rouen to join Mr. Fisbee. The "Herald" boomed the oil-field; people swarmed into town; the hotel was crowded; strangers became no sensation whatever. A capitalist bought the whole north side of the Square to erect new stores, and the Carlow Bank began the construction of a new bank building of Bedford stone on Main Street. Then it was whispered, next affirmed, that the "Herald" had succeeded in another of its enterprises, and Main Street was to be asphalted. That was the end of the "old days" of Plattville.

There was a man who had laid the foundation upon which the new Plattville was to be built; he who, through the quiet labor of years, had stamped his spirit upon the people, as their own was stamped upon him; but he lay sick in his friend's house and did not care. One day Meredith found him propped up in bed, reading a letter— reading it listlessly, and with a dull eye.

"PLATTVILLE, *September 1st.*

"*Dear Mr. Harkless*: Yours of the 30th received. Every one here is very glad to know that your health is so far improved as to admit of your writing; and it is our strongest hope that you will soon be completely recovered.

"New subscriptions are coming in at a slightly advanced rate since my last letter; you will see they are distributed over several counties, when you examine the books on your return; and I am glad to state that with our arrangement for Gainesville the 'Herald' is now selling every morning at a prominent store in all the towns within the radius we determined on. Our plan of offering the daily with no advance on the price of the former tri-weekly issue proves a success. I now propose making the issue a quarto every day (at the same price) instead of once a week. I think our experience warrants the experiment. It is my belief that our present circulation will be increased forty per cent. Please advise me if you approve. Of course this would mean a further increase of our working force, and we should have to bring another man from Rouen—possibly two more—but I think we need not fear such enlargements.

"I should tell you that I have taken you at your word entrusting me with the entire charge of your interests here, and I had the store-room adjoining the office put in shape, and offered it to the telegraph company for half the rent they were paying in

188

their former quarters over the post-office. They have moved in; and this, in addition to giving us our despatches direct, is a reduction of expense.

"Mr. Watts informs me that the Standard's offer is liberal and the terms are settled. The boom is not hollow, it is simply an awakening; and the town, so long a dependent upon the impetus of agriculture or its trade, is developing a prosperity of its own on other lines as well. Strangers come every day; oil has lubricated every commercial joint. Contracts have been let for three new brick business buildings to be erected on the east side of the Square. The value of your Main Street frontage will have doubled by December, and possibly you may see fit to tear away the present building and put up another, instead; the investment might be profitable. The 'Herald' could find room on the second and third floors, and the first could be let to stores.

"I regret that you find your copy of the paper for the 29th overlooked in the mail and that your messenger could find none for you at the newspaper offices in Rouen. Mr. Schofield was given directions in regard to supplying you with the missing issue at once.

"I fear that you may have had difficulty in deciphering some of my former missives, as I was unfamiliar with the typewriter when I took charge of the 'Herald'; however, I trust that you find my later letters more legible.

"The McCune people are not worrying us; we are sure to defeat them. The papers you speak of were found by Mr. Parker in your trunk, and are now in my hands.

"I send with this a packet of communications and press clippings indicative of the success of the daily, and in regard to other innovations. The letters from women commendatory of our 'Woman's Page,' thanking us for various house-keeping receipts, etc., strike me as peculiarly interesting, as I admit that a 'Woman's Page' is always a difficult matter for a man to handle without absurdity.

"Please do not think I mean to plume myself upon our various successes; we attempted our innovations and enlargements at just the right time—a time which you had ripened by years of work and waiting, and at the moment when you had built up the reputation of the 'Herald' to its highest point. Everything that has been done is successful only because you paved the way, and because every one knows it is your paper; and the people believe that whatever your paper does is interesting and right.

"Trusting that your recovery will be rapid, I am

"Yours truly,

"H. FISBEE."

Harkless dropped the typewritten sheets with a sigh.

"I suppose I ought to get well," he said wearily.

"Yes," said Meredith, "I think you ought; but you're chock full of malaria and fever and all kinds of meanness, and——"

"You 'tend to your own troubles," returned the other, with an imitation of liveliness. "I—I don't think it interests me much," he said querulously. He was often querulous of late, and it frightened Tom. "I'm just tired. I am strong enough—that is, I think I am till I try to move around, and then I'm like a log, and a lethargy gets me—that's it; I don't think it's malaria; it's lethargy."

"Lethargy comes from malaria."

"It's the other way with me. I'd be all right if I only could get over this—this tiredness. Let me have that pencil and pad, will you, please, Tom?"

He set the pad on his knee, and began to write languidly:

"ROUEN, *September 2d.*

"*Dear Mr. Fisbee*: Yours of the 1st to hand. I entirely approve all arrangements you have made. I think you understand that I wish you to regard *everything* as in your own hands. You are the editor of the 'Herald' and have the sole responsibility for everything, including policy, until, after proper warning, I relieve you in person. But until that time comes, you must look upon me as a mere spectator. I do not fear that you will make any mistakes; you have done very much better in all matters than I could have done myself. At present I have only one suggestion: I observe that your editorials concerning Halloway's renomination are something lukewarm.

"It is very important that he be renominated, not altogether on account of assuring his return to Washington (for he is no Madison, I fear), but the fellow McCune must be so beaten that his defeat will be remembered for twenty years. Halloway is honest and clean, at least, while McCune is corrupt to the bone. He has been bought and sold, and I am glad the proofs of it are in your hands, as you tell me Parker found them, as directed, in my trunk, and gave them to you.

"The papers you hold drove him out of politics once, by the mere threat of publication; you should have printed them last week, as I suggested. Do so at once; the time is short. You have been too gentle; it has the air of fearing to offend, and of catering, as if we were afraid of antagonizing people against us; as though we had a personal stake in the convention. Possibly you consider our subscription books as such; I do not. But if they are, go ahead twice as hard. What if it does give the enemy a weapon in case McCune is nominated; if he is (and I begin to see a danger of it) we will be with the enemy. I do not carry my partisanship so far as to help elect Mr. McCune to Congress. You have been as non-committal in your editorials as if this were a fit time for delicacy and the cheaper conception of party policy. My

190

notion of party policy—no new one—is that the party which considers the public service before it considers itself will thrive best in the long run. The 'Herald' is a little paper (not so little nowadays, after all, thanks to you), but it is an honest one, and it isn't afraid of Rod McCune and his friends. He is to be beaten, understand, if we have to send him to the penitentiary on an old issue to do it. And if the people wish to believe us cruel or vengeful, let them. Please let me see as hearty a word as you can say for Halloway, also. You can write with ginger; please show some in this matter.

"My condition is improved.

"I am, very truly yours,

"JOHN HARKLESS."

When the letter was concluded, he handed it to Meredith. "Please address that, put a 'special' on it, and send it, Tom. It should go at once, so as to reach him by to-night."

"H. Fisbee?"

"Yes; H. Fisbee."

"I believe it does you good to write, boy," said the other, as he bent over him. "You look more chirrupy than you have for several days."

"It's that beast, McCune; young Fisbee is rather queer about it, and I felt stirred up as I went along." But even before the sentence was finished the favor of age and utter weariness returned, and the dark lids closed over his eyes. They opened again, slowly, and he took the others hand and looked up at him mournfully, but as it were his soul shone forth in dumb and eloquent thanks.

"I—I'm giving you a jolly summer, Tom," he said, with a quivering effort to smile. "Don't you think I am? I don't—I don't know what I should have —done——"

"You old Indian!" said Meredith, tenderly.

Three days later, Tom was rejoiced by symptoms of invigoration in his patient. A telegram came for Harkless, and Meredith, bringing it into the sick room, was surprised to find the occupant sitting straight up on his couch without the prop of pillows. He was reading the day's copy of the "Herald," and his face was flushed and his brow stern.

"What's the matter, boy?"

191

"Mismanagement, I hope," said the other, in a strong voice. "Worse, perhaps. It's this young Fisbee. I can't think what's come over the fellow. I thought he was a rescuing angel, and he's turning out bad. I'll swear it looks like they'd been—well, I won't say that yet. But he hasn't printed that McCune business I told you of, and he's had two days. There is less than a week before the convention, and—" He broke off, seeing the yellow envelope in Meredith's hand. "Is that a telegram for me?" His companion gave it to him. He tore it open and read the contents. They were brief and unhappy.

"Can't you do something? Can't you come down? It begins to look the other way. "K. H."

"It's from Halloway," said John. "I have got to go. What did that doctor say?"

"He said two weeks at the earliest, or you'll run into typhoid and complications from your hurts, and even pleasanter things than that. I've got you here, and here you stay; so lie back and get easy, boy."

"Then give me that pad and pencil." He rapidly dashed off a note to H. Fisbee:

"*September 5th.*

"H. FISBEE,

"Editor 'Carlow Herald.'

"*Dear Sir:* You have not acknowledged my letter of the 2d September by a note (which should have reached me the following morning), or by the alteration in the tenor of my columns which I requested, or by the publication of the McCune papers which I directed. In this I hold you grossly at fault. If you have a conscientious reason for refusing to carry out my request it should have been communicated to me at once, as should the fact—if such be the case—that you are a personal (or impersonal, if you like) friend of Mr. Rodney McCune. Whatever the motive, ulterior or otherwise, which prevents you from operating my paper as I direct, I should have been informed of it. This is a matter vital to the interests of our community, and you have hitherto shown yourself too alert in accepting my slightest suggestion for me to construe this failure as negligence. Negligence I might esteem as at least honest and frank; your course has been neither the one nor the other.

"You will receive this letter by seven this evening by special delivery. You will print the facts concerning McCune in to-morrow morning's paper.

"I am well aware of the obligations under which your extreme efficiency and your thoughtfulness in many matters have placed me. It is to you I owe my unearned profits from the transaction in oil, and it is to you I owe the 'Herald's' extraordinary present circulation, growth of power and influence. That power is still under my direction, and is an added responsibility which shall not be misapplied.

"You must forgive me if I write too sharply. You see I have failed to understand your silence; and if I wrong you I heartily ask your pardon in advance of your explanation. Is it that you are sorry for McCune? It would be a weak pity that could keep you to silence. I warned him long ago that the papers you hold would be published if he ever tried to return to political life, and he is deliberately counting on my physical weakness and absence. Let him rely upon it; I am not so weak as he thinks. Personally, I cannot say that I dislike Mr. McCune. I have found him a very entertaining fellow; it is said he is the best of husbands, and a friend to some of his friends, and, believe me, I am sorry for him from the bottom of my heart. But the 'Herald' is not.

"You need not reply by letter. To-morrow's issue answers for you. Until I have received a copy, I withhold my judgment.

"JOHN HARKLESS."

The morrow's issue—that fateful print on which depended John Harkless's opinion of H. Fisbee's integrity—contained an editorial addressed to the delegates of the convention, warning them to act for the vital interest of the community, and declaring that the opportunity to be given them in the present convention was a rare one, a singular piece of good fortune indeed; they were to have the chance to vote for a man who had won the love and respect of every person in the district—one who had suffered for his championship of righteousness—one whom even his few political enemies confessed they held in personal affection and esteem—one who had been the inspiration of a new era—one whose life had been helpfulness, whose hand had reached out to every struggler and unfortunate—a man who had met and faced danger for the sake of others—one who lived under a threat for years, and who had been almost overborne in the fulfilment of that threat, but who would live to see the sun shine on his triumph, the tribute the convention would bring him as a gift from a community that loved him. His name needed not to be told; it was on every lip that morning, and in every heart.

Tom was eagerly watching his companion as he read. Harkless fell back on the pillows with a drawn face, and for a moment he laid his thin hand over his eyes in a gesture of intense pain.

"What is it?" Meredith said quickly.

"Give me the pad, please."

"What is it, boy?"

The other's teeth snapped together.

"What is it?" he cried. "What is it? It's treachery, and the worst I ever knew. Not a word of the accusation I demanded—lying *praises* instead! Read that editorial—there, *there!*" He struck the page with the back of his hand, and threw the paper to Meredith. "Read that miserable lie! 'One who has won the love and respect of every person in the district!'—'One who has suffered for his championship of righteousness!' *Righteousness!* Save the mark!"

"What does it mean?"

"Mean! It means McCune—Rod McCune, 'who has lived under a threat for years'—*my* threat! I swore I would print him out of Indiana if he ever raised his head again, and he knew I could. 'Almost overborne in the fulfilment of that threat!' *Almost!* It's a black scheme, and I see it now. This man came to Plattville and went on the 'Herald' for nothing in the world but this. It's McCune's hand all along. He daren't name him even now, the coward! The trick lies between McCune and young Fisbee—the old man is innocent. Give me the pad. Not *almost* overborne. There are three good days to work in, and, by the gods of Perdition, if Rod McCune sees Congress it will be in his next incarnation!"

He rapidly scribbled a few lines on the pad, and threw the sheets to Meredith. "Get those telegrams to the Western Union office in a rush, please. Read them first."

With a very red face Tom read them. One was addressed to H. Fisbee:

"You are relieved from the cares of editorship. You will turn over the management of the 'Herald' to Warren Smith. You will give him the McCune papers. If you do not, or if you destroy them, you cannot hide where I shall not find you.

"JOHN HARKLESS."

The second was to Warren Smith:
"Take possession 'Herald.' Dismiss H. Fisbee. This your authority. Publish McCune papers so labelled which H. Fisbee will hand you. Letter follows. Beat McCune.

"JOHN HARKLESS."

The author of the curt epistles tossed restlessly on his couch, but the reader of them stared, incredulous and dumfounded, uncertain of his command of gravity. His jaw fell, and his open mouth might have betokened a being smit to imbecility; and, haply, he might be, for Helen had written him from Plattville, pledging his honor to secrecy with the first words, and it was by her command that he had found excuses for not supplying his patient with all the papers which happened to contain references to the change of date for the Plattville convention. And Meredith had known for some time where James Fisbee had found a "young relative" to be the savior of the "Herald" for his benefactor's sake.

"You mean—you—intend to—you discharge young Fisbee?" he stammered at last.

"Yes! Let me have the answers the instant they come, will you, Tom?" Then Harkless turned his face from the wall and spoke through his teeth: "I mean to see H. Fisbee before many days; I want to talk to him!"

But, though he tossed and fretted himself into what the doctor pronounced a decidedly improved state, no answer came to either telegram that day or night. The next morning a messenger boy stumbled up the front steps and handed the colored man, Jim, four yellow envelopes, night messages. Three of them were for Harkless, one was for Meredith. Jim carried them upstairs, left the three with his master's guest, then knocked on his master's door.

"What is it?" answered a thick voice. Meredith had not yet risen.

"A telegraph. Mist' Tawm."

There was a terrific yawn. "O-o-oh! Slide it—oh—under the—door."

"Yessuh."

Meredith lay quite without motion for several minutes, sleepily watching the yellow rhomboid in the crevice. It was a hateful looking thing to come mixing in with pleasant dreams and insist upon being read. After a while he climbed groaningly out of bed, and read the message with heavy eyes, still half asleep. He read it twice before it penetrated:

"Suppress all newspapers to-day. Convention meets at eleven. If we succeed a delegation will come to Rouen this afternoon. They will come.

"HELEN."

Tom rubbed his sticky eyelids, and shook his head violently in a Spartan effort to rouse himself; but what more effectively performed the task for him were certain sounds issuing from Harkless's room, across the hall. For some minutes, Meredith had been dully conscious of a rustle and stir in the invalid's chamber, and he began to realize that no mere tossing about a bed would account for a noise that reached him across a wide hall and through two closed doors of thick walnut. Suddenly he heard a quick, heavy tread, shod, in Harkless's room, and a resounding bang, as some heavy object struck the floor. The doctor was not to come till evening; Jim had gone down-stairs. Who wore shoes in the sick man's room? He rushed across the hall in his pyjamas and threw open the unlocked door.

The bed was disarranged and vacant. Harkless, fully dressed, was standing in the middle of the floor, hurling garments at a big travelling bag.

The horrified Meredith stood for a second, bleached and speechless, then he rushed upon his friend and seized him with both hands.

"Mad, by heaven! Mad!"

"Let go of me, Tom!"

"Lunatic! Lunatic!"

"Don't stop me one instant!"

Meredith tried to force him toward the bed. "For mercy's sake, get back to bed. You're delirious, boy!"

"Delirious nothing. I'm a well man."

"Go to bed—go to bed."

Harkless set him out of the way with one arm. "Bed be hanged!" he cried. "I'm going to Plattville!"

Meredith wrung his hands. "The doctor——"!

"Doctor be damned!"

"Will you tell me what has happened, John?"

His companion slung a light overcoat, unfolded, on the overflowing, misshapen bundle of clothes that lay in the bag; then he jumped on the lid with both feet and kicked the hasp into the lock; a very elegantly laundered cuff and white sleeve dangling out from between the fastened lids. "I haven't one second to talk, Tom; I have seventeen minutes to catch the express, and it's a mile and a half to the station; the train leaves here at eight fifty, I get to Plattville at ten forty-seven. Telephone for a cab for me, please, or tell me the number; I don't want to stop to hunt it up."

Meredith looked him in the eyes. In the pupils of Harkless flared a fierce light. His cheeks were reddened with an angry, healthy glow, and his teeth were clenched till the line of his jaw stood out like that of an embattled athlete in sculpture; his brow was dark; his chest was thrown out, and he took deep, quick breaths; his shoulders were squared, and in spite of his thinness they looked massy. Lethargy, or malaria, or both, whatever were his ailments, they were gone. He was six feet of hot wrath and cold resolution.

Tom said: "You are going?"

196

"Yes," he answered, "I am going."

"Then I will go with you."

"Thank you, Tom," said the other quietly.

Meredith ran into his own room, pressed an electric button, sprang out of his pyjamas like Aphrodite from the white sea-foam, and began to dive into his clothes with a panting rapidity astonishingly foreign to his desire. Jim appeared in the doorway.

"The cart, Jim," shouted his master. "We want it like lightning. Tell the cook to give Mr. Harkless his breakfast in a hurry. Set a cup of coffee on the table by the front door for me. Run like the deuce! We've got to catch a train.—That will be quicker than any cab," he explained to Harkless. "We'll break the ordinance against fast driving, getting down there."

Ten minutes later the cart swept away from the house at a gait which pained the respectable neighborhood. The big horse plunged through the air, his ears laid flat toward his tail; the cart careened sickeningly; the face of the servant clutching at the rail in the rear was smeared with pallor as they pirouetted around curves on one wheel—to him it seemed they skirted the corners and Death simultaneously—and the speed of their going made a strong wind in their faces.

Harkless leaned forward.

"Can you make it a little faster, Tom?" he said.

They dashed up to the station amid the cries of people flying to the walls for safety; the two gentlemen leaped from the cart, bore down upon the ticket-office, stormed at the agent, and ran madly at the gates, flourishing their passports. The official on duty eyed them wearily, and barred the way.

"Been gone two minutes," he remarked, with a peaceable yawn.

Harkless stamped his foot on the cement flags; then he stood stock still, gazing at the empty tracks; but Meredith turned to him, smiling.

"Won't it keep?" he asked.

"Yes, it will keep," John answered. "Part of it may have to keep till election day, but some of it I will settle before night. And that," he cried, between his teeth, "and that is the part of it in regard to young Mr. Fisbee!"

"Oh, it's about H. Fisbee, is it?"

"Yes, it's H. Fisbee."

"Well, we might as well go up and see what the doctor thinks of you; there's no train."

"I don't want to see a doctor again, ever—as long as I live. I'm as well as anybody."

Tom burst out laughing, and clapped his companion lightly on the shoulder, his eyes dancing with pleasure.

"Upon my soul," he cried, "I believe you are! It's against all my tradition, and I see I am the gull of poetry; for I've always believed it to be beyond question that this sort of miracle was wrought, not by rage, but by the tenderer senti—" Tom checked himself. "Well, let's take a drive."

"Meredith," said the other, turning to him gravely, "you may think me a fool, if you will, and it's likely I am; but I don't leave this station except by train. I've only two days to work in, and every minute lessens our chances to beat McCune, and I have to begin by wasting time on a tussle with a traitor. There's another train at eleven fifty-five; I don't take any chances on missing that one."

"Well, well," laughed his friend, pushing him good-humoredly toward a door by a red and white striped pillar, "we'll wait here, if you like; but at least go in there and get a shave; it's a clean shop. You want to look your best if you are going down to fight H. Fisbee."

"Take these, then, and you will understand," said Harkless; and he thrust his three telegrams of the morning into Tom's hand and disappeared into the barber-shop. When he was gone, Meredith went to the telegraph office in the station, and sent a line over the wire to Helen:

"Keep your delegation at home. He's coming on the 11.55."

Then he read the three telegrams Harkless had given him. They were all from Plattville:

"Sorry cannot oblige. Present incumbent tenacious. Unconditionally refuses surrender. Delicate matter. No hope for K. H. But don't worry. Everything all right.

"WARREN SMITH."

"Harkless, if you have the strength to walk, come down before the convention. Get here by 10.47. Looks bad. Come if it kills you.

198

"K. H."

"You entrusted me with sole responsibility for all matters pertaining to 'Herald.' Declared yourself mere spectator. Does this permit your interfering with my policy for the paper? Decline to consider any proposition to relieve me of my duties without proper warning and allowance of time.

"H. FISBEE."

CHAPTER XIX

THE GREAT HARKLESS COMES HOME

The accommodation train wandered languidly through the early afternoon sunshine, stopping at every village and almost every country post-office on the line; the engine toot-tooting at the road crossings; and, now and again, at such junctures, a farmer, struggling with a team of prancing horses, would be seen, or, it might be, a group of school children, homeward bound from seats of learning. At each station, when the train came to a stand-still, some passenger, hanging head and elbows out of his window, like a quilt draped over a chair, would address a citizen on the platform:

"Hey, Sam, how's Miz Bushkirk?"

"She's wal."

"Where's Milt, this afternoon?"

"Warshing the buggy." Then at the cry, "All 'board"—"See you Sunday over at Amo."

"You make Milt come. I'll be there, shore. So long."

There was an impatient passenger in the smoker, who found the stoppages at these wayside hamlets interminable, both in frequency and in the delay at each of them; and while the dawdling train remained inert, and the moments passed inactive, his eyes dilated and his hand clenched till the nails bit his palm; then, when the trucks groaned and the wheels crooned against the rails once more, he sank back in his seat with sighs of relief. Sometimes he would get up and pace the aisle until his companion reminded him that this was not certain to hasten the hour of their arrival at their destination.

"I know that," answered the other, "but I've got to beat McCune."

"By the way," observed Meredith, "you left your stick behind."

"You don't think I need a club to face——"

Tom choked. "Oh, no. I wasn't thinking of your giving H. Fisbee a thrashing. I meant to lean on."

"I don't want it. I've got to walk lame all my life, but I'm not going to hobble on a stick." Tom looked at him sadly; for it was true, and the Cross-Roaders might hug themselves in their cells over the thought. For the rest of his life John Harkless was to walk with just the limp they themselves would have had, if, as in former days, their sentence had been to the ball and chain.

The window was open beside the two young men, and the breeze swept in, fresh from the wide fields, There was a tang in the air; it soothed like a balm, but there was a spur to energy and heartiness in its crispness, the wholesome touch of fall. John looked out over the boundless aisles of corn that stood higher than a tall man could reach; long waves rippled across them. Here, where the cry of the brave had rung in forest glades, where the painted tribes had hastened, were marshalled the tasselled armies of peace. And beyond these, where the train ran between shadowy groves, delicate landscape vistas, framed in branches, opened, closed, and succeeded each other, and then the travellers were carried out into the level open again, and the intensely blue September skies ran down to the low horizon, meeting the tossing plumes of corn.

It takes a long time for the full beauty of the flat lands to reach a man's soul; once there, nor hills, nor sea, nor growing fan leaves of palm shall suffice him. It is like the beauty in the word "Indiana." It may be that there are people who do not consider "Indiana" a beautiful word; but once it rings true in your ears it has a richer sound than "Vallombrosa."

There was a newness in the atmosphere that day, a bright invigoration, that set the blood tingling. The hot months were done with, languor was routed. Autumn spoke to industry, told of the sowing of another harvest, of the tawny shock, of the purple grape, of the red apple, and called upon muscle and laughter; breathed gaiety into men's hearts. The little stations hummed with bustle and noise; big farm wagons rattled away and raced with cut-under or omnibus; people walked with quick steps; the baggage-masters called cheerily to the trainmen, and the brakemen laughed good-bys to rollicking girls.

As they left Gainesville three children, clad in calico, barefoot and bareheaded, came romping out of a log cabin on the outskirts of the town, and waved their hands to the passengers. They climbed on the sagging gate in front of their humble domain, and laughed for joy to see the monstrous caravan come clattering out of the unknown, bearing the faces by. The smallest child, a little cherubic tow-head, whose cheeks were smeared with clean earth and the tracks of forgotten tears, stood upright on a fence-post, and blew the most impudent of kisses to the strangers on a journey.

Beyond this they came into a great plain, acres and acres of green rag-weed where the wheat had grown, all so flat one thought of an enormous billiard table, and now, where the railroad crossed the country roads, they saw the staunch brown thistle, sometimes the sumach, and always the graceful iron-weed, slender, tall, proud, bowing a purple-turbaned head, or shaking in an agony of fright when it stood too close to the train. The fields, like great, flat emeralds set in new metal, were bordered with golden-rod, and at sight of this the heart leaped; for the golden-rod is a symbol of stored granaries, of ripe sheaves, of the kindness of the season generously given and abundantly received; more, it is the token of a land of promise and of bounteous fulfilment; and the plant stains its blossom with yellow so that when it falls it pays tribute to the ground which has nourished it.

From the plain they passed again into a thick wood, where ruddy arrows of the sun glinted among the boughs; and, here and there, one saw a courtly maple or royal oak wearing a gala mantle of crimson and pale brown, gallants of the forest preparing early for the October masquerade, when they should hold wanton carnival, before they stripped them of their finery for pious gray.

And when the coughing engine drew them to the borders of this wood, they rolled out into another rich plain of green and rust-colored corn; and far to the south John Harkless marked a winding procession of sycamores, which, he knew, followed the course of a slender stream; and the waters of the stream flowed by a bank where wild thyme might have grown, and where, beyond an orchard and a rose-garden, a rustic bench was placed in the shade of the trees; and the name of the stream was Hibbard's Creek. Here the land lay flatter than elsewhere; the sky came closer, with a gentler benediction; the breeze blew in, laden with keener spices; there was the flavor of apples and the smell of the walnut and a hint of coming frost; the immeasurable earth lay more patiently to await the husbandman; and the whole world seemed to extend flat in line with the eye—for this was Carlow County.

All at once the anger ran out of John Harkless; he was a hard man for anger to tarry with. And in place of it a strong sense of home-coming began to take possession of him. He was going home. "Back to Plattville, where I belong," he had said; and he said it again without bitterness, for it was the truth. "Every man cometh to his own place in the end."

Yes, as one leaves a gay acquaintance of the playhouse lobby for some hard-handed, tried old friend, so he would wave the outer world God-speed and come back to the old ways of Carlow. What though the years were dusty, he had his friends and his memories and his old black brier pipe. He had a girl's picture that he should carry in his heart till his last day; and if his life was sadder, it was infinitely richer for it. His winter fireside should be not so lonely for her sake; and losing her, he lost not everything, for he had the rare blessing of having known her. And what man could wish to be healed of such a hurt? Far better to have had it than to trot a smug pace unscathed.

He had been a dullard; he had lain prostrate in the wretchedness of his loss. "A girl you could put in your hat—and there you have a strong man prone." He had been a sluggard, weary of himself, unfit to fight, a failure in life and a failure in love. That was ended; he was tired of failing, and it was time to succeed for a while. To accept the worst that Fate can deal, and to wring courage from it instead of despair, that is success; and it was the success that he would have. He would take Fate by the neck. But had it done him unkindness? He looked out over the beautiful, "monotonous" landscape, and he answered heartily, "No!" There was ignorance in man, but no unkindness; were man utterly wise he were utterly kind. The Cross-Roaders had not known better; that was all.

202

The unfolding aisles of corn swam pleasantly before John's eyes. The earth hearkened to man's wants and answered; the clement sun and summer rains hastened the fruition. Yonder stood the brown haystack, garnered to feed the industrious horse who had earned his meed; there was the straw-thatched shelter for the cattle. How the orchard boughs bent with their burdens! The big red barns stood stored with the harvested wheat; and, beyond the pasture-lands, tall trees rose against the benign sky to feed the glance of a dreamer; the fertile soil lay lavender and glossy in the furrow. The farmhouses were warmly built and hale and strong; no winter blast should rage so bitterly as to shake them, or scatter the hospitable embers on the hearth. For this was Carlow County, and he was coming home.

They crossed a by-road. An old man with a streaky gray chin-beard was sitting on a sack of oats in a seatless wagon, waiting for the train to pass. Harkless seized his companion excitedly by the elbow.

"Tommy!" he cried. "It's Kim Fentriss—look! Did you see that old fellow?"

"I saw a particularly uninterested and uninteresting gentleman sitting on a bag," replied his friend.

"Why, that's old Kimball Fentriss. He's going to town; he lives on the edge of the county."

"Can this be true?" said Meredith gravely.

"I wonder," said Harkless thoughtfully, a few moments later, "I wonder why he had them changed around."

"Who changed around?"

"The team. He always used to drive the bay on the near side, and the sorrel on the off."

"And at present," rejoined Meredith, "I am to understand that he is driving the sorrel on the near side, and bay on the off?"

"That's it," returned the other. "He must have worked them like that for some time, because they didn't look uneasy. They're all right about the train, those two. I've seen them stand with their heads almost against a fast freight. See there!" He pointed to a white frame farmhouse with green blinds. "That's Win Hibbard's. We're just outside of Beaver."

"Beaver? Elucidate Beaver, boy!"

"Beaver? Meredith, your information ends at home. What do you know of your own State if you are ignorant of Beaver. Beaver is that city of Carlow County next in importance and population to Plattville."

Tom put his head out of the window. "I fancy you are right," he said. "I already see five people there."

Meredith had observed the change in his companion's mood. He had watched him closely all day, looking for a return of his malady; but he came to the conclusion that in truth a miracle had been wrought, for the lethargy was gone, and vigor seemed to increase in Harkless with every turn of the wheels that brought them nearer Plattville; and the nearer they drew to Plattville the higher the spirits of both the young men rose. Meredith knew what was happening there, and he began to be a little excited. As he had said, there were five people visible at Beaver; and he wondered where they lived, as the only building in sight was the station, and to satisfy his curiosity he walked out to the vestibule. The little station stood in deep woods, and brown leaves whirled along the platform. One of the five people was an old lady, and she entered a rear car. The other four were men. One of them handed the conductor a telegram.

Meredith heard the official say, "All right. Decorate ahead. I'll hold it five minutes."

The man sprang up the steps of the smoker and looked in. He turned to Meredith: "Do you know if that gentleman in the gray coat is Mr. Harkless? He's got his back this way, and I don't want to go inside. The—the air in a smoker always gives me a spell."

"Yes, that's Mr. Harkless."

The man jumped to the platform. "All right, boys," he said. "Rip her out."

The doors of the freight-room were thrown open, and a big bundle of colored stuffs was dragged out and hastily unfolded. One of the men ran to the further end of the car with a strip of red, white and blue bunting, and tacked it securely, while another fastened the other extremity to the railing of the steps by Meredith. The two companions of this pair performed the same operation with another strip on the other side of the car. They ran similar strips of bunting along the roof from end to end, so that, except for the windows, the car was completely covered by the national colors. Then they draped the vestibules with flags. It was all done in a trice.

Meredith's heart was beating fast. "What's it all about?" he asked.

"Picnic down the line," answered the man in charge, removing a tack from his mouth. He motioned to the conductor, "Go ahead."

The wheels began to move; the decorators remained on the platform, letting the train pass them; but Meredith, craning his neck from the steps, saw that they jumped on the last car.

"What's the celebration?" asked Harkless, when Meredith returned.

"Picnic down the line," said Meredith.

"Nipping weather for a picnic; a little cool, don't you think? One of those fellows looked like a friend of mine. Homer Tibbs, or as Homer might look if he were in disgrace. He had his hat hung on his eyes, and he slouched like a thief in melodrama, as he tacked up the bunting on this side of the car." He continued to point out various familiar places, finally breaking out enthusiastically, as they drew nearer the town, "Hello! Look there—beyond the grove yonder! See that house?"

"Yes, John."

"That's the Bowlders'. You've got to know the Bowlders."

"I'd like to."

"The kindest people in the world. The Briscoe house we can't see, because it's so shut in by trees; and, besides, it's a mile or so ahead of us. We'll go out there for supper to-night. Don't you like Briscoe? He's the best they make. We'll go up town with Judd Bennett in the omnibus, and you'll know how a rapid-fire machine gun sounds. I want to go straight to the 'Herald' office," he finished, with a suddenly darkening brow.

"After all, there may be some explanation," Meredith suggested, with a little hesitancy. "H. Fisbee might turn out more honest than you think."

Harkless threw his head back and laughed; it was the first time Meredith had heard him laugh since the night of the dance in the country. "Honest! A man in the pay of Rodney McCune! Well, we can let it wait till we get there. Listen! There's the whistle that means we're getting near home. By heaven, there's an oil-well!"

"So it is."

"And another—three—five—seven—seven in sight at once! They tried it three miles south and failed; but you can't fool Eph Watts, bless him! I want you to know Watts."

They were running by the outlying houses of the town, amidst a thousand descriptive exclamations from Harkless, who wished Meredith to meet every one in Carlow. But he came to a pause in the middle of a word.

"Do you hear music?" he asked abruptly. "Or is it only the rhythm of the ties?"

"It seems to me there's music in the air," answered his companion. "I've been fancying I heard it for a minute or so. There! No—yes. It's a band, isn't it?"

"No; what would a band——"

The train slowed up, and stopped at a watertank, two hundred yards east of the station, and their uncertainty was at an end.

From somewhere down the track came the detonating boom of a cannon. There was a dash of brass, and the travellers became aware of a band playing "Marching through Georgia." Meredith laid his hand on his companion's shoulder. "John," he said, "John——" The cannon fired again, and there came a cheer from three thousand throats, the shouters all unseen.

The engine coughed and panted, the train rolled on, and in another minute it had stopped alongside the station in the midst of a riotous jam of happy people, who were waving flags and banners and handkerchiefs, and tossing their hats high in the air, and shouting themselves hoarse. The band played in dumb show; it could not hear itself play. The people came at the smoker like a long wave, and Warren Smith, Briscoe, Keating, and Mr. Bence of Gaines were swept ahead of it. Before the train stopped they had rushed eagerly up the steps and entered the car.

Harkless was on his feet and started to meet them. He stopped.

"What does it mean?" he said, and began to grow pale. "Is Halloway—did McCune—have you——"

Warren Smith seized one of his hands and Briscoe the other. "What does it mean?" cried Warren; "it means that you were nominated for Congress at five minutes after one-o'clock this afternoon."

"On the second ballot," shouted the Judge, "just as young Fisbee planned it, weeks ago."

It was one of the great crowds of Carlow's history. They had known since morning that he was coming home, and the gentlemen of the Reception Committee had some busy hours; but long before the train arrived, everything was ready. Homer Tibbs had done his work well at Beaver, and the gray-haired veterans of a battery Carlow had sent out in '61 had placed their worn old gun in position to fire salutes. At one-o'clock, immediately after the nomination had been made unanimous, the Harkless Clubs of Carlow, Amo, and Gaines, secretly organized during the quiet agitation preceding the convention, formed on parade in the court-house yard, and, with the Plattville Band at their head, paraded the streets to the station, to make sure of being on hand when the train arrived—it was due in a couple of hours. There they were joined by an increasing number of glad enthusiasts, all noisy, exhilarated, red-faced with shouting, and patriotically happy. As Mr. Bence, himself the spoiled child of another county, generously said, in a speech, which (with no outrageous pressure) he was induced to make during the long wait: "The favorite son of Carlow is returning to his Lares and Penates like another Cincinnatus accepting the call of the people; and, for the first time in sixteen years, Carlow shall have a representative to bear the banner of this district and the flaming torch of Progress sweeping on to Washington and triumph like a speedy galleon of old. And his friends are here to take his hand and do him homage, and the number of his friends is as the number given in the last census of the population of the counties of this district!"

And, indeed, in this estimate the speaker seemed guilty of no great exaggeration. A never intermittent procession of pedestrians and vehicles made its way to the station; and every wagon, buckboard, buggy, and cut-under had its flags or bunting, or streamer of ribbons tied to the whip. The excitement increased as the time grew shorter; those on foot struggled for better positions, and the people in wagons and carriages stood upon seats, while the pedestrians besieged them, climbing on the wheels, or balancing recklessly, with feet on the hubs of opposite wagons. Everybody was bound to see *him*. When the whistle announced the coming of the train, the band began to play, the cannon fired, horns blew, and the cheering echoed and reechoed till heaven's vault resounded with the noise the people of Carlow were making.

There was one heart which almost stopped beating. Helen was standing on the front seat of the Briscoe buckboard, with Minnie beside her, and, at the commotion, the horses pranced and backed so that Lige Willetts ran to hold them; but she did not notice the frightened roans, nor did she know that Minnie clutched her round the waist to keep her from falling. Her eyes were fixed intently on the smoke of the far-away engine, and her hand, lifted to her face in an uncertain, tremulous fashion, as it was one day in a circus tent, pressed against the deepest blush that ever mantled a girl's cheek. When the train reached the platform, she saw Briscoe and the others rush into the car, and there ensued what was to her an almost intolerable pause of expectation, while the crowd besieged the windows of the smoker, leaning up and climbing on each other's shoulders to catch the first glimpse of *him*. Briscoe and a red-faced young man, a stranger to Plattville, came down the steps, laughing like boys, and then Keating and Bence, and then Warren Smith. As the lawyer reached the platform, he turned toward the door of the car and waved his hand as in welcome.

"Here he is, boys!" he shouted, "Welcome Home!" At that it was as if all the noise that had gone before had been mere leakage of pent-up enthusiasm. A thousand horns blared deafeningly, the whistles of the engine and of Hibbard's mill were added to the din, the court-house bell was pealing out a welcome, and the church bells were ringing, the cannon thundered, and then cheer on cheer shook the air, as John Harkless came out under the flags, and passed down the steps of the car.

When Helen saw him, over the heads of the people and through a flying tumult of flags and hats and handkerchiefs, she gave one frightened glance about her, and jumped down from her high perch, and sank into the back seat of the buckboard with her burning face turned from the station and her eyes fixed on the ground. She wanted to run away, as she had run from him the first time she had ever seen him. Then, as now, he came in triumph, hailed by the plaudits of his fellows; and now, as on that long-departed day of her young girlhood, he was borne high over the heads of the people, for Minnie cried to her to look; they were carrying him on their shoulders to his carriage. She had had only that brief glimpse of him, before he was lost in the crowd that was so glad to get him back again and so proud of him; but she had seen that he looked very white and solemn.

Briscoe and Tom Meredith made their way through the crowd, and climbed into the buckboard. "All right, Lige," called the judge to Willetts, who was at the horses' heads. "You go get into line with the boys; they want you. We'll go down on Main Street to see the parade," he explained to the ladies, gathering the reins in his hand.

He clucked to the roans, and by dint of backing and twisting and turning and a hundred intricate manoeuvres, accompanied by entreaties and remonstrances and objurgations, addressed to the occupants of surrounding vehicles, he managed to extricate the buckboard from the press; and once free, the team went down the road toward Main Street at a lively gait. The judge's call to the colts rang out cheerily; his handsome face was one broad smile. "This is a big day for Carlow," he said; "I don't remember a better day's work in twenty years."

"Did you tell him about Mr. Halloway?" asked Helen, leaning forward anxiously.

"Warren told him before we left the car," answered Briscoe. "He'd have declined on the spot, I expect, if we hadn't made him sure it was all right with Kedge."

"If I understood what Mr. Smith was saying, Halloway must have behaved very well," said Meredith.

The judge laughed. "He saw it was the only way to beat McCune, and he'd have given his life and Harkless's, too, rather than let McCune have it."

"Why didn't you stay with him, Tom?" asked Helen.

"With Halloway? I don't know him."

"One forgives a generous hilarity anything, even such quips as that," she retorted. "Why did you not stay with Mr. Harkless?"

"That's very hospitable of you," laughed the young man. "You forget that I have the felicity to sit at your side. Judge Briscoe has been kind enough to ask me to review the procession from his buckboard and to sup at his house with other distinguished visitors, and I have accepted."

"But didn't he wish you to remain with him?"

"But this second I had the honor to inform you that I am here distinctly by his invitation."

"*His?*"

"Precisely, his. Judge Briscoe, Miss Sherwood will not believe that you desire my presence. If I intrude, pray let me—" He made as if to spring from the buckboard, and the girl seized his arm impatiently.

"You are a pitiful nonsense-monger!" she cried; and for some reason this speech made him turn his glasses upon her gravely. Her lashes fell before his gaze, and at that he took her hand and kissed it quickly.

"No, no," she faltered. "You must not think it. It isn't—you see, I— there is nothing!"

"You shall not dull the edge of my hilarity," he answered, "especially since so much may be forgiven it."

"Why did you leave Mr. Harkless?" she asked, without raising her eyes.

"My dear girl," he replied, "because, for some inexplicable reason, my lady cousin has not nominated me for Congress, but instead has chosen to bestow that distinction upon another, and, I may say, an unworthier and unfitter man than I. And, oddly enough, the non-discriminating multitude were not cheering for me; the artillery was not in action to celebrate me; the band was not playing to do me honor; therefore why should I ride in the midst of a procession that knows me not? Why should I enthrone me in an open barouche—a little faded and possibly not quite secure as to its springs, but still a barouche—with four white horses to draw it, and draped with silken flags, both barouche and steeds? Since these things were not for me, I flew to your side to dissemble my spleen under the licensed prattle of a cousin."

"Then who *is* with him?"

"The population of this portion of our State, I take it."

"Oh, it's all right," said the judge, leaning back to speak to Helen. "Keating and Smith and your father are to ride in the carriage with him. You needn't be afraid of any of them letting him know that H. Fisbee is a lady. Everybody understands about that; of course they know it's to be left to you to break it to him how well a girl has run his paper." The old gentleman chuckled, and looked out of the corner of his eye at his daughter, whose expression was inscrutable.

"I!" cried Helen. "*I* tell him! No one must tell him. He need never know it."

Briscoe reached back and patted her cheek. "How long do you suppose he will be here in Plattville without it's leaking out?"

"But they kept guard over him for months and nobody told him."

"Ah," said Briscoe, "but this is different."

"No, no, no!" she exclaimed. "It *must* be kept from him somehow!"

"He'll know it by to-morrow, so you'd better tell him this evening."

"This evening?"

"Yes. You'll have a good chance."

"I will?"

"He's coming to supper with us. He and your father, of course, and Keating and Bence and Boswell and Smith and Tom Martin and Lige. We're going to have a big time, with you and Minnie to do the honors; and we're all coming into town afterwards for the fireworks; I'll let him drive you in the phaeton. You'll have plenty of time to talk it over with him and tell him all about it."

Helen gave a little gasp. "Never!" she cried. "Never!"

The buckboard stopped on the "Herald" corner, and here, and along Main Street, the line of vehicles which had followed it from the station took their places. The Square was almost a solid mass of bunting, and the north entrance of the court-house had been decorated with streamers and flags, so as to make it a sort of stand. Hither the crowd was already streaming, and hither the procession made its way. At intervals the cannon boomed, and Schofields' Henry was winnowing the air with his bell; nobody had a better time that day than Schofields' Henry, except old Wilkerson, who was with the procession.

In advance, came the boys, whooping and somersaulting, and behind them, rode a band of mounted men, sitting their horses like cavalrymen, led by the sheriff and his deputy and Jim Bardlock; then followed the Harkless Club of Amo, led by Boswell, with the magnanimous Halloway himself marching in the ranks; and at sight of this the people shouted like madmen. But when Helen's eye fell upon his fat, rather unhappy face, she felt a pang of pity and unreasoning remorse, which warned her that he who looks upon politics when it is red must steel his eyes to see many a man with the heart-burn. After the men of Amo, came the Harkless Club of Gainesville, Mr. Bence in the van with the step of a grenadier. There followed next, Mr. Ephraim

Watts, bearing a light wand in his hand and leading a detachment of workers from the oil-fields in their stained blue overalls and blouses; and, after them, came Mr. Martin and Mr. Landis at the head of an organization recognized in the "Order of Procession," printed in the "Herald," as the Business Men of Plattville. They played in such magnificent time that every high-stepping foot in all the line came down with the same jubilant plunk, and lifted again with a unanimity as complete as that of the last vote the convention had taken that day. The leaders of the procession set a brisk pace, and who could have set any other kind of a pace when on parade to the strains of such a band, playing such a tune as "A New Coon in Town," with all its might and main?

But as the line swung into the Square, there came a moment when the tune was ended, the musicians paused for breath, and there fell comparative quiet. Amongst the ranks of Business Men ambled Mr. Wilkerson, singing at the top of his voice, and now he could be heard distinctly enough for those near to him to distinguish the melody with which it was his intention to favor the public:

> "Glory! Glory! Hallelujah!
> As we go marching on."

The words, the air, that husky voice, recalled to the men of Carlow another day and another procession, not like this one. And the song Wilkerson was singing is the one song every Northern-born American knows and can sing. The leader of the band caught the sound, signalled to his men; twenty instruments rose as one to twenty mouths; the snare-drum rattled, the big drum crashed, the leader lifted his baton high over his head, and music burst from twenty brazen throats:

"Glory! Glory! Hallelujah!"

Instantaneously, the whole procession began to sing the refrain, and the people in the street, and those in the wagons and carriages, and those leaning from the windows joined with one accord, the ringing bells caught the time of the song, and the upper air reverberated in the rhythm.

The Harkless Club of Carlow wheeled into Main Street, two hundred strong, with their banners and transparencies. Lige Willetts rode at their head, and behind him strode young William Todd and Parker and Ross Schofield and Homer Tibbs and Hartley Bowlder, and even Bud Tipworthy held a place in the ranks through his connection with the "Herald." They were all singing.

And, behind them, Helen saw the flag-covered barouche and her father, and beside him sat John Harkless with his head bared.

She glanced at Briscoe; he was standing on the front seat with Minnie beside him, and both were singing. Meredith had climbed upon the back seat and was nervously fumbling at a cigarette.

"Sing, Tom!" the girl cried to him excitedly.

"I should be ashamed not to," he answered; and dropped the cigarette and began to sing "John Brown's Body" with all his strength. With that she seized his hand, sprang up beside him, and over the swelling chorus her full soprano rose, lifted with all the power in her.

The barouche rolled into the Square, and, as it passed, Harkless turned, and bent a sudden gaze upon the group in the buckboard; but the western sun was in his eyes, and he only caught a glimpse of a vague, bright shape and a dazzle of gold, and he was borne along and out of view, down the singing street.

"Glory! Glory! Hallelujah!
Glory! Glory! Hallelujah!
Glory! Glory! Hallelujah!

    As we go marching on!"

The barouche stopped in front of the courthouse, and he passed up a lane they made for him to the steps. When he turned to them to speak, they began to cheer again, and he had to wait for them to quiet down.

"We can't hear him from over here," said Briscoe, "we're too far off. Mr. Meredith, suppose you take the ladies closer in, and I'll stay with the horses. You want to hear his speech."

"He is a great man, isn't he?" Meredith said to Helen, gravely, as he handed her out of the buckboard. "I've been trying to realize for the last few minutes, that he is the same old fellow I've been treating so familiarly all day long."

"Yes, he is a great man," she answered. "This is only the beginning."

"That's true," said Briscoe, who had overheard her. "He'll go pretty far. A man that people know is steady and strong and level-headed can get whatever he wants, because a public man can get anything, if people know he's safe and honest and they can rely on him for *sense*. It sounds like a simple matter; but only three or four public men in the country have convinced us that they are like that. Hurry along, young people."

Crossing the street, they met Miss Tibbs; she was wiping her streaming eyes with the back of her left hand and still mechanically waving her handkerchief with her right. "Isn't it beautiful?" she said, not ceasing to flutter, unconsciously, the little square of cambric. "There was such a throng that I grew faint and had to come away. I don't mind your seeing me crying. Pretty near everybody cried when he walked up to the steps and we saw that he was lame."

212

Standing on the outskirts of the crowd, they could hear the mellow ring of Harkless's voice, but only fragments of the speech, for it was rather halting, and was not altogether clear in either rhetoric or delivery; and Mr. Bence could have been a good deal longer in saying what he had to say, and a thousand times more oratorical. Nevertheless, there was not a man or woman present who did not declare that it was the greatest speech ever heard in Plattville; and they really thought so—to such lengths are loyalty and friendship sometimes carried in Carlow and Amo and Gaines.

He looked down upon the attentive, earnest faces and into the kindly eyes of the Hoosier country people, and, as he spoke, the thought kept recurring to him that this was the place he had dreaded to come back to; that these were the people he had wished to leave—these, who gave him everything they had to give—and this made it difficult to keep his tones steady and his throat clear.

Helen stood so far from the steps (nor could she be induced to penetrate further, though they would have made way for her) that only fragments reached her, but what she heard she remembered:

"I have come home . . . Ordinarily a man needs to fall sick by the wayside or to be set upon by thieves, in order to realize that nine-tenths of the world is Samaritan, and the other tenth only too busy or too ignorant to be. Down here he realizes it with no necessity of illness or wounds to bring it out; and if he does get hurt, you send him to Congress. . . . There will'be no other in Washington so proud of what he stands for as I shall be. To represent you is to stand for realities—fearlessness, honor, kindness. . . . We are people who take what comes to us, and it comes bountifully; we are rich—oh, we are all Americans here! . . . This is the place for a man who likes to live where people are kind to one another, and where they have the old-fashioned way of saying 'Home.' Other places, they don't seem to get so much into it as we do. And to come home as I have to-day. . . . I have come home. . . ."

Every one meant to shake hands with him, and, when the speech was over, those nearest swooped upon him, cheering and waving, and grasping at his hand. Then a line was formed, and they began to defile by him, as he stood on the steps, and one by one they came up, and gave him hearty greetings, and passed on through the court-house and out at the south door. Tom Meredith and Minnie Briscoe came amongst the others, and Tom said only, "Good old boy," as he squeezed his friend's hand; and then, as he went down the hall, wiping his glasses, he asked Minnie if she believed the young man on the steps had risen from a sick bed that morning.

It was five-o'clock when Harkless climbed the stairs to the "Herald" office, and his right arm and hand were aching and limp. Below him, as he reached the landing, he could see boys selling extras containing his speech (taken by the new reporter), and long accounts of the convention, of the nominee's career, and the celebration of his home-coming. The sales were rapid; for no one could resist the opportunity to read in print descriptions of what his eyes had beheld and his ears had heard that day.

Ross Schofield was the only person in the editorial room, and there was nothing in his appearance which should cause a man to start and fall back from the doorway; but that was what Harkless did.

"What's the matter, Mr. Harkless?" cried Ross, hurrying forward, fearing that the other had been suddenly reseized by illness.

"What are those?" asked Harkless, with a gesture of his hand which seemed to include the entire room.

"Those!" repeated Ross, staring blankly.

"Those rosettes—these streamers—that stovepipe—all this blue ribbon."

Ross turned pale. "Ribbon?" he said, inquiringly. "Ribbon?" He seemed unable to perceive the decorations referred to.

"Yes," answered John; "these rosettes on the chairs, that band, and——"

"Oh!" Ross exclaimed. "That?" He fingered the band on the stovepipe as if he saw it for the first time. "Yes; I see."

"But what are they for?" asked Harkless, touching one of the streamers curiously.

"Why—it's—it's likely meant for decorations."

John picked up the ink-well, staring in complete amazement at the hard knot of ribbon with which it was garnished.

"They seem to have been here some time."

"They have; I reckon they're almost due to be called in. They've be'n up ever sence—sence——"

"Who put them up, Ross?"

"We did."

"What for?"

Ross was visibly embarrassed. "Why—fer—fer the other editor."

"For Mr. Fisbee?"

"Land, no! You don't suppose we'd go to work and bother to brisken things up fer that old gentleman, do you?"

"I meant young Mr. Fisbee—he is the other editor, isn't he?"

"Oh!" said Ross, coughing. "Young Mr. Fisbee? Yes; we put 'em up fer him."

"You did! Did he appreciate them?"

"Well—he seemed to—kind of like 'em."

"Where is he now? I came here to find him."

"He's gone."

"Gone? Hasn't he been here this afternoon?"

"Yes; some 'the time. Come in and stayed durin' the leevy you was holdin', and saw the extra off all right."

"When will he be back?"

"Sence it's be'n a daily he gits here by eight, after supper, but don't stay very late; the new man and old Mr. Fisbee and Parker look after whatever comes in late, unless it's something special. He'll likely be here by half-past eight at the farthest off."

"I can't wait till then." John took a quick turn about the room. "I've been wanting to see him every minute since I got in," he said impatiently, "and he hasn't been near me. Nobody could even point him out to me. Where has he gone? I want to see him *now*."

"Want to discharge him again?" said a voice from the door, and turning, they saw that Mr. Martin stood there observing them.

"No," said Harkless; "I want to give him the 'Herald.' Do you know where he is?"

Mr. Martin stroked his beard deliberately. "The person you speak of hadn't ort to be very hard to find—in Carlow. The committee was reckless enough to hire that carriage of yours by the day, and Keating and Warren Smith are setting in it up at the corner, with their feet on the cushions to show they're used to ridin' around with four white horses every day in the week. It's waitin' till you're ready to go out to Briscoe's. It's an hour before supper time, and you can talk to young Fisbee all you want. He's out there."

As they drove along the pike, Harkless's three companions kept up a conversation sprightly beyond the mere exhilaration of the victorious; but John sat almost silent, and, in spite of their liveliness, the others eyed him a little anxiously now and then, knowing that he had been living on excitement through a physically exhausting day, and they were fearful lest his nerves react and bring him to a breakdown. But the healthy flush of his cheek was reassuring; he looked steady and strong, and they were pleased to believe that the stirring-up was what he needed.

It had been a strange and beautiful day to him, begun in anger, but the sun was not to go down upon his wrath; for his choleric intention had almost vanished on his homeward way, and the first words Smith had spoken had lifted the veil of young Fisbee's duplicity, had shown him with what fine intelligence and supreme delicacy and sympathy young Fisbee had worked for him, had understood him, and had *made* him. If the open assault on McCune had been pressed, and the damnatory evidence published in Harkless's own paper, while Harkless himself was a candidate and rival, John would have felt dishonored. The McCune papers could have been used for Halloway's benefit, but not for his own; he would not ride to success on another man's ruin; and young Fisbee had understood and had saved him. It was a point of honor that many would have held finicky and inconsistent, but one which young Fisbee had comprehended was vital to Harkless.

And this was the man he had discharged like a dishonest servant; the man who had thrown what was (in Carlow's eyes) riches into his lap; the man who had made his paper, and who had made him, and saved him. Harkless wanted to see young Fisbee as he longed to see only one other person in the world. Two singular things had happened that day which made his craving to see Helen almost unbearable—just to rest his eyes upon her for a little while, he could ask no more. And as they passed along that well-remembered road, every tree, every leaf by the wayside, it seemed, spoke to him and called upon the dear memory of his two walks with her—into town and out of town, on show-day. He wondered if his heart was to project a wraith of her before him whenever he was deeply moved, for the rest of his life. For twice to-day he had seen her whom he knew to be so far away. She had gone back to her friends in the north, Tom had said. Twice that afternoon he had been momentarily, but vividly, conscious of her as a living presence. As he descended from the car at the station, his eyes, wandering out over the tumultuous crowd, had caught and held a picture for a second—a graceful arm upraised, and a gloved hand pressed against a blushing cheek under a hat such as is not worn in Carlow; a little figure poised apparently in air, full-length above the crowd about her; so, for the merest flick of time he had seen her, and then, to his straining eyes, it was as though she were not. She had vanished. And again, as his carriage reached the Square, a feeling had come to him that she was near him; that she was looking at him; that he should see her when the carriage turned; and in the same instant, above the singing of a multitude, he heard her voice as if there had been no other and once more his dazzled eyes beheld her for a second; she was singing, and as she sang she leaned toward him from on high with the most ineffable look of tenderness and pride and affection he had ever seen on a woman's face; such a look, he thought, as she would wear if she came to love some archangel (her love should be no less) with all of her heart and soul and strength. And so he knew he had seen a vision. But it was a cruel one to visit a man who loved her. He had summoned his philosophy and his courage in his interview with himself on the way to Carlow, and they had answered; but nothing could answer if his eyes were to play him tricks and bring her visibly before him, and with such an expression as he had seen upon her face. It was too real. It made his eyes yearn for the sight of her with an ache that was physical. And even at that moment, he saw, far ahead of them on the road, two figures standing in front of the brick house. One was unmistakable at any distance. It was that of old Fisbee; and the other was a girl's: a light, small figure without a hat, and the low, western sun dwelt on a head that shone with gold. Harkless put his hand over his eyes with a pain that was like the taste of hemlock in nectar.

"Sun in your eyes?" asked Keating, lifting his hat, so as to shield the other's face.

"Yes."

When he looked again, both figures were gone. He made up his mind that he would think of the only other person who could absorb his attention, at least for a time; very soon he would stand face to face with the six feet of brawn and intelligence and manhood that was young Fisbee.

"You are sure he is there?" he asked Tom Martin.

"Yes," answered Martin, with no need to inquire whom the editor meant. "I reckon," he continued, solemnly, peering at the other from under his rusty hat-brim, "I reckon when you see him, maybe you'll want to put a kind of codicil to that deed to the 'Herald.'"

"How's that, Martin?"

"Why, I guess maybe you'll—well, wait till you see him."

"I don't want to wait much longer, when I remember what I owe him and how I have used him, and that I have been here nearly three hours without seeing him."

As they neared the brick house Harkless made out, through the trees, a retreative flutter of skirts on the porch, and the thought crossed his mind that Minnie had flown indoors to give some final directions toward the preparation of the banquet; but when the barouche halted at the gate, he was surprised to see her waving to him from the steps, while Tom Meredith and Mr. Bence and Mr. Boswell formed a little court around her. Lige Willetts rode up on horse back at the same moment, and the judge was waiting in front of the gate. Harkless stepped out of the barouche and took his hand.

"I was told young Fisbee was here."

"Young Fisbee is here," said the judge.

"Where, please, Briscoe?"

"Want to see him right off?"

"I do, very much."

"You'll withdraw his discharge, I expect, now?"

"Ah!" exclaimed the other. "I want to make him a present of the 'Herald,' if he'll take it." He fumed to Meredith, who had come to the gate. "Tom, where is he?"

Meredith put his hand on his friend's shoulder, and answered: "I don't know. God bless you, old fellow!"

"The truth is," said the judge, as they entered the gate, "that when you drove up, young Fisbee ran into the house. Minnie—" He turned, but his daughter had disappeared; however, she came to the door, a moment later, and shook her head mysteriously at her father.

"Not in the house," she said.

Mr. Fisbee came around the corner of the porch and went toward Harkless. "Fisbee," cried the latter, "where is your nephew?"

The old man took his hand in both his own, and looked him between the eyes, and thus stood, while there was a long pause, the others watching them.

"You must not say that I told you," he said at last. "Go into the garden."

But when Harkless's step crunched the garden path there was no one there. Asters were blooming in beds between the green rose-bushes, and their many-fingered hands were flung open in wide surprise that he should expect to find young Fisbee there. It was just before sunset. Birds were gossiping in the sycamores on the bank. At the foot of the garden, near the creek, there were some tall hydrangea bushes, flower-laden, and, beyond them, one broad shaft of the sun smote the creek bends for a mile in that flat land, and crossed the garden like a bright, taut-drawn veil. Harkless passed the bushes and stepped out into this gold brilliance. Then he uttered a cry and stopped.

Helen was standing beside the hydrangeas, with both hands against her cheeks and her eyes fixed on the ground. She had run away as far as she could run; there were high fences extending down to the creek on each side, and the water was beyond.

"*You!*" he said. "*You—you!*"

She did not lift her eyes, but began to move away from him with little backward steps. When she reached the bench on the bank, she spoke with a quick intake of breath and in a voice he scarcely heard. It was the merest whisper, and her words came so slowly that sometimes minutes separated them.

"Can you—will you keep me—on the 'Herald'?"

"Keep you——"

"Will you—let me—help?"

He came near her. "I don't understand. Is it you—you—who are here again?"

"Have you—forgiven me? You know now why I wouldn't—resign? You forgive my—that telegram?"

"What telegram?"

"That one that came to you—this morning."

"*Your* telegram?"

"Yes."

"Did you send me one?"

"Yes."

"It did not come to me."

"Yes—it did."

"But there—What was it about?"

"It was signed," she said, "it was signed—" She paused and turned half way, not lifting the downcast lashes; her hand, laid upon the arm of the bench, was shaking; she put it behind her. Then her eyes were lifted a little, and, though they did not meet his, he saw them, and a strange, frightened glory leaped in his heart. Her voice fell still lower and two heavy tears rolled down her cheeks. "It was signed," she whispered, "it was signed—'H. Fisbee.'"

He began to tremble from head to foot. There was a long silence. She had turned quite away from him. When he spoke, his voice was as low as hers, and he spoke as slowly as she had.

"You mean—then—it was—you?"

"Yes."

"You!"

"Yes."

"And you have been here all the time?"

"All—all except the week you were—hurt, and that—that one evening."

The bright veil which wrapped them was drawn away, and they stood in the silent, gathering dusk.

He tried to loosen his neck-band; it seemed to be choking him. "I—I can't—I don't comprehend it. I am trying to realize what it——"

"It means nothing," she answered.

"There was an editorial, yesterday," he said, "an editorial that I thought was about Rodney McCune. Did you write it?"

"Yes."

"It was about—me—wasn't it?"

"Yes."

"It said—it said—that I had won the love of every person in Carlow County."

Suddenly she found her voice. "Do not misunderstand me," she said rapidly. "I have done the little that I have done out of gratitude." She faced him now, but without meeting his eyes. "I told you, remember, that you would understand some day what I meant by that, and the day has come. I owed you more gratitude than a woman ever owed a man before, I think, and I would have died to pay a part of it. I set every gossip's tongue in Rouen clacking at the very start, in the merest amateurish preparation for the work Mr. Macauley gave me. That was nothing. And the rest has been the happiest time in my life. I have only pleased myself, after all!"

"What gratitude did you owe me?"

"What gratitude? For what you did for my father."

220

"I have only seen your father once in my life—at your table at the dance supper, that night."

"Listen. My father is a gentle old man with white hair and kind eyes. You saw my uncle, that night; he has been as good to me as a father, since I was seven years old, and he gave me his name by law and I lived with him. My father came to see me once a year; I never came to see him. He always told me everything was well with him; that his life was happy. Once he lost the little he had left to him in the world, his only way of making his living. He had no friends; he was hungry and desperate, and he wandered. I was dancing and going about wearing jewels—only—I did not know. All the time the brave heart wrote me happy letters. I should have known, for there was one who did, and who saved him. When at last I came to see my father, he told me. He had written of his idol before; but it was not till I came that he told it all to me. Do you know what I felt? While his daughter was dancing cotillions, a stranger had taken his hand— and—" A sob rose in her throat and checked her utterance for a moment; but she threw up her head and met his eyes proudly. "Gratitude, Mr. Harkless!" she cried. "I am James Fisbee's daughter."

He fell back from the bench with a sharp exclamation, and stared at her through the gray twilight. She went on hurriedly, again not looking at him:

"When you showed me that you cared for me—when you told me that you did— I—do you think I wanted to care for you? I wanted to do something to show you that I could be ashamed of my vile neglect of him—something to show you his daughter could be grateful. If I had loved you, what I did would have been for that—and I could not have done it. And how could I have shown my gratitude if I had done it for love? And it has been such dear, happy work, the little I have done, that it seems, after all, that I have done it for love of myself. But—but when you first told me—" She broke off with a strange, fluttering, half inarticulate little laugh that was half tears; and then resumed in another tone: "When you told me you cared that night—that night we were here—how could I be sure? It had been only two days, you see, and even if I could have been sure of myself, why, I couldn't have told you. Oh! I had so brazenly thrown myself at your head, time and again, those two days, in my—my worship of your goodness to my father and my excitement in recognizing in his friend the hero of my girlhood, that you had every right to think I cared; but if—but if I had —if I had—loved you with my whole soul, I could not have—why, no woman could have—I mean the sort of girl I am couldn't have admitted it—must have denied it. And what I was trying to do for you when we met in Rouen was—was courting you. You surely see I couldn't have done it if I had cared. It would have been brazen! And do you think that then I could have answered—'Yes'—even if I wanted to—even if I had been sure of myself? And now—" Her voice sank again to a whisper. "And now——"

From the meadows across the creek, and over the fields, came a far tinkling of farm-bells. Three months ago, at this hour, John Harkless had listened to that sound, and its great lonesomeness had touched his heart like a cold hand; but now, as the mists were rising from the water and the small stars pierced the sky one by one, glinting down through the dim, immeasurable blue distances, he found no loneliness in heaven or earth. He leaned forward toward her; the bench was between them. The last light was gone; evening had fallen.

"And now—" he said.

She moved backward as he leaned nearer.

"You promised to remember on the day you understood," she answered, a little huskily, "that it was all from the purest gratitude."

"And—and there is nothing else?"

"If there were," she said, and her voice grew more and more unsteady, "if there were, can't you see that what I have done—" She stopped, and then, suddenly, "Ah, it would have been *brazen*!"

He looked up at the little stars and he heard the bells, and they struck into his heart like a dirge. He made a singular gesture of abnegation, and then dropped upon the bench with his head bowed between his hands.

She pressed her hand to her bosom, watching him in a startled fashion, her eyes wide and her lips parted. She took a few quick, short steps toward the garden, still watching him over her shoulder.

"You mustn't worry," he said, not lifting his bent head, "I know you're sorry. I'll be all right in a minute."

She gave a hurried glance from right to left and from left to right, like one in terror seeking a way of escape; she gathered her skirts in her hand, as if to run into the garden; but suddenly she turned and ran to him—ran to him swiftly, with her great love shining from her eyes. She sank upon her knees beside him. She threw her arms about his neck and kissed him on the forehead.

"Oh, my dear, don't you see?" she whispered, "don't you see—don't you see?"

When they heard the judge calling from the orchard, they went back through the garden toward the house. It was dark; the whitest asters were but gray splotches. There was no one in the orchard; Briscoe had gone indoors. "Did you know you are to drive me into town in the phaeton for the fireworks?" she asked.

"Fireworks?"

"Yes; the Great Harkless has come home."

222

Even in the darkness he could see the look the vision had given him when the barouche turned into the Square. She smiled upon him and said, "All afternoon I was wishing I could have been your mother."

He clasped her hand more tightly. "This wonderful world!" he cried. "Yesterday I had a doctor—a doctor to cure me of love-sickness!"

They went on a little way. "We must hurry," she said. "I am sure they have been waiting for us." This was true; they had.

From the dining-room came laughter and hearty voices, and the windows were bright with the light of many lamps. By and by, they stood just outside the patch of light that fell from one of the windows.

"Look," said Helen. "Aren't they good, dear people?"

"The beautiful people!" he answered.